PENGUIN  C

UTILITARIANISM AND

JOHN STUART MILL (1806–73) was educated by his father and through his influence obtained a clerkship at India House. He formed the Utilitarian Society which met to read and discuss essays, and in 1825 he edited Bentham's *Treatise upon Evidence*. In 1826 he suffered an acute mental crisis and found that poetry helped him recover the will to live, particularly the work of Wordsworth. Having reconsidered his aims and those of the Benthamite school, he met Harriet Taylor and she inspired a great deal of his philosophy. They married in 1851. *Utilitarianism* was published in 1861 but before that Mill published his *System of Logic* (1843), *Principles of Political Economy* (1848) and *On Liberty* (1839). His other works include his classic *Autobiography* (1873). Mill retired in 1858 and became the independent MP for Westminster from 1865 to 1868. During the rest of his life he spent about half of each year in France and died in Avignon.

JEREMY BENTHAM (1748–1832) was educated at Westminster and Queen's College, Oxford. He was called to the bar but found the work morally and intellectually distasteful and set out to theorize a simple and equitable legal system. The law of utility, for which he is best remembered, states that the goodness of a law can be measured in accordance with the measure in which it subserves the happiness of the individual. His democratic views are expressed in his *Constitutional Code* (1830). With J. S. Mill he founded the *Westminster Review*, the organ of his philosophical radicals. True to his principles, Bentham left his body to be dissected and his remains are on view at University College, London.

ALAN RYAN is Professor of Politics at Princeton University and a Fellow of New College, Oxford. He was educated at Christ's Hospital and Balliol College, Oxford. At the age of fifteen he was asked to write an essay on Mill's *Liberty* and concluded that Mill was more than a match for his innumerable critics and a writer with much to say to the twentieth century. *The Philosophy of John Stuart Mill* (1970) and *J. S. Mill* (1974), defended that conclusion at greater length. Alan Ryan's other books include *Property and Political Theory* (1984) and *Bertrand Russell: A Political Life* (1988). He jointly edited *The Blackwell Encyclopedia of Political Thought* (1987).

UTILITARIANISM
AND OTHER ESSAYS

J. S. Mill and Jeremy Bentham

EDITED BY ALAN RYAN

Penguin Books

PENGUIN BOOKS

Published by the Penguin Group
Penguin Books Ltd, 27 Wrights Lane, London W8 5TZ, England
Penguin Books USA Inc., 375 Hudson Street, New York, New York 10014, USA
Penguin Books Australia Ltd, Ringwood, Victoria, Australia
Penguin Books Canada Ltd, 10 Alcorn Avenue, Toronto, Ontario, Canada M4V 3B2
Penguin Books (NZ) Ltd, 182–190 Wairau Road, Auckland 10, New Zealand

Penguin Books Ltd, Registered Offices: Harmondsworth, Middlesex, England

First published 1987
10

Introduction copyright © Alan Ryan, 1987
All rights reserved

Filmset in Bembo Linotron
Printed in England by Clays Ltd, St Ives plc

Contents

Introduction

Mill's *Utilitarianism* is one of the best known of all philosophical texts. Any student of philosophy and almost any student of English literature and English history will at least have glanced at it, and will have heard something about the philosophical and political movement to which its author belonged. Since it is short, readable, polemical and eloquent, it has always offered an easy way into the complexities of moral philosophy and into the creed of the utilitarian movement. But it has only kept that place because utilitarianism itself is the best known of all moral theories. It is doubtless an exaggeration to suggest that 'the greatest happiness principle' is widely accepted as an ultimate moral principle by plain men and philosophers alike; it is certainly an exaggeration believed more readily by the opponents of utilitarianism than by its defenders.[1] But much of what utilitarians argue has an immediate appeal to contemporary common sense. The idea that it is at least some argument in favour of a course of action that it gives happiness, the thought that numbers make a difference to the merits of any action or policy because they make a difference to how much happiness or misery it causes, the belief that basic morality is a matter of preventing us being a nuisance to our fellows and by extension getting us to do them some positive good – all these are familiar utilitarian claims and commonplaces of everyday argument.

Most people have a good idea what is meant when, say, one politician accuses another of sacrificing justice for merely utilitarian considerations, or someone declares that city planners have sacrificed aesthetics to utility; but if they had accused each other of preferring 'teleological' to 'deontological' considerations, not one person in a hundred would have had the least idea what they were arguing about. This is far from saying that many people

7

have a very clear idea of what was at stake in nineteenth-century arguments between utilitarians and their critics. Innumerable students of English literature go through their whole lives believing that the portrait of Mr Gradgrind in Dickens's *Hard Times* is the last word on utilitarianism and on utilitarianism's impact on education, on imagination, and on individual character. But Mill's essay makes it clear that Dickens was attacking a straw man; utilitarianism proposed as its ideal the happiness of fully developed human beings, not the commercial success of the stunted creatures Mr Gradgrind set out to produce. Mill attacked 'that creature Dickens' for his disparaging view of female emancipation in *Bleak House* but generally thought well enough of him to feel his death as a personal loss; there appears to be no evidence of his reading *Hard Times*, and therefore no knowing what he made of it.[2]

John Stuart Mill and Jeremy Bentham

Utilitarianism is associated above all with two men – Jeremy Bentham (1748–1832) and John Stuart Mill (1806–1873). There were other distinguished utilitarians, among them Mill's father and John Austin; since then there have been innumerable moral philosophers, philosophers of law and economic theorists who would have described themselves as utilitarians. None the less, it is Bentham's brutally clear statement of 'the greatest happiness theory' and Mill's anxious reflections upon that theory which between them define utilitarianism. Bentham was the son of a Tory lawyer and was almost as precocious as J. S. Mill; he went to Westminster School at seven and Queen's College, Oxford at the age of fifteen. He loathed both places, and all his life resented the hypocrisy of a university which forced its students to swear their belief in the Thirty-nine Articles of the Church of England but really cared for nothing but its own privileges. He was called to the bar in 1768, but almost immediately decided that the practice of the law was less important than its reform. For the next sixty-four years he wrote increasingly complicated proposals for that reform.

His earliest works are generally his most readable. Certainly that is true of the *Fragment on Government* of 1776 in which he demolished Blackstone's *Commentaries on the Laws of England* together with the doctrine of the social contract and the theory of natural right. Its publication coincided neatly with the American Revolution, a revolution aimed at drawing up a new social contract for the protection of the natural rights of Americans. In 1789 he published his *Introduction to the Principles of Morals and Legislation*, seven chapters of which are printed here. (It had been written some time before 1780, according to his preface.) It has always been taken to be the definitive statement of Bentham's utilitarianism; it is certainly the clearest and plainest statement. It in turn coincided with the outbreak of the French Revolution, though this was inspired by principles which Bentham dismissed as nonsense.

Much of Bentham's energy was devoted to his project for a new design of reformatory, which he named the *Panopticon* on the strength of the prison's main feature – a central observatory which would enable the gaoler to keep an eye on all his prisoners at any hour of the day or night and without their being aware of it. (The prison was designed on a star plan, with corridors radiating out from this central office.) Bentham offered his design to the government in the early 1790s, but nothing ever came of it, and after years of argument he was paid £23,000 for the time and expense the scheme had cost him. The effect on him of what he thought was ill-treatment by successive governments was to turn him from a believer in benevolent despotism into a believer in radical democracy. In early life, he had thought that an enlightened monarchy would be only too willing to institute legal reforms along utilitarian lines; the *Panopticon* affair disillusioned him, and he concluded that only a government which was answerable to the electorate at frequent intervals and constantly under its eye would be reliably benevolent.[3]

Bentham became a friend of James Mill in 1808, when J. S. Mill was two years old. For ten years, the Mill family spent part of every summer with Bentham, and for many years they lived near him in Queen's Square, Westminster. James Mill was widely thought of as Bentham's mouthpiece, the man who turned

Bentham's doctrine into the basis of a political movement.[4] Whether he always felt at ease in this role is doubtful, for he was a strong-minded man of a fierce and independent temper. Bentham's existence was not very much affected by the increasing awe in which he was held by the radicals; he continued to write ever more difficult essays on ever more difficult subjects until he died a fortnight after the passing of the Reform Act of 1832. His influence on the English radicals and on an international public came through pamphlets and through letters – his impact in Spain, Greece and Latin America is still to be properly chronicled and assessed. Although Bentham always took a close interest in J. S. Mill's education, there is no evidence that he played any role in its design; but whoever designed it, J. S. Mill's education is justly famous.[5] He was taught Greek at three, read the Roman historians before he was ten, embarked on logic at twelve and in his early teens learned economics by assisting his father in the composition of his *Elements of Political Economy*.

John Stuart Mill joined his father in the East India Company in 1823, and rose steadily to become its chief official – the so-called 'Examiner of India Correspondence' – shortly before the Indian Mutiny of 1857 finally persuaded the British Government that India could not be governed by the ghost of a trading company. But unlike James Mill, he took little interest in India; his impact on nineteenth-century Britain was the result of a formidable intellect and a capacity for writing lucid, authoritative accounts of complicated doctrine. He had something close to a God-given talent for the textbook – but not the usual, second-hand object; his talent was for the first-hand rendered comprehensible and comprehensive. Within a couple of decades of his youthful assaults on the intellectual conservatism of English universities, they were employing his *System of Logic* (1843) and his *Principles of Political Economy* (1848) as the required reading for their young men.

Mill was no 'ivory tower' intellectual. He grew up with the 'Philosophical Radicals', middle-class reformers of a generally utilitarian persuasion who had since the end of the Napoleonic Wars demanded parliamentary reform, legal reform, greater democracy and accountability in all aspects of politics and administration.[6] Although he came to think their views altogether too narrow, he never deserted the radical cause; in the 1830s he edited the *London and Westminster Review*, and if he attacked his own side with as much gusto as he attacked his opponents, it was always in the name of an enlarged radicalism. He went on to defend the French Revolution of 1848 against all its English critics, and added chapters in defence of socialism and co-operativism to his *Principles of Political Economy*. After he had retired from the East India Company, he served briefly as MP for Westminster (1865–8), and in the debates on the second Reform Bill came closer to gaining the vote for women than anyone before or after him until the case was conceded in 1918. He had long been known to favour the abolition of every legal disability suffered by women, and in *Considerations on Representative Government* (1862) treated the opponents of female suffrage as so far beneath contempt as to deserve no argument whatever. *The Subjection of Women* (1869) revealed the extent of his feminism, though it disappointed those of his friends who would have liked a more uninhibited defence of easy divorce. After losing Westminster at the general election of 1868, Mill retired to Avignon. Harriet Taylor, whom he had met in 1830, and married in 1851 on the death of her husband, had died there in 1858, and Mill died there himself in May 1873.

Mill was unusual in the Victorian age in never suffering a crisis of religious faith – unless we count the breakdown he suffered in 1826 when he turned against his father and Bentham. In conventional terms, he was brought up an agnostic, and remained one all his life. He published posthumously 'Three Essays on Religion' (written at various times between 1854 and 1869) which argued that there was no reason to suppose Christianity true, though some reason to think there might be a less than omnipotent deity playing some part in human affairs. The real message of the essays was that the religious sentiment might be applied to this-worldly matters, that 'the religion of humanity' could and should be inculcated in a society which was already less than wholly Christian.

'Utilitarianism' – its Audience and its Purpose

Of all Mill's works, three have no difficulty in finding a modern audience. Mill's *Autobiography* (published posthumously, written in two instalments in 1853–4 and 1869–70) gives a moving account of the education he enjoyed (or suffered) at the hands of his father, of the nervous breakdown which followed, of his recovery under the impulse of Wordsworth's poetry, and of the Platonic but passionate friendship with Harriet Taylor which simultaneously restored his emotional health and drove him out of polite society. *Liberty* (1858) is such a deeply felt defence of the right of individuals to be left alone unless they are causing real damage to other people that hardly anyone puts it down without reading it straight through. Even those who find the arguments unconvincing find it hard to resist the manner. *Utilitarianism* (1863) is rather different. It has less of the personal appeal which makes the *Autobiography* and *Liberty* so compelling; but it is a model of philosophical exposition. It seizes the reader's attention, invites him to consider argument after argument, every one of them lucidly expressed, energetically defended and its rivals briskly seen off. As much as Plato, who can seize our attention across two and a half millennia by sheer argumentative energy, Mill never lets go of the reader.

Nevertheless, *Utilitarianism* is a curiosity. It is certainly a 'philosophical classic' – that is, it is widely read, it is the definitive statement of a distinctive doctrine, it is frequently controverted, and as frequently rises phoenix-like from its own ashes to be defended and controverted again. Yet *Utilitarianism* is unusual in the degree to which it has become a classic through the efforts of its opponents rather than those of its friends, and its use for the past eighty years as a set book in introductory courses in moral philosophy means that it is better known for its supposed faults than for its many actual virtues. That it has become a philosophical classic at all is slightly odd, for Mill never had it in mind to write a treatise on moral philosophy and he never did so.

His contribution to the reinterpretation of 'the utilitarian philosophy' is scattered piecemeal throughout his work. He attacked what he thought of as the debased and time serving utilitarianism of William Paley in a youthful essay on the teaching of philosophy in the University of Cambridge;[7] he came to terms with Bentham in two essays devoted to him,[8] as well as in a companion essay on Coleridge, and in another (printed here) which he devoted to one of Bentham's critics and a long-standing antagonist of his own, William Whewell, the Master of Trinity College, Cambridge; he explained the difference between argument in scientific and in practical matters, first in an essay on the nature of economics,[9] then in the last chapter of his *System of Logic*; and he discussed the freedom of the will and the nature of moral responsibility, both in the *Logic* and in his *Examination of Sir William Hamilton's Philosophy*. It is arguable that his essay on *Liberty* contributes as much to our understanding of Mill's moral philosophy as *Utilitarianism* does – indeed, I shall argue so below.

Utilitarianism was written as a series of essays in *Fraser's Magazine*; they appeared in October, November and December 1861 and the three essays were recast as five chapters when they were republished as a book in 1863. *Fraser's Magazine* was an intelligently written monthly review, not an academic journal – it was another twenty years before philosophical journals became part of the academic scene. Its readership was mildly radical, but not, so to speak, a 'committed' readership. Mill's essays, therefore, were not written with the weight of reference of his attack on Sir William Hamilton, nor were they as ambitious as his *Logic*. The *Logic* had been a 'manifesto' of the empirical and inductive approach to science and social science; it was intended to be comprehensive in its scope – and so it was.[10] *Utilitarianism* is not like that. Mill was not in any case a 'professional philosopher' – the breed hardly existed as a part of English academic life – and on this occasion particularly he was trying to persuade a lay audience of what seemed to him to be some fairly elementary truths. Whether he ever saw at all deeply into the logical puzzles which entangle utilitarian ethics, and whose solution and restatement provide contemporary students with their bread and butter, is problematic. What is perfectly clear is that *Utilitarianism* is not written to clear the logical puzzles which have intrigued Mill's critics and commentators. It is written to persuade the readers of *Fraser's Magazine* that there can be morality without religion, that a utilitarian is as well able as anyone else to do his duty just because it is his duty and without ulterior motives, that making utility or pleasure the ultimate test of good and bad conduct is far from espousing a 'pig philosophy' whose highest ideal is the contentment of the swinish multitude.

The character of Mill's short essay is best appreciated by contrasting it with two works of his which were avowedly systematic and comprehensive treatises – his *Logic* and his *Principles of Political Economy* – and with Henry Sidgwick's *Methods of Ethics*. All three are strikingly different in tone and approach, as well as in their bulk. At some sixty pages, *Utilitarianism* is barely a tenth of their length. More importantly, it is brisk and polemical throughout, where they are magisterial, and ready to canvass any number of objections and alternatives. It is a highly selective snapshot of the field of ethics, avowedly intended to answer what Mill supposed to be the most common misconceptions of the utilitarian philosophy. Sidgwick's *Methods of Ethics* was written to be just the sort of systematic treatise *Utilitarianism* was not; it was a piece of professional philosophy. Certainly, it also defended utilitarianism; but its caution, its canvassing of endless small problems, its continual adjustment of the utilitarianism it defended to difficulties which its application to practice showed up, all stamp it as an academic treatise, a work of the study, and not an exercise in practical persuasion. Mill's essay was written to strike a blow in his lifelong campaign against what he thought of as the irrational conservatism of his opponents and the dangerous narrowness of his allies.

Mill wrote as a polemicist, even if he was a polemicist whose main aim was to reconcile the disciples of Bentham and the followers of Coleridge. His essays on Bentham and Coleridge are the work of a man concerned with the broad intellectual and political culture of the age, not the work of a philosopher in the academic twentieth-century sense. There is nothing of what today is described as 'conceptual analysis' either in the essays or in *Utilitarianism*, nor are they restricted to narrowly 'moral' topics. It is not just that Bentham was a legal reformer, and Coleridge a poet – Coleridge's philosophical writings on morals and politics are as voluminous as Mill's. It is rather that Mill wrote to defend utilitarianism as a guide to practice in all walks of life; to do that he certainly had to interpret the principle of utility in such a way as to clear it of confusion and to render it acceptable to his readers. But essays in persuasion are not on all fours with essays in analysis, and to understand Mill, it is necessary to understand what his purposes were. To understand those, we must look briefly at the history of utilitarian ethics, and at Mill's biography.

Precursors and Opponents

Mill thought that he had been the first person to employ the term 'utilitarianism' when he coined the term 'utilitarian' to describe the allegiances of himself and his friends in the 1820s. He was certainly not the first, for Bentham himself had done so in 1781; but if he was less original than he supposed, it is none the less worth noticing that writers whom the twentieth century unhesitatingly describes as 'utilitarians' were not themselves conscious of defending an '-ism'. Eighteenth-century rationalists and reformers, such as Beccaria and Helvetius, who argued that the test of institutions was their contribution to human happiness or the *utilité générale* now seem to us to have been Mill's forerunners and early defenders of utilitarianism. But this is largely an illusion fostered by hindsight. It is not merely that they themselves evidently were not conscious of playing such a part, any more than Galileo was conscious of being a precursor of Newton. The crucial point is that they were neither appealing to, nor concerned to construct, a systematic moral theory which needed to be articulated, clarified and defended. Even William Godwin, whose *Political Justice* is a systematic moral and political treatise and gives an account of what he called 'political justice' that identifies political justice with the pursuit of the greatest happiness, was not a fully fledged utilitarian.[11]

This may seem a perverse judgement, when Godwin derived from this account of justice extreme conclusions which are often cited to show the difficulties utilitarianism can face. So, for instance, Godwin argues that gratitude is not a virtue – if justice demands that we pursue the greatest happiness, I do no more

15

than my duty in bestowing a gift on the person to whom it does most good; since I do no more than my duty, he or she has no call to be grateful. Conversely, if I bestow it where it does less than the most good, I am failing in my duty and gratitude is even more out of place; it would be very much like expressing gratitude for a gift of stolen goods. By the same token, family loyalties are misguided. In a memorable passage, Godwin raised the question whether I ought in a fire to save Archbishop Fenelon or Archbishop Fenelon's chambermaid, *supposing that the chambermaid is my mother or my sister*.[12] The answer was clear; I ought to rescue the Archbishop because he would do more good than the chambermaid. The fact that I was related to her was neither here nor there. In later editions, Godwin slightly softened the argument and agreed that the domestic affections could themselves contribute to the greatest happiness. Still, there is no doubt that he took the greatest happiness to be the test of the justice of my actions – does it not follow that he was a 'utilitarian' in the full sense of the term?

There is no conclusive answer to the question, but there are strong reasons for saying that he was not. For one thing, he talked constantly of the 'justice' of our actions, and his theory was couched in terms of 'rights'. A self-conscious utilitarian is, as we shall see, aware that considerations of justice fit rather awkwardly into utilitarianism; and utilitarians would be cautious about employing the concept of rights – Bentham, indeed, thought that except in legal contexts, all talk of rights was nonsense. For another, Godwin gave pride of place in his scheme to the doctrine that individuals possess what he calls 'the right of private judgement', the right to act only on their own view of what is right and wrong. What he called 'the unspeakably beautiful doctrine' that every individual be guided by his or her own judgement and by nothing else meant that Godwin was a 'philosophical anarchist'; governments were intrinsically illegitimate since they claimed the right to violate the most precious right their subjects possessed. It is a doctrine which is exceedingly hard to reconcile with utilitarianism, though one which is not too hard to trace back to Godwin's background as a Dissenting minister. Finally, Godwin's conception of moral judgement and moral argument owes everything to eighteenth-century rationalism and nothing to nineteenth-century utilitarianism. He held that justice was grounded in the nature of things and in the eternal reason which underpinned the organization of the universe; this was at least a rationalistic view of ethics and perhaps a view which presupposed some kind of theism. In all these ways, Godwin's ethics is far removed from Mill's.[13]

Hume is another seeming ancestor of utilitarianism who turns out on closer inspection to be something rather different. Hume certainly held many views which utilitarians hold, and his cast of mind is one which many utilitarians have found sympathetic. Hume was entirely opposed to contractarian theories of government; he did not think that governments had acquired their authority over their subjects through any sort of social contract in fact – most governments, he said, had originated in force and fraud; and he was sure that any such contract would have been futile in principle – since only those who actually signed would have been bound by it, leaving their descendants as free as ever. Moreover, it was no easier to explain why we ought to take any notice of promises which we ourselves had made than to explain why we ought to take any notice of the wishes of our government. All authority needed explanation; and an explanation which made sense of the obligation to keep promises would make equally good sense of the obligation to obey government – but without deriving the latter obligation from the former.

Hume explained both in terms of the contribution of conventions and conventionally accepted institutions to general utility. Did this make him a utilitarian? Again, not entirely. What Hume was interested in was the way in which the mind leaped from factual premises to moral judgements – I observe that a friend has broken a promise; I judge that he has done wrong; but what takes me from the observation to the judgement? Hume saw that this was not a *logical* process, strictly considered.[14] That is, if I say 'he said that he would take his aunt to hospital; he did not do so; nothing prevented him from doing so; I approve very much of his behaviour' I might be expressing an odd moral position, but I would not be contradicting myself. For Hume, an inference was a matter of reason only if self-contradiction was involved in denying the inference. So ethics was not a matter of reason. It must, therefore, be a matter of feeling. In Hume's view, what launched moral judgements was the dictate of a moral sense. This moral sense was simply one of the human faculties, and Hume's account of its workings is presented as a psychological description. Hume's aim was not to present us with a standard by which we could *test* our existing moral intuitions and remodel them where necessary. If he had any aim other than that of gratifying a legitimate curiosity about the nature of moral attitudes, it was that of curbing sectarian strife by inducing in his readers some scepticism about the claims of revealed religion and some tolerance towards the variety of moral outlooks to be found among mankind. Mill neither believed in a moral sense, nor contented himself with describing its deliverances. Utilitarianism – at least in so far as Mill subscribed to it – was a reforming doctrine, and although Bentham and Mill accepted a view of human psychology much like that of Hume, both Bentham and Mill were hostile to any suggestion that we possess a 'moral sense'.

Mill's view was that it was true as a matter of psychological fact that we possess distinctively moral reactions to the objects of approval and disapproval. To that extent, no one could deny that we possess a 'moral sense'. 'It is a fact in human nature, that we have moral judgements and moral feelings. We judge certain actions and dispositions to be right, others wrong; this we call approving and disapproving them. We have also feelings of pleasure in the contemplation of the former class of actions and dispositions – feelings of dislike and aversion to the latter; which feelings, as everybody must be conscious, do not exactly resemble any other of our feelings of pain or pleasure.'[15] The important question, however, was not whether we had such sensations, but how they related to the distinction between moral and immoral actions or dispositions. What Mill was invariably at odds with was the claim that the distinction between the moral and the immoral is a 'peculiar and inscrutable property in the acts themselves, which we perceive by a sense, as we perceive colours by sight'. There were two distinct questions to be answered; one, whether there are distinctively moral reactions, the other, what the test is of the morality and immorality of conduct or character.

Only if the second question is kept distinct from the first can we answer the question whether a person's moral reactions are rightly focused. Mill's complaint against all 'intuitive' theories of morality was that they made criticism impossible by making our moral reactions self-justifying; if moral distinctions are just what our moral sense perceives when it is working properly, there is no room for argument about whether we might be wrong.

Mill regarded William Paley as an unequivocal utilitarian because he denied the conclusions of the intuitive theory of ethics. He was not, however, a utilitarian of Mill's persuasion in one crucial respect. Paley treated the contribution of actions and dispositions to the general happiness as an index of their morality or immorality, but not because the general happiness is itself the ultimate goal. Rather, the general happiness is an index of God's wishes; what *makes* actions and sentiments right or wrong is that God commands or forbids them. Their status as moral or immoral is a matter of divine legislation. This doctrine, as may well be imagined, Mill will not entertain for one moment. Although he disagreed with Kant on almost every issue in philosophy, they stood together in insisting that questions of good and evil cannot be reduced to divine prescription and proscription. It must always be possible for us to ask whether God's commands are themselves good; and if an evil deity commanded us to do his bidding, the moral course would be to resist. Mill did not object to linking God and utility; if God was moved by the general happiness to issue a moral code and support it with sanctions, so much the better. But the goodness of God, and of his code, depended upon the standard to which he and it referred, not upon God's own say-so.

Paley was further lowered in Mill's eyes by the mean-spirited account of virtue which he derived from his deplorable account of morality and immorality. For Paley held that action out of a regard for the general welfare was not virtuous; to act virtuously demanded reference to God's commandments, and the reference required was that we must act in order to secure our own eternal happiness. Altruistically doing good for the sake of others was not virtuous. God tells us what to do, and attaches to his commandments a promise of rewards and a threat of punishment. Paley takes the surprising position that to be virtuous is to act self-centredly out of a regard to these threats. Mill takes the common-sensical view that this sort of selfish behaviour may be better than nothing but can hardly be the height of virtue. Virtue demands that we act out of respect for the law and its purposes, not out of a desire to save our own skins. Add to this Paley's notorious willingness to invoke his doctrines to justify mental reservations by clergymen who found it hard to believe the Thirty-nine Articles of the Church of England, and his defence of the political and moral laxity of eighteenth-century public life, and Mill's unwillingness to have utilitarianism tarred with the sins of Paley is understandable. None the less, Paley was unequivocally a utilitarian, even in Mill's eyes. But he was, as Mill said, simply a very bad one.

Mill was more willing to acknowledge as utilitarian precursors some thinkers who were doubtfully utilitarian at all. He described Aristotle as a 'judicious utilitarian' and declared that the teachings of Jesus contained the perfection of the utilitarian doctrine. How sincere he was in that latter declaration is an open question; there is some distance between claiming that 'love thy neighbour as thyself' is a good utilitarian principle and claiming that Jesus was a utilitarian. Polemically, of course, Mill was well advised to imply that Jesus had been a utilitarian; it cleared utilitarianism of the taint of atheism. Philosophically it was rather less plausible. Indeed, the ethics of both Aristotle and Jesus illustrate quite neatly one way in which utilitarianism is distinctive and Aristotle and Jesus are not utilitarians.

Aristotle shared a number of views with all utilitarians. His ethical theory was teleological, not deontological. That is, the fundamental concept in Aristotle's ethics was goodness rather than duty; 'teleological' theories, as the name suggests, are theories which focus on the goals or ends of conduct, 'deontological' theories, as again the name suggests, are theories which concentrate on whether conduct conforms to rules or orders. Aristotle's interest lay in the question of what kind of good different sorts of conduct aimed at. And Mill's description of him as a utilitarian might be thought to be justified by Aristotle's claim that the ultimate goal in ethics was 'eudaemonia' or 'well-being' – as for his judiciousness, nobody has ever doubted that a man who looked for virtue in the pursuit of the mean between two extremes was a paragon of judiciousness.

Granted that he was judicious, was he a judicious utilitarian, however? The answer is that he was not. He was not, because he had a very different conception of what ethics was about from any that Mill entertained. Aristotle was interested first and foremost in what 'good' conduct did for the agent whose conduct was in question. It was not the 'good' he did to others which was central; nor was it always the good he would do himself, considered in an instrumental way. What he was interested in was how the virtues such as generosity, courage, and (what most people think an odd candidate for a virtue) pride contributed to leading 'a good life'. It is noteworthy that it is a good life on which he focuses, rather than on a life of goodness; 'goodness' in that sense already has overtones of living for others and self-sacrifice which are entirely foreign to Aristotle. What Aristotle relies on is the thought that nature destines men to live in society and to live the kind of social and intellectual life that a moderately well off and well educated Athenian citizen would lead. (Nature has lives planned for women, slaves and non-Greeks, too, and these have their own goodness, but of a more limited kind. It is not a reproach to a woman that she cannot lead the best life; but it would be a reproach if she did not lead a womanly life. Mill fought all his life for equality for women, looked forward to the day when India attained self-government, and thought that citizenship should be extended to everyone who was literate and employable; he was fiercely hostile to the idea that Nature planned anything for us, and was at odds with everything in Aristotle except his exaltation of the life of the active citizen and his insistence that we can pursue our own happiness in pursuing ideal ends such as knowledge and self-improvement.) The goodness of our lives was a matter of their matching the natural model; certainly, a man who leads a good life will in general and on average be happy – or 'eudaemonic' – but happiness is not the standard of goodness. In a sense there is no general standard of goodness in Aristotle, because goodness is a matter of functioning properly in the way Nature intends. The connection between happiness and goodness is that happiness is the effect of good functioning for a human being, rather than the test of good functioning.

It is clearer still that the attempt to pass off Jesus as a utilitarian is special pleading – at any rate in the way in which Mill does it. For Jesus comes to reveal God's law; it is true that the law so revealed is an expansion from the Mosaic Law of the Old Testament, and the God revealed in His law is the God of Love rather than the God of Wrath. None the less, the most one can say is that God so organizes the world that those who obey His law will be rewarded with happiness and eternal life. What constitutes moral goodness is obedience to God's commandments, and the test of an individual's goodness of conduct is his or her conformity to those commandments. There is no question of testing the merits of divine commandment by asking whether those commandments make good sense as utilitarian precepts. We may trust that they somehow do, because we believe in a God of Love who cares for His creation, but we are not invited to pronounce on the merits of divine legislation. Among genuine utilitarians there were few real Christians; Mill and his father were agnostics, and so was Bentham, though they all had a high regard for Jesus and a correspondingly low opinion of St Paul.

An exception was John Austin. He believed that the obligatoriness of morality was a matter of divine legislation. Moral obligation was the obligation to obey the divine *fiat* – a close analogue to Austin's account of the obligatoriness of domestic law, where obligation was the counterpart of the authority of the sovereign, and his authority was no more than his ability to impose his rules on the people over whom he was sovereign. But Austin was a utilitarian because he thought that the point of divine legislation was to promote happiness. He, therefore, could distinguish between the *obligatoriness* of moral rules and their *goodness*; their obligatoriness was a matter of their being laid down by the ultimate sovereign; their goodness was a matter of their being such that if we obeyed them general happiness would be promoted. Austin, therefore, escapes Mill's objections to Paley, because he opens a sufficient gap between something's being commanded by God and its being good to do it. Mill, however, drew no such distinction; or, to be more accurate, he never employed it for this purpose. He took it for granted that moral obligatoriness and moral goodness were logically so related that the foundation of the obligation to be moral lay in the goodness of the rules which utilitarianism dictated.

The paradigm of deontological and non-utilitarian moral theories was the moral theory presented in Immanuel Kant's *Groundwork of the Metaphysics of Morals* – a work which Mill found quite preposterously unpersuasive.[16] Kant insisted that the goodness of moral action was wholly a matter of its motive, and that the only morally acceptable motive was respect for the moral law. In other words, morality was a matter of doing our duty just because it was our duty and for no other reason whatever. This is a deontological theory of the purest kind, for it makes dutiful conduct the central feature of ethics, and looks for a distinctively moral form of goodness in conduct, which it finds in dutifulness. So, if I promise to give someone five pounds I may not ask whether they need it, whether I like the use to which they will put it, whether I can afford it as readily as when I made the promise; all I may do is hand over the money just because I have promised. The attractions of this view are obvious. Most of us do think that 'I promised' is very nearly conclusive as a reason for doing what we promised; most of us admire people who are scrupulous about keeping promises, who do not look for ways of wriggling out of their obligations and so on. Even where we are willing to admit that we may take consequences into account in deciding whether to keep a promise, most of us feel that failing to keep it is somehow wrong, even if on balance we ought not to keep it.

The repulsive features of Kant's views are equally obvious. A man who visits a detested relative because he has promised to do so is a morally good man, because he is doing his duty; but the man who visits a much-loved relative out of spontaneous good nature is not morally good because he has obeyed the inducements of inclination. Most of us have clear views about which of the two we would rather have as a friend, and think that Kant devalues good nature and overvalues rigorousness. There are contexts in which Kant's views seem even stranger. Lying, for instance, is absolutely impermissible; but what of the traditional dilemma of the man who is asked by a would-be murderer for the whereabouts of his intended victim. Most of us would think lying a positive good on such an occasion; Kant merely wriggles uncomfortably and suggests ways of evading telling a direct lie.

The explanation of Kant's discomfort comes in another anti-utilitarian feature of his theory. If we ask how we are to know what rules to obey, the utilitarian has an answer and so does Kant. The utilitarian's answer is that we ask which rules would best promote the general happiness; Kant's answer is that we must ask what rules we could lay down as lawgivers to all rational creatures without involving ourselves in contradiction. It is easy to see why the obligation to keep promises and tell the truth figures so prominently in Kant. The rule 'always tell lies' is self-defeating. Unless most people most of the time tell the truth, there can be no lying, because lying is parasitic upon the near universality of truth telling. Similarly, the rule 'break promises' is self-defeating. Unless there was a general understanding that promises are to be kept, there would be no such thing as a promise to be broken. My saying 'yes, I will lend you five pounds tomorrow' would be no guide to my conduct and so the very expression would become senseless. What Kant does not seem to notice is that it is only a rule with the same universality – but a negative universality – as the rules prescribing the telling of truth and the keeping of prom-ises which is vulnerable to this argument. A rule which says 'keep your promises unless . . .' may be more complicated to develop, but it is no more self-destructive than the rule which says 'keep promises'. Nor would most of us think a man unduly lacking in scruples if his maxim of action was 'return what you have bor-rowed unless there is a high risk of damage'; it is the man who returned his neighbour's shotgun without thinking whether his neighbour might be contemplating homicide whom we should think a menace to society.[7]

It is unfair to Kant to introduce him here only in his character as a target of Mill's objections; none the less, to discover what utilitarianism was, no method is so effective as that of contrast – seeing what utilitarians were eager to emphasize that it was not.

The unfairness is somewhat mitigated by two other considerations. The first is that Kant's insistence that the virtuous man
acted on principle and not for the sake of consequences was so
widely believed by Mill's readers that Mill found himself obliged
to give an account of how it could be true but consistent with a
consequentialist, utilitarian morality. The other is that if Mill
was brutal in his dismissal of Kant's attempt to derive moral
obligations from the requirement that morality should not contradict itself, he was tougher still on his utilitarian forerunners,
including the greatest and the closest of them.

Bentham's utilitarianism

Bentham was for Mill the purest representative of what was right
with utilitarianism and what was incomplete or wrong with it.
Bentham's views define utilitarianism for us almost as much as
they did for Mill. When Mill was in revolt against the education
he had received at the hands of his father and Bentham, and com-
plained of the narrow and over-simplified picture of human
nature and society prevalent among the philosophical radicals, it
was Bentham's position which was always singled out for discussion. As the extract from Bentham's *Principles of Morals and
Legislation* shows, Bentham fulfils all the requirements of the pure
utilitarian. He was hostile to moral-sense theories, to theories of
natural law, and to all theories which allowed anyone to treat his
or her own views as beyond the reach of argument and contradiction. He held, quite unequivocally, that pleasure was the only
thing good in itself, and that states of affairs were to be judged
by how much pleasure (or pain) they gave to those involved; the
ultimate standard therefore could only be the general happiness.
As for what prompted men and women to do their duty, the
motives under which they acted were reducible to the pursuit of
pleasure and the avoidance of pain. In one of the most famous
phrases in the history of ethics, Bentham began his *Principles* by
summing up these claims, 'Nature has placed mankind under the
governance of two sovereign masters, *pain* and *pleasure*. It is for
them alone to point out what we ought to do, as well as to deter-

mine what we shall do. On the one hand the standard of right and wrong, on the other the chain of causes and effects, are fastened to their throne.'[18]

Bentham paid little attention to the task of proving utilitarianism true. Indeed, he held that it was both unnecessary and impossible to prove the principle of utility, for reasons which Mill reiterated many years later in *Utilitarianism*. Bentham asks of the principle, 'Is it susceptible of any direct proof?' and replies, 'It should seem not: for that which is used to prove everything else cannot itself be proved: a chain of proofs must have their commencement somewhere. To give such proof is as impossible as it is needless.'[19] What Bentham appears to expect is that readers who clear their minds of prejudice will see that there is no real competitor to the principle. This is why he begins by spelling out what the principle of utility is: 'that principle which approves or disapproves of every action whatever, according to the tendency which it appears to have to augment or diminish the happiness of the party whose interest is in question: or, what is the same thing in other words, to promote or oppose that happiness.'[20] Bentham also appears to think that words like *ought*, *right*, *wrong*, and the like are meaningful only when they are used with reference to utility. 'Of an action that is conformable to the principle of utility, one may always say either that it is one that ought to be done, or at least that it is not one that ought not to be done. One may say also, that it is right that it should be done; at least that it is not wrong that it should be done: that it is a right action; at least that it is not a wrong action. When thus interpreted, the words *ought*, and *right* and *wrong*, and others of that stamp, having a meaning: when otherwise, they have none.'[21]

Mill's 'Remarks on Bentham's Philosophy' complain, and rightly, that Bentham is altogether too quick and too casual on this point. It is one thing to claim that we can only argue about the rightness and wrongness of actions if we adopt some calculable standard such as the principle of utility; it is quite another to claim that 'right' means 'conformable to utility'. Similarly, it is one thing to claim that argument and the achievement of consistency are only possible if we adopt the principle of utility, and quite another to claim that nobody really accepts any other principle.

As Mill says, it is all too apparent that many people do accept other principles. It is one thing to claim that if people are clear-headed they will come to adopt utility as their guide, and quite another to claim that unless they accept it they are talking literal nonsense.[22]

Bentham's casualness may have stemmed from his conviction that no sensible person could disagree with him. Certainly, he defended utility by attacking what he thought of as its absurd rivals. One such argument is both subtle and effective; people who object to the evil results of utilitarianism are themselves utilitarians, for they are employing the utilitarian standard to criticize the effects of its being employed. What such critics are objecting to is not the principle of utility but to misapplications of it.[23] But Bentham's way with his opponents is commonly quicker still; he argues, in essence, that anyone who does not accept the principle of utility must end by supposing that his own sentiments ought to be a sufficient guide to all mankind. This he christens 'ipse dixitism', that is, the view that mankind ought to follow the principles I follow, simply because it is I who utter them. The other title he confers on this way of proceeding is 'the principle of caprice'. Unlike many philosophers, who have thought an appeal to individual conscience the truest part of moral argument, Bentham asks us all to consider whether an appeal to the dictates of our own consciences is not 'despotical and hostile to all the rest of the human race' and 'anarchical' in addition, because liable to result in as many answers as there are questioners.[24]

As if suspecting that opponents will be unconvinced by so short a way with them, Bentham devoted one of the most amusing chapters of the *Principles* to listing and demolishing 'principles adverse to that of utility'. The argument in all cases is the same, however. Principles which are different from that of utility fall into three errors – though they may, on re-interpretation fall into one, two or all three simultaneously. One error besets moral principles which are genuinely opposed to utility, but cannot consistently be pursued; the principle of asceticism falls into this category. A man may think that the avoidance of pleasure is a proper rule for his private conduct, but he cannot try to legislate on the strength of it – Bentham thought that legislation was inevitably connected with giving people inducements to conform to what the legislator enacted, and those inducements had to be connected with their happiness.[25] So utility creeps back in. In any case asceticism is incoherent because it bears the record of its history as a moral principle within itself. Mankind began by adopting ascetic and self-denying principles in order to gain everlasting life from some deity or other; that was a utilitarian reason, rather than the adoption of pure asceticism. Only the habit of self-mortification institutionalized in monasteries and the like gained any currency for the idea that pain is good in itself. Asceticism is vulnerable to the question, 'What good does it do to pursue ascetic principles?' and any coherent answer is a utilitarian one. The second vice of non-utilitarian principles is that they aim at no fixed outcome. If Bentham is right in objecting to asceticism on the ground that anti-utilitarian principles are incoherent, it takes little further argument to show that principles which coincide on and off with the dictates of utility are coherent when they coincide and incoherent when they do not.[26] What he labels the 'principle of sympathy and antipathy' aims at no fixed outcome; as the name suggests, it erects our sympathies and antipathies into the standard of judgement. As our sympathies and antipathies alter, so do the standards we apply. This vice is connected with the last, which is that all such principles simply throw us back on the sentiments of the persons whose judgements are at issue. The various phrases which cover this fact are listed by Bentham in an extended footnote – theories of the moral sense, or of common sense, or the rule of right, or the fitness of things, or the law of nature, or the law of reason, of right reason and so endlessly on, all suffer the one crucial deficiency, which is that they refer to no fixed and external standard.[27]

One can see here the impact on Bentham's theory of morality of his hostility to the cumbersome irrationality and inhumanity of the English legal system. The aim of Bentham's entire existence was to bring order and good sense to the chaotic jumble which passed for the law. Often Bentham's aims were utilitarian in the narrow sense; that is, he was appalled at the complexity, the delay and the expense of civil litigation. Only the lawyers profited from the system; ordinary people could not know whether their property was theirs to call their own without risking its loss at the hands of the lawyers, and did not know when they might inadvertently commit some crime or other. His ultimate ambition was to construct a code of such simplicity that everyone might carry an abridgement of it in his pocket, and know his rights and duties as easily as he might nowadays look up the time of a train. To construct a simple code was itself a very complicated business; unless we were clear what had to be included and excluded, we should infallibly make a bad job of its construction. Unless we had a perfectly clear view of the springs of human action, and the nature of our raw material, we should fail to rear the fabric of felicity. So, it is easy to see that in Bentham's eyes the point of the principle of utility was to provide the fixed standard by which the goodness and badness of law was to be estimated, and that almost everything paled into insignificance beside the task of showing the simplicity and clarity of the utilitarian guide and denouncing the mass of sentimentality and subjectivity which passed for its rivals. Mill, complaining of the narrowness and over-simplicity of Bentham's view of the world none the less agreed that 'the most permanently valuable part of his works' was 'the uniform and unflinching application of his own greatest-happiness principle' to 'practical ethics and legislation'.[28]

It is this which leads to two characteristic features of Bentham's utilitarianism. The first is his emphasis on the importance of calculating the 'pay-off' from different policies and therefore from different regulations, different punishments and all the rest of it. Committed as he was to the view that it is pleasure and pain which do prompt our actions and to the principle that the pleasure and pain of those whose interests are at stake is the standard of what ought to prompt our actions, he moved inexorably to a view of law and morality which stressed the role of punishment and reward in squaring the individual's happiness with that of humanity generally. He began by distinguishing 'the four sanctions or sources of pain and pleasure' with which the lawgiver had to work – the physical, the political, the moral and the religious. Physical sanctions work through natural causes, political sanctions are imposed by judges and magistrates, moral sanctions are the sanctions of public opinion and popular sentiment, while religious sanctions are those which may or may not befall us at the hands of God. Bentham's point, predictably enough, is that when the lawgiver employs the physical and political sanctions, he will find that the moral and religious sanctions are at work also. 'In every inch of his career are the operations of the political magistrate liable to be aided or impeded by these two foreign powers: who, one or other of them, or both, are sure to be either his rivals or his allies. Does it happen to him to leave them out of his calculations? He will be sure almost to find himself mistaken in the result.'[29]

In working out their interaction with the physical sanctions at his command, the lawgiver makes use of the 'felicific calculus'. That is, he must calculate the combined effect of the features of a situation which dictate how productive it is of happiness or unhappiness. What Bentham supposed was that we could calculate the value of a pleasure or a pain according to various factors, of which he listed seven. The intrinsic properties of a pleasure are '1. Its *intensity*; 2. Its *duration*; 3. Its *certainty* or *uncertainty*; 4. Its *propinquity* or *remoteness*.' But we must also take into account the chance of a pain being followed by another pain or a pleasure by another pleasure. Accordingly two further factors are '5. Its *fecundity*, or the chance it has of being followed by sensations of the same kind: that is, pleasures, if it be a pleasure: pains, if it be a pain. 6. Its *purity*, or the chance it has of *not* being followed by sensations of the *opposite* kind: that is, pains, if it be a pleasure: pleasures, if it be a pain.' Finally, there is the question of how many people share the pleasure or pain, so the final factor is '7. Its *extent*, that is, the number of persons to whom it *extends*; or (in other words) who are affected by it.'[30] Much ink has been spilled over the question of how seriously Bentham intended us to take this as a calculus. It is obvious that there is no ready way to (say) trade off the intensity of a pain against its duration, or to find some unit of valuation in which to trade either against its probability. Whether this is fatal to Bentham's project is contentious. One might say that the recent development of the theory of games is proof that Bentham's project was entirely rational;

one might on the other hand argue that the theory of games is irrelevant to moral philosophy precisely because it is really a branch of probability theory and tells us nothing about happiness and misery, virtue and vice. Happily, we can set this argument to one side here. It is enough to notice that Mill at any rate never thought of Bentham as trying to give moral evaluation the certainty of a mathematical calculus; so far as Mill was concerned, it was characteristic of Bentham that he should exaggerate a reasonable concern for clarity and objectivity in ethical argument into the wholly implausible suggestion that we might make precise calculations of the worth of actions and characters.

But, this brings us to the second characteristic feature of Bentham's utilitarianism, and one which was much more salient for Mill's criticism of his work. Bentham's interest was largely in law; the good side of this, as Mill always insisted, was that Bentham was concerned with the detail of legislation, with the following through of cause and effect to discover just what consequences we might expect from a given law, or from the breach of it. This was what Mill called the discovery of *axiomata media* (the expression was originally Bacon's), or middle-range principles. The 'greatest happiness principle' is too abstract and remote a principle to guide us. Moreover, says Mill, 'happiness' is simply too indefinite a goal to take as our target. But it would be irrational to try to decide every case on its merits without some principled way of telling what merits it has. Accordingly, all the interesting work is done at the middle level; Bentham's genius was to bring order into this middle range – to see clearly what was at stake in systems of election, in rules for the establishment and transfer of property rights, and so on.[31]

And this was the area in which Bentham's mind functioned most like a lawyer's. He was concerned with ensuring that people acted to promote security, predictability, and efficiency. It was not the law's business to make us sensitive, subtle, poetically minded; it was the law's business to keep us from behaving in such a way as would make us a thorough nuisance to our neighbours and to establish rules which allow us to co-operate with each other. So Bentham's theory of punishment and Bentham's attitude to motive and intention were wholly external and consequentialist. A motive, considered in its narrowest extent, was whatever perception of pleasure and pain moved people to act. Given Bentham's view that pleasure and pain were the only intrinsic good and evil, it followed that whatever was wrong with a 'mischievous' motive must lie in its consequences. The pleasure I get from the thought of your misery is intrinsically just one more pleasure; what is wrong with malice is that it leads us to act to bring about the ill in which we take that pleasure.[32] This makes Bentham's thinking on crime and punishment a strange mixture of the liberal and the illiberal.

The liberal aspect of the matter is that Bentham wished to keep the law from scrutinizing what goes on in our minds. So long as we do not make ourselves a menace to others, we should be left alone. This, of course, would lead to a tolerant attitude to what are commonly called 'victimless crimes' – homosexual relations between consenting adults, say, or smoking dope, or prostitution. It is no accident that much of the pressure for liberalization of the law in the twentieth century has come from a 'Benthamite' direction – from reformers who have taken it for granted that the general welfare is the proper object of the law, and that individual virtue is not, and who have asked whether the costs of prohibition and enforcement have produced any corresponding good.[33] In Britain at least legal reform has come through this humanitarian pressure rather than through an insistence on 'human rights'. Homosexual law reform, to take an obvious instance, was not the result of a popular conviction that homosexuals had the same natural right to implement their tastes as heterosexuals had; it was the result of a growing belief that the damage done by prohibition was greater than any good it did. By the same token, the legal side of the growth of the welfare state reflects a Benthamite belief that the rights of property owners may be reduced without undue risk, so long as the process is slow, steady and predictable; and this improvement in the legal position of the property-less and the worsening of the advantages of the propertied is justified if the overall welfare demands it.

This 'liberal' aspect of Benthamite utilitarianism is not its only aspect. There are two features worth observing. First, the uncon-cern with individual character save in its predictable effects also implies an unconcern for how individuals are treated, save for the effects of that. Bentham's *Panopticon*, the projected prison in which all inmates would be under the eye of their warders twenty-four hours a day, and in which every aspect of their behaviour would be controlled, is the epitome of benign illiberalism. 'Call them men, call them monks, call them soldiers, call them machines; I care not so long as they be happy ones,' said Bentham. Readers of *Brave New World* shudder at the words. Bentham described his projected prison as a 'mill for grinding rogues honest', and that cheerfully external and inhumane view of the criminal sums up what liberals fear in his ideas. Certainly Bentham did not advocate violent or cruel measures of punishment – they would do more harm than good, and the fear they induced in the law-abiding would be worse than anything they might achieve. But there is nothing to inhibit governments from, say, imposing indeterminate sentences allowing officials to keep a man in prison until they were satisfied with his behaviour.[34]

Second, in spite of Bentham's antipathy to natural rights, it may be that a belief in natural rights may be more reliably humane than a reliance on utility. Suppose a country contained many citizens who were racially prejudiced. If we calculate the utility of resisting them or appeasing them, we might decide that appeasing them was the better prospect. But liberals generally think that the prejudiced simply have no right to have their prejudices gratified and that those against whom they are prejudiced do have a right not to be the object of prejudice. As one recent writer puts it, the rights of the targets of prejudice 'trump' any calculations of overall utility.[35] There are several ways of putting this point; one way is to appeal to our intuition that making such a calculation is a way of sacrificing innocent individuals for the sake of others; another is to claim that counting the views of the prejudiced is a form of 'double-counting', because their utilities are dependent on the utilities of others. Without considering the merits of these suggestions, we can at least acknowledge that Bentham's disregard of the content of people's aspirations and his interest only in the effects of behaviour on overall utility is decidedly two-edged in its implications.

Mill's education – and his disillusionment with 'Benthamism'

This perception made Mill a relentless critic of Bentham. In a roundabout way it was the most important product of Mill's extraordinary education. Mill's education was not quite the relentless exercise in Benthamite indoctrination which legend suggests, but Bentham took a close interest in John Stuart Mill's progress, and James Mill wrote to Bentham of his hopes that the boy would be brought up a credit to them both. By the time Mill came to read Bentham at the age of sixteen he was already a utilitarian, and felt that Bentham had simply put into words what a rational person would believe already. But in his late teens, Mill worked for two years as amanuensis or as what a later age would have called an editorial assistant to Bentham; Bentham was preparing his *Rationale of Judicial Evidence*, and Mill's task was to collect Bentham's notes, collate them, try to reconstruct what the preferred version ought to look like and reduce the great man's chaotic writings to order. There is much that is comic in the spectacle of Bentham trying to bring order into English law amidst such disorder in his own study; for Mill, however, it meant two years of appallingly hard work, at a time when he was already emotionally and intellectually drained by the education he had received from his father.[36]

That education, detailed at length in his *Autobiography*, amounted to an experiment by the father on the son; James Mill wanted to see how much he could teach his son if he had him to himself, undistracted by schools and the company of other children. There is no doubt that the result was intellectually impressive; but by the time John Stuart Mill was twenty he was more than ready for rebellion – though he did not know it. In 1826, he fell into an acute depression; as he says, 'it occurred to me to put the question directly to myself, "Suppose that all your objects in life were realized; that all the changes in institutions and opinions which you are looking forward to, could be effected at this very instant: would this be a great joy and happiness to you?" And an irrepressible self-consciousness distinctly answered, "No!"'[37] The futility of a life devoted to the greatest happiness and itself barren of even the least happiness struck him forcibly. For what happened next we have only Mill's own word; none of his friends reported that he was ill, or moody, or lethargic, and the crisis was an interior one. How long it lasted is obscure; trying to fit dates to Mill's narrative is an ungrateful task. But that is beside the point. The point is what Mill made of the experience.

He decided that his depression was symbolic of what was wrong with Benthamism. Benthamism was arid, and emotionally unappealing; it was a cold, analytical, critical doctrine, which might do valuable service in helping men to manage the business arrangements of life with greater efficiency, but which could do nothing to help us find a meaning in life and inspire us to take any moral goal seriously. Mill did not write his *Autobiography* until thirty years after the event – he revised a good deal of his account of his early years a little before he died, but the account of his breakdown dates from 1854–55 – and his account of events carries a heavy weight of theory as well as some strong feeling. Mill's feelings are not hard to share; he thought that he had been brought up to be a calculating machine, and that he had never been taught to develop himself in his own way. The analytical side of his nature had been over-developed and the poetic side starved. This was undoubtedly unfair to James Mill, in the sense that his son's education included a great deal of poetry and other literature – but that was not how his son felt. James Mill's dominating personality had left his son feeling that he had no character of his own. Characteristically, Mill records that the event which brought him out of his depression was a sudden surge of emotion; he was reading Marmontel's *Memoirs*, and came across the passage where the hero's father has died and young Marmontel resolves to be everything to his family and so replace his father. 'A vivid conception of the scene and its feelings came over me, and I was moved to tears. From this moment my burthen grew lighter. The oppression of the thought that all feeling was dead within me, was gone. I was no longer hopeless: I was not a stock or a stone.'[38]

Reflecting on all this, Mill contrasted the men of the eighteenth century and the men of the nineteenth. The men of the eighteenth century were sceptical, unemotional, objective in their outlook.

They saw the folly and superstition of the *ancien régime* but they did not see the emotional supports which tradition and religious sentiment had provided. As he says in 'Coleridge', what Coleridge asks of an institution is 'what does it mean?' – looking, of course, not for the literal meaning, but looking to uncover the attachment which it sustains. Mill resolved to try to combine the virtues of the eighteenth century and the insights of the nineteenth. He would not succumb to mere eclecticism, sticking together whatever scraps of doctrine he could. He would think systematically, but broadly. As he said of this time, he took for his motto Goethe's 'many-sidedness', the conviction that any new intellectual system must be much richer than what he had been brought up on. Yet at the same time it must be as intellectually rigorous as that on which he had been brought up. If Francis Place thought that Mill had become a metaphysical mystic (a mistake made by Carlyle as well), Mill knew better.[39]

The essays on Bentham and Coleridge

This is why the essays on Bentham and Coleridge form admirable companion pieces. If Mill seems much friendlier to Coleridge, it must be remembered that Mill was writing in a 'Benthamite' journal and could expect his readers to be more hostile to Coleridge. Mill's comparison is straightforward. Bentham is tidy-minded, admirable as a reformer and as a legal systematizer, but entirely useless as a guide for the rest of life. He was a man of the study, who had few deep feelings himself and little general culture – his indifference to poetry is well known. Accordingly, it never struck him to point out that his doctrines were meant for a limited purpose, that of legal reform, and that we must look elsewhere for an insight into the meaning of life. Mill mocks Bentham's view of human motivation; everything is reduced to self-interest of one sort and another, and no account is taken of such central motives as the artist's passion for order, the hero's contempt for cowardly ways of carrying on, the insistence that we are acting subjects not passive objects.[40]

This leads to an important objection to Bentham. He was

unaware of the variety of considerations which morality in its largest sense embraces; he did not see that we may evaluate actions for their nobility and their sympathy as well as for their effects on other people's welfare. A man may, as Brutus did, kill his sons for the sake of the republic; this is noble, but not sympathetic – we admire him for the toughness with which he stuck to his principles, but we do not find him lovable. Morality in its narrowest sense – the avoidance of damage to the interests of others and meeting our obligations towards them – is a 'business' matter. The wider sense embraces far more than business matters; what Bentham never understood was that it did not matter only what we do, it mattered what sort of people we were. This in turn implies the rejection of Bentham's view that the only appraisal of motives which made sense was an appraisal of their predictable effects; a person who does his duty always and everywhere, but only because he is too feeble and cowardly to challenge other people's expectations, is justly the object of contempt. It is this insistence which links 'Bentham' to *Liberty*; for that essay is also devoted to the proposition that there is much more to life than morality narrowly construed, and that one of the most important of those wider ends is the cultivation of a strong-minded, independent, and adventurous individual character. From de Tocqueville, but also from his revolt against his father's overbearing personality, Mill acquired a horror of sheep-like passivity and a passion for personal independence.[41]

The difficulty was to find room for it in a utilitarian ethic. Bentham's doctrine has the overwhelming virtue of clarity. The object is to maximize happiness; the instrument for achieving it is the pressure of law and opinion on individuals; we cannot complain of individuals who always do what is for the best in utilitarian terms. As Bentham himself observed, he would cheerfully have thrown away free will if in so doing he could throw away the freedom to do wrong. This may be repulsive in various respects, but it is quite clear. Mill's difficulty is that he wanted much of the substance of the romantic insistence on variety, individuality and freedom, but believed all his life that the psychological theory to which his father and Bentham subscribed was the only possible basis of social science and moral theory alike.

So we find Mill praising Coleridge for his emphasis on history and culture; and we find him insisting that the poet's imagination has an indispensable contribution to make to moral and political theory. Coleridge, for instance, held views about the basis of political cohesion which Mill never ceased to praise. Bentham's political theory had a mysterious vacuum at its centre – if men were generally self-interested, which is why law is necessary and democracy desirable, the attachment of individuals to the laws and institutions of their country was somewhat mysterious. Why did they not go along with such laws as suited them and break the law when it was more convenient to do so? It was no use saying that they would be punished for doing so, since punishment also depended on those whose task it was to apprehend and punish offenders doing so without calculating whether it was in their interest to do it. If I know that those who are supposed to punish me will only do so if it is in their interest to do it, I shall have no great fear of punishment. To invoke the fear of punishment presupposes that *some* people at least will act altruistically. Bentham's only retort to such arguments was to suppose that it was a fact of human nature that many people derived pleasure themselves from contemplating the welfare of others, so that for many people at least there was no tension between self-interest and altruism. This retort in turn concedes too much or too little. If pressed, it subverts the distinction between self-interest and altruism on which the entire argument for the necessity of law and the virtues of democracy is founded. Otherwise, it seems to make the possibility of a stable society and polity hinge on an unexplained accident in human nature.

Coleridge's insistence that the social tie was stronger and more subtle than that seemed to Mill to be the beginnings of wisdom; to see the strength of social cohesion as the result of a complicated historical development was a further virtue; to see it implicated in all manner of intellectual and emotional commitments was evidently right and showed up Bentham's ideas for the over-simplifications they were. Coleridge's effect on Mill's views on democracy and much else was powerful. Mill's *Considerations on Representative Government* insisted that the discussion of forms of government could only proceed on the basis of a philosophy of history and an account of human progress which would determine the form of government most apt to develop the abilities already present in a society and to bring into existence those required for further progress. Similarly, *Liberty* reflected Mill's debts to Coleridge, not only as we have seen already in the sense that Mill's conception of what was worthwhile in human character owed so much to Coleridge and Wordsworth, but also in Mill's insistence that his views were adapted to the peculiarities of the English and to the demands of the age. *Liberty* was not a timeless plea for freedom for everyone; it was an argument aimed at and intended for an increasingly comfortable and conformist Victorian England.

But in accepting so much, Mill rejected a great deal. He remained an obdurate empiricist in psychology and epistemology. Coleridge's conception of the 'active mind' was wholly foreign to Mill, who emphatically subscribed to 'the school of Locke'; and this meant that there could be no question of Mill accepting Coleridge's view that all serious inquiry reveals the idea or essence of a phenomenon. Mill's view of science, whether natural science or social science, could be summed up in the empiricist claim that all science tells us about the world is what regular laws it obeys – and these laws are not derived from essences, but are simply regular sequences of cause and effect. In much the same spirit of refusing to go beyond the limits of his empiricist upbringing, Mill insisted that Coleridge's insights into social and political life were not embedded in a sound view of social science generally. In political economy, for instance, his views were those of 'an arrant driveller'.

On no subject does Mill stand his ground more fiercely than on the freedom of the will. During the depression of 1826–27, he had been oppressed by the spectre of necessity – as one might expect in a young man who felt that he was a construction of his father's, like a machine. If we were simply the product of experience and of the actions of others, in what sense were we responsible for ourselves and our characters? Mill was friendly with disciples of Robert Owen, who were so impressed by the possibilities of educating mankind in any way we chose that they concluded that the whole idea of individual responsibility was nonsensical. Our characters were not of our own making, so our actions were not in any deep sense 'our own' either. Part of what prompted them was an attachment to non-violence; they were disposed in advance to be sceptical of the value of punishment, and the denial of the reality of individual responsibility was one plank in the intellectual case against punishment.[42]

Mill's task was to rescue enough freedom to make it credible that we were responsible beings without succumbing to the intuitionist claim that we have an immediate and infallible consciousness of the freedom of the will. His problem was that the associationist psychology in which he was reared and to which he continued to subscribe was a doctrine which explained human behaviour in just the same way that physics or chemistry explained the behaviour of any natural phenomenon. All explanation was causal; all causation was what Mill called 'physical' causation. On this view the relation between an act of will and the action to which it gave rise was exactly like the relationship between a spark falling into a barrel of gunpowder and the subsequent explosion. But this was what the Owenites believed. Mill argued that what distressed people was the mere word 'necessity'; to say that our actions were the necessary results of our beliefs and desires gave the misleading impression that we just could not help doing what we do. Plausibly enough, Mill insisted that the distinction between what we can help doing and what we cannot help doing is not the same thing as the distinction between what is and what is not caused. We (generally) can help ourselves, and that is enough to support the ordinary conception of free will and responsibility.[43] Once arrived at this view, Mill stood by it without flinching, as is evident from the similarity of his discussion of freedom and necessity in the *Logic* to that in the *Examination of Sir William Hamilton's Philosophy*, and the casual way in which he distinguishes the subject of *Liberty* from 'the so-called Liberty of the Will, so unfortunately opposed to the misnamed doctrine of Philosophical Necessity.'[44]

Mill's task, therefore, was to reconcile the insights of Coleridge with the rationalism of Bentham. Commentators who see the problem in these terms commonly go on to claim that it is simply impossible; real imagination, spontaneity, freedom and the rest cannot be squared with the mechanical psychology of Bentham and James Mill. Others, however, suggest that a sufficiently complex reinterpretation of utilitarianism can, so to speak, re-absorb the psychological foundations appropriate to such an open-ended and historical moral theory.[45] Whatever the truth about that, it is undeniable that one of the intellectual charms of Mill's mature moral and political theory is its strenuous attachment to both its rationalist and its romantic origins.

Whewell and Intuitionism routed

Utilitarianism begins with an attack on ethical intuitionism – on the doctrine that moral principles are necessary, self-evident, and true *a priori*. The long critical essay on 'Whewell on Moral Philosophy' which he wrote a decade earlier had also been an extended account of the shortcomings of ethical intuitionism, and a defence of Bentham against one of his nineteenth-century critics. William Whewell was the Master of Trinity College, Cambridge; he was a conservative in politics though something of an educational reformer. He was also the most distinguished historian of science and mathematics of his age, and a philosopher of science who anticipated many of the most interesting ideas of the late twentieth century. He was a polymath whose abilities had provoked the quip that 'knowledge was his *forte* and omniscience his foible'. Mill had unashamedly pillaged his *History of the Inductive Sciences* (published in 1837) for examples of scientific theorizing when he was writing his *System of Logic*; more importantly, he had taken Whewell's *Philosophy of the Inductive Sciences* (published in 1840) as a stalking horse throughout that work.

Whewell defended an intuitionist account of science, that is, he argued that scientific theories can be seen to be true at the point where we have scrutinized the evidence and cleared our minds of all confusion and see clearly that *the world cannot be otherwise* than the theory dictates. Similarly, methodological principles such as the claim that every event has a cause are known to be true because it is *inconceivable* that they be false. The role of experiment and testing in science is not – as it is for Mill – simply to eliminate unsuccessful hypotheses; the eventual goal is to leave in sole possession of the field a theorem which is self-evident, and true *a priori*. Without going far into the matter it is easy to see that such a doctrine would be congenial to a theist who sees the world as conforming to the requirements of a rational God; it is equally easy to see that an agnostic would have much the same motive for resisting it. Mill was a lifelong enemy of intuitionism. It seemed to him to be the chief support of outmoded doctrine, to encourage mankind in its favourite intellectual vice – that of supposing any view held firmly enough needed no empirical grounding – and in its favourite delusion – that of mistaking habit for nature. 'There never was such an instrument devised for consecrating all deep-seated prejudices.'[46]

Mill thought that no truth about the world was *a priori* or self-evident; he even went to the length of claiming that the truths of arithmetic *might* turn out to be false in some remote portion of the universe. The idea that a favoured belief was self-evident was an incapacity of the mind; we see something happen over and over again, and think it *inconceivable* that it should fail to happen. But 'inconceivability' does not refer to the quality of the truth in question; it simply means that we are incapable of thinking of its opposite. The King of Siam believed his Dutch visitor until he told him of ice strong enough to bear an elephant; then he knew the Dutchman for a liar, because it was inconceivable that water should bear an elephant. Mill's ultimate target was always the intuitive theory of ethics; in *Liberty* as in *Utilitarianism*, he begins by complaining of so-called philosophers who encourage people to believe that they cannot be in error about anything they feel strongly enough about. Just as intuitionism in science elevates habit into authority, so does intuitionism in ethics. In both it is obnoxious; but in morals it is practically obnoxious as well as intellectually obnoxious. Mill's review of Whewell's moral philosophy had an easier target than Mill's attack on his philosophy of science. Whewell was a very distinguished historian and philosopher of science and vastly less impressive on ethics. But Mill hammered away at Whewell on his better defended flank precisely because it was on the attractions of intuitionism in mathematics and physics that moral intuitionism relied.

In the opening chapter of *Utilitarianism*, Mill observes that intuitive morality runs into a difficulty, in that it needs to be derived from some first principle or other, and yet no intuitionist has ever produced a principle which is half as acceptable as the particular precepts usually derived from it. Readers familiar with twentieth-century intuitionism will notice Mill's assumption that the object of intuition is a moral *principle* rather than the goodness or badness, rightness or wrongness of a particular action. Because Mill was dealing with disciples of Kant, such as Coleridge and Whewell, he was dealing with writers who thought that morality was based on principles of something like the scope of scientific theories. Among twentieth-century intuitionists, G. E. Moore thought of goodness as a non-natural property of actions and states of affairs, whose presence we perceived by some sort of intuition, while H. A. Prichard thought the property of rightness was similarly perceived. Mill treats such views as so obviously fatuous that he does not suppose any of his opponents could hold them. What he is concerned to do is show that the intuitionists, with their emphasis on self-evidence and non-contradiction, cannot produce any substantial principles whatever. Two pages of his review of Whewell are devoted to showing the difficulty he gets into; here Mill refers in passing to Kant, whose injunction 'So act, then the rule on which thou actest would admit of being adopted as a law by all rational beings' fails to rule out 'the most outrageously immoral rules of conduct' until Kant moves off the ground of consistency and considers the *consequences* of our adopting these rules. But once consequences are brought into the argument, we are on utilitarian ground.[47]

Utilitarianism defended

Mill's contention is that if morality is to be the subject of argument and discussion, it must be because moral rules have a point or a purpose; they must aim at something. The goodness of all subordinate rules of conduct consists in their efficacy in achieving this good end. That the end itself is good cannot be shown by the same kind of argument, for the ultimate good cannot be proved to be a good by being proved to be instrumental to some further good. This, of course, is the same argument as Bentham's. But, says Mill, this does not mean that there cannot be something equivalent to proof here. 'Considerations may be presented capable of determining the intellect either to give or withhold its assent to the doctrine; and this is equivalent to proof.'[48] We shall shortly see what those are, but it is easy to see at once that Mill is giving hostages to fortune by so saying – for the intellectual purist will insist that the only thing equivalent to proof is proof. The intellect may be swayed by all sorts of things from alcohol to passion; but a well-conducted intellect will distinguish proof from all counterfeits.

Like Bentham, Mill supposed both that most of mankind will generally be guided by utilitarian considerations, and that much of the hostility to utilitarianism which philosophers and popular writers display is the result of misunderstanding. Mill's brisk contempt for the misrepresentations of his opponents is inimitable; but the claims he makes must be part of any rational defence of utilitarianism. So, he insists that 'utility' is not to be contrasted with pleasure, although common speech frequently does contrast the useful with the enjoyable; 'utility' is identical with pleasure (and the absence of pain). Turning about to confront Carlyle, who had dismissed utilitarianism as a philosophy for pigs, Mill insists that the pursuit of pleasure is not the pursuit of the pleasures of the pig or the sybarite. If men were only capable of the pleasures of which the pig is capable, then the charge would be justified; but then, by the same token, no moral theory would be listened to which exhorted mankind to adopt higher standards than the pig, and whatever was good for pigs would be good enough for us. Expanding on this claim, Mill draws his famous and contentious distinction between quantitative and qualitative assessments of pleasure. 'It is quite compatible with the principle of utility to recognize the fact, that some *kinds* of pleasure are more desirable and more valuable than others. It would be absurd that while, in estimating all other things, quality is considered as well as quantity, the estimation of pleasures should be supposed to depend on quantity alone.'[49] As to how we are to tell whether a pleasure is of a high or a low quality, Mill declares that the only method is the considered judgement of those who know both the higher and lower pleasures. Better Socrates dissatisfied than a fool satisfied; if the fool disagrees, we discount it because he only knows one side of the question.

Mill's insistence on this point is part of his emphasis on what he thought Bentham had neglected. Nobility of character is to be prized, and the man whose happiness lies in the pursuit of an ideal character is to be commended. But it is not simply a matter of admiring the man whose sources of happiness are nobler and more enlightened than most; if that point amounts to criticism of Bentham, Mill follows him in reminding us that what is at stake is not only the happiness of the agent, but the happiness of everyone whose interests are in question. This, too, is an argument for encouraging aspirations to nobility of character. Its wider spread would be the most important means we could have to the achievement of happiness generally.

Mill turns from that straightforward point to tackle Carlyle again; Carlyle's doctrine of *Entsagen* or renunciation irritated Mill thoroughly, for it was the corruption of a wise insight into an absurd piece of rhetoric. Both for the individual and humanity generally, the ability to do without happiness was valuable. Individuals would be happier in the long run if they were better rather than worse at putting up with periods of unhappiness – but the *point* of renunciation was not renunciation itself, but the greater happiness it might lead to. The human race would be happier if more of its members were capable of self-sacrifice, for then more of us would do good to others at the cost of our own welfare and if our judgement was sound this would make for an increase overall. We should be better able to co-operate with each other, to aid each other in adversity and so on. What made no sense to Mill was the thought that we should all pursue self-abnegation for its own sake. This was pointless in the same way that St Simeon's life on his pillar was pointless. The disinterested pursuit of virtue was a good thing to cultivate, but only because the ultimate test of what was worth cultivating was its tendency to promote happiness.

If Mill was willing to say this much in criticism of Bentham's view that there was nothing to be said about the intrinsic goodness and badness of individual character and motive, he was not willing to add much more. For the most part, we should be glad if people do what they ought, no matter their motives; we certainly should not suppose that actions are only good if done from a sense of duty, nor should we think that only a good man can do his duty. Here Mill is once again elaborating his earlier criticism of Bentham and his opponents; unlike Bentham, Mill wants to emphasize that we judge men as well as actions, and that we should distinguish a variety of forms of assessment of men and their actions – not everything is a matter of duty done or duty neglected. But, it is the greatest happiness principle that provides the basis of all these assessments; Mill does not rely on utilitarianism to supply a theory of duty and turn elsewhere for insights into nobility or lovableness of character. As he says in the *System of Logic*, the philosophy of practice needs an ultimate end, and if the right one is chosen it will serve as the first principle in all kinds of activity and their appraisal.[50]

Other criticisms of utilitarianism which rest, as he thinks, on mistaking what it is, are even more briefly dismissed. To the complaint that utilitarianism is godless Mill replies that anyone who believes that God desires the happiness of his creation is devoutly utilitarian. To the complaint that utilitarianism is a doctrine of Expediency not Right, he retorts that 'expedient' usually means 'expedient for me, but not for anyone else' and in that sense expediency is a vice by utilitarian standards as much as by any other. But if we take expediency in an enlarged sense, namely as what is expedient for all, then utilitarianism unapologetically explains right and wrong in terms of their universal expediency. In dismissing those who object that utilitarianism demands we make calculations we cannot make, Mill makes an important observation. He says, first, that the objection is simply silly – everyone agrees that prudence is possible, which it would not be if the consequences of our actions were genuinely incalculable, so nobody really believes that the calculations demanded by utility are impossible. In any case, says Mill, the long experience of mankind has given us plenty of experience by which to decide which rules and practices tend to the general benefit and which do not. We do not have to wait until we are tempted to lie or pick a pocket before working out that the world would go better if rules against lying were strictly adhered to and theft was strictly repressed. 'Nobody argues that the art of navigation is not founded on astronomy, because sailors cannot wait to calculate the Nautical Almanack. Being rational creatures, they go to sea with it ready calculated; and all rational creatures go out upon the sea of life with their minds made up on the common questions of right and wrong, as well as on many of the far more difficult questions of wise and foolish.' In other words, we do not look directly to this greatest happiness principle to tell us what to do, but refer the question to 'secondary principles'.[51]

The mention of secondary principles is a reminder of what Mill had said about Bentham, that his genius did not lie in a discovery which he had never pretended to make, but in the application of a settled standard to secondary principles. The distinction between ultimate principles and secondary ones is an essential element in the claim that utilitarianism is an instrument of moral progress. Bentham wished to reform the law by asking of its secondary principles whether they served some useful purpose. Mill, in turn, thought that moral progress was achieved by taking our ordinary moral principles and asking whether they served any useful purpose. Only by distinguishing middle-level rules from the ultimate end of all action can we find room for moral progress. Intuitionists who thought that we just 'see' the truth of their favoured principles are the enemies of progress and conspire to freeze morality at whatever stage it has currently reached. We must return below to the question of how we validate rules by means of the principle of utility, and what sort of rules they are that are thus validated, for it is the issue which has obsessed Mill's readers for the past thirty years. What we may notice now, however, is that the 'greatest happiness principle' stands at several removes from the direct assessment of our actions and our characters. For, all the principle itself claims is that the only thing valuable in itself is happiness, and that the 'interests' of sentient creatures are to be explained in terms of their pleasures and their freedom from pain. How we bring that claim to bear on morality, nobility and prudence is a further, contentious issue.

Bentham, as we saw, defended the principle of utility by clarifying it rather than by direct argument; Mill does not follow him the whole way, but it is certainly true that the third and fourth chapters of *Utilitarianism* are slight in comparison with the chapter that elucidates the meaning of the principle, and the chapter which reconciles the claims of utility with the claims of justice. And this is somewhat surprising, since the fourth chapter of *Utilitarianism* contains Mill's notorious proof of the principle of utility. Before offering that, Mill turns to the 'Ultimate Sanction' of the principle – whatever it is that induces us to do our duty. Mill's problem is twofold. The opponents of utilitarianism said with some plausibility that the plain man did his duty because it just looked to him as if he had to; conscience spoke and he obeyed. Give him the idea that he had to calculate what he ought to do and he would soon lose the idea that he had to do his duty at all. To this Mill has a ready answer; social training induces in all of us a desire to keep the rules that others lay down. We may begin by behaving well only as a means to keeping the good opinion of others, but soon we get to the point where the mere thought of behaving badly is painful to us. A society can secure conscientious acceptance of practically any moral principle whatever, and there is nothing to prevent it securing acceptance of utilitarian standards. Moreover, as society advances and we become more and more mutually dependent, we become emotionally dependent on each other, too, and therefore the readier to accept whatever social standards are strenuously inculcated in the members of our society.

As Mill's essays on religion argued, there is no reason to doubt that something very like the pressure of supernatural sanctions could be put behind utilitarian ethics. The difficulty for Mill is that this argument may go altogether too far; public opinion is a valuable ally of utilitarianism, but may be simply despotic. Mill, after all, defends utilitarianism because it is a progressive doctrine; we can revise its secondary principles and improve them. But this will not be possible if the hold of those principles on our minds is too absolute. So Mill has to steer a cautious course; and *Liberty* shows what we might call the other face of the argument in chapter three of ,*Utilitarianism*, the proposition that it is so easy to provide a sanction for ethical beliefs that it is the more vital that individuals are encouraged to preserve some intellectual independence and a strong sense of where it is wrong and oppressive to enforce rules of conduct. And here, too, we can see Mill borrowing from and going beyond Bentham; like Bentham, he explains conscience as the internalization of social pressure; like Bentham, he thinks it contrary to utility to lay down rules for our 'self-regarding' conduct. Unlike Bentham, he thinks the pressure of public opinion so dangerous that we need a countervailing doctrine of individuality and independence of mind to ensure that social pressure is kept within bounds.

Mill begins his discussion of the proof of utility with an important disclaimer. 'It has already been remarked, that questions of ultimate ends do not admit of proof, in the ordinary acceptation of the term.'[52] This, he says, is true of all first principles, but if they concern matters of fact they may be susceptible of direct inspection – what about the first principles of practice? Then he produces his famous claim. 'The only proof capable of being given that an object is visible, is that people actually see it. The only proof that a sound is audible, is that people hear it: and so of the other sources of our experience. In like manner, I apprehend, the sole evidence it is possible to produce that anything is desirable, is that people do actually desire it.'[53] On these three sentences a greater weight of critical abuse has fallen than on almost any other passage of philosophical writing. One way and another, every critic has made the same point. That is that the analogy between being visible and being desirable does not hold up, and Mill commits a perfect howler in relying on it. Visible means 'can be seen' and of course the fact that something is seen is a knock-down proof that it can be seen. But desirable means 'ought to be desired', and from the fact that someone does desire whatever it might be nothing whatever follows about whether he ought to desire it.

Mill moves on to claim that what lies behind the desirability of happiness is a psychological impossibility, namely the impossibility of desiring anything other than happiness as an ultimate end. That, however, would result in a different 'proof', namely the argument that it was no use suggesting anything other than happiness as the ultimate test, because nobody could consistently employ anything else. We have seen already that something like this view was held by Bentham, and it is evidently one which would sit naturally with his defence of utility; if mankind could not but pursue happiness, all they needed was to be clear in their own minds about what they were doing. 'Proof' of the principle of utility would indeed be both impossible and unnecessary. Mill, however, seems to have cut himself off from that line of thought when he rebuked Bentham for supposing that his opponents were not really committed to different principles from his own.

In any case Mill has a further hurdle to surmount, because he has to answer the question, *whose* happiness do we inevitably pursue? The greatest happiness principle says that the ultimate test of our actions is the happiness of all sentient beings; if the argument that we cannot pursue anything but happiness means anything it must mean that each of us can only pursue his own happiness. Having argued that we desire nothing but happiness, Mill says: '. . . we have not only all the proof which the case admits of, but all that it is possible to require, that happiness is a good: that each person's happiness is a good to that person, and the general happiness, therefore, a good to the aggregate of all persons.'[54] From the first appearance of the essay, Mill's critics objected that this was another howler; we cannot move from the proposition that *my* happiness is a good for me to the proposition that the universal happiness is a good for everybody and therefore for me too. The 'aggregate of all persons' to whom the general happiness is a good is, of course, not itself a person and cannot be happy in the same sense that an individual can be happy.

Mill answered one of his critics, but only in private and in a letter to him.[55] There Mill said that he had no intention of trying to prove that each person's happiness was somehow identical with the happiness of the whole. He had intended to say no more than that since everybody had to admit that he or she thought his or her own happiness a good, it was impossible to deny that the happiness of others was a good, too. Of course, said Mill, he had not meant to claim that in pursuing my own happiness I commit myself to thinking the happiness of others is a good for me; but I do commit myself to it being a good. If that letter had been more widely known, the critical literature would have been somewhat thinner; on the other hand, the casual way Mill responded to his critics is itself somewhat dispiriting.

Most of Mill's attention is directed to the claim that the only thing desirable in itself is happiness. He recurs to the familiar objection that some people pursue virtue entirely disinterestedly, and repeats the familiar reply – a person who pursues virtue for its own sake is a man who finds his happiness in the pursuit of virtue, or at any rate is a man who would be made miserable by not pursuing virtue. To pursue anything for its own sake is not in the least inconsistent with pursuing happiness. To love music for its own sake is not inconsistent with being made happy by music; so, the pursuit of virtue for its own sake is perfectly explicable. We may begin by pursuing it only as a means to an end – to gain the approval of others, say – but we end by pursuing it for itself. The phenomenon is familiar in less admirable cases; the miser begins like everyone else by desiring money as a means to the goods it buys, but he ends by desiring money for its own sake. But he is still pursuing happiness in so doing, for he would be made utterly wretched by the loss of his money.

The ramifications of this argument would embrace almost the whole of the philosophy of mind. There is evidently something wrong-headed about it, but at the same time something right. The general claim that pursuing anything for its own sake is the same thing as pursuing it for the happiness it brings is plainly false. For some things, such as music, it is true enough, for the end or purpose of music is (or is plausibly said to be) enjoyment; but, virtue is hardly in the same category, and it is vitally important to Mill that it should be. Yet, what Mill has a hold on throughout this chapter is something which his critics and opponents generally overlook. That is, he sees that if we offer anyone a practical goal of some sort, they may properly ask why they should pursue it; in order to show that they in particular should pursue it we have to show how it latches on to what they already regard as worth pursuing.[56] If we tell someone to oil a ratchet, we must be able to go on to explain why the ratchet needs the oil, and why his projects, whatever they are, will be advanced by a ratchet which works better rather than worse. Similarly in the larger business of life, we must be able to show anyone with whom we are debating that what he or she ought to do is implied by what he or she already values. It is this point that Mill's untidily expressed 'proof' tries to make; ethics must start from what people do desire; talk of the desirable makes no sense unless it is grounded in what is desired. The flaw comes when he claims that what is desired is illuminatingly described as happiness.

Mill's discussion of the relationship between justice and utility occupies more than a third of the entire essay. There are two good reasons for this. The first is that there is a *prima facie* contrast between justice and utility which is universally recognized. The old tag 'let justice be done though the heavens fall' presupposes just this contrast. We can all visualize situations in which the general welfare could be promoted by injustice – when the conviction of an innocent man, say, might calm an angry crowd, when reneging on an onerous contract would release large amounts of money for charitable purposes, when appointing an unqualified but agreeable applicant for a post over the head of a more qualified one would give general pleasure. In recent years, the stock objection to utilitarianism has been that it allows the unjust sacrifice of innocent persons in order to promote the general welfare.[57] Mill was aware of the common view that utility and justice might conflict and that where they did, it was justice which must take precedence. He set out to explain how it was that what are commonly called the rules of justice do indeed take precedence over all others, but not because justice comes from any source other than utility. His second reason for paying particular attention to the idea of justice was that his intuitionist opponents, who believed that our moral sense simply discriminated right from wrong, the obligatory from the forbidden, relied heavily on examples taken from the sphere of justice. If Mill could show how justice was derived from utility and yet had this peculiarly stringent character, he would have defeated the enemy at his strongest point.

Mill proceeds by listing the various elements that come into issues of justice and injustice. It is unjust to violate someone's legal rights, but justice is not exhausted by law, since some legal rights ought not to have been given to their holders in the first place; this introduces the notion of moral rights, which unjust laws infringe. Again, it is part of justice to give each person what he or she deserves, to keep agreements, to display impartiality, and as a corollary to treat people equally unless some very good reason justifies inequality. In this diversity, there is no common feature in the various elements of justice, says Mill; but there is one common feature in our reaction to them. The idea of justice is related to that of a debt, and that in turn to what may be exacted from someone by punishment in case of default. This alone, however, does not pick out the realm of justice in particular. All morality involves the idea of punishment. Punishability is what distinguishes the realm of morality from the realms of prudence and worthiness – we punish breaches of obligation, but not the failure to be prudent or noble.

What picks out justice is the thought that the breach of duty in cases of injustice is breach of a duty to some particular and assignable individual – 'the two essential ingredients in the sentiment of justice are, the desire to punish a person who has done harm, and the knowledge or belief that there is some definite individual or individuals to whom harm has been done.'[58] The question then arises of how we have come to pick out this aspect of morality and to dignify it with a particular label and to strengthen it with more stringent demands for compliance with its rules. Mill's reply is that justice concerns security. The idea that we all have rights which others are obliged not to violate is, so to speak, a projection of our need to be secure against attack. Is security basic? It evidently is, for whatever other goods we may or may not wish to pursue, security is essential to them; whether our desires are expansive and far-reaching or relatively modest, security remains essential, since none of them can be satisfied without security of life and limb. Human beings are creatures who live in anticipation of the future; for them, therefore, security is far and away the fundamental good.

Adopting this naturalistic approach to our concern for justice enables Mill to turn aside almost all his critics. It is now clear why we distinguish justice from the rest of morality, and clear why we attach special importance to its enforcement. It is also clear why we believe that everyone can act justly; justice demands of us only that we do not make others insecure – benevolent behaviour goes far beyond that. We can see why charity is something other than the payment of a debt, why it is admirable but not obligatory. Moreover, we can also see why we are torn between saying that justice can occasionally be overridden by other claims and saying that it can never be overridden. So, if we justify stealing a car to take a dying man to hospital we are uncertain whether to say that we have violated the owner's rights in a good cause, and have therefore sacrificed justice to utility, or to say that in such an exceptional case we have not really violated his rights at all and have done no injustice to anyone. In arguing this, Mill can strike one last blow at the moral-sense theorists. They claim that right and wrong impose themselves upon us with absolute clarity; but, says Mill, nothing is more obvious than that arguments about justice are as wrapped in controversy as all other moral arguments. The rights and wrongs of socialism, say, are fought out on the terrain of justice, but whether it is private property or common ownership that is more in accordance with a strict concern for right remains a wide open question. It is apparent that different factors press us in different directions; inspection of the situation will not tell us how to balance one against another. Once again, it is only considerations of utility which are of any assistance, even if they too give uncertain guidance.

With this, Mill rests his case. To pursue the subsequent history of the argument would turn this introduction into a book. But three topics demand some discussion before we end. The first is Mill's success or failure in explaining justice in terms of utility; the second is Mill's account of what morality *is* and of the place of rules in morality; the last is Mill's view of rationality in ethics and of the scope of rational argument in ethical matters.

The final chapter of *Utilitarianism* is persuasively done. There is much to be said for Mill's account of the *point* of rights and their relation to security. Contemporary writers like John Rawls and Ronald Dworkin give an almost identical account of our reasons for saying that individuals have rights, and, like Mill, they link rights to the need for security and predictability, and to the thought that each of us is entitled to equal treatment in the sense of not being merely a means to the ends of others. This raises two questions; the first whether this accounts for everything that needs accounting for under the heading of 'justice', the second whether it is plausibly derived from utility. On the first point, it seems that the subject of rights overlaps with, but is not identical with, the range of issues of justice. Suppose a man is murdered; we say his right to life has been wantonly violated; and it is plain that security against being done to death is one of our vital interests. None the less, we do not ordinarily think that being murdered is a case of unjust treatment. (It might be part of an injustice, such as being executed after an unfair trial, but in that case it is the unfairness of the proceedings which is the ground of the complaint of injustice.) Conversely, a boy who runs a race at a great pace but trips just before the end will often be sympathized with as the victim of injustice; we feel that he deserved to win. We certainly do not feel that he had a right to win. In other words, justice in particular seems to involve issues of fairness in the distribution of goods and evils even more than it involves rights. 'Giving to everyone what is due to them' is still the most immediately appealing definition of justice. This is far from saying that Mill's account is just wrong; it might well be that further analysis would show ways of incorporating 'giving what is due' into a utilitarian framework, and it is quite clear that Mill would not much have minded a critic who said that his account did not analyse the ordinary view of justice but offered a tidied and rationalized account of some of it. For if utilitarianism reforms our ordinary views as well as defending and explaining them, it is open to Mill to claim that what can be derived from utility is (only) the rational kernel of the idea of justice. John Rawls is every bit as vulnerable as Mill was to the charge that his account of justice embraces more and less than the ordinary idea of justice, and he has replied much as Mill would have done. As to whether we really can derive justice from utility, that depends on whether we want more than a derivation of rights from security. Security is plainly at home in a utilitarian schema, and if we are content with the rationalized account of justice given by Mill, then we must agree with him that justice is a branch of utility. But many of Mill's readers feel that there is something missing, and that what is missing is what is implicit in Kant's dictum that we may never treat anyone as a mere means to the ends of others. Mill agrees that 'each to count for one and only for one' is a utilitarian principle, but he glosses it as the proposition that every unit of pleasure is as valuable as every other unit of pleasure, no matter whose pleasure it is. Again, it is clear that the gloss is utilitarian; if we did not count equal pleasure equally we should not be utilitarians at all.[59] But, it is not clear that the gloss seizes on the point at issue. For that point is that people are to be treated with respect for their personhood, and not treated as things. The happiness it yields them or anyone else is beside the point.

To rescue Mill from this criticism we must attend to the second issue, the place of rules in Mill's moral thinking and the analysis he gives of what morality is. An obvious criticism of utilitarianism runs as follows: the greatest happiness principle requires us to maximize happiness, and defines concepts such as right and wrong, ought and ought not by reference to the obligation to maximize utility. Suppose I go to the cinema and watch a film which bores and irritates me. I have failed to maximize utility; have I broken an obligation? That is, was it my *duty* to see the film which gave me the most pleasure? Only by so doing could I satisfy the greatest happiness principle, but is this conclusive? Neither Mill nor Bentham gives an entirely satisfactory answer. What is plain is that both took it for granted that *morality* did not apply to such cases; I might be condemned as imprudent if I regularly went to see the wrong film, but however often I did it I could not be said to be doing wrong, or acting wickedly. So the question arises of how utility is brought to bear on *moral* assessments as opposed to prudential ones.

It has been suggested that *rules* are crucial, in that Mill supposed that what was validated by the principle was rules rather than particular judgements – a thing he often says, as we have seen. But this does not help unless we can get further with the analysis of rules; for my failing to see the best film violates the *rule* 'choose the film most likely to give you pleasure' and we still think the rule belongs to prudence rather than morality. What Mill appears to think is that the scope of morality is defined by asking a somewhat roundabout question, namely, 'would it be maximally expedient to promote the pursuit of the general happiness by punishing breaches of a rule to the effect that . . .?' It would not

56

be sensible to punish people for failing to see the best possible film; it is entirely sensible to punish people for stealing their neighbour's chattels or failing to fulfil their contracts. Now we have the basis of a theory in which rules play a part. All utilitarian answers yield a·rule in the sense of yielding a rule of thumb; generally, it would be absurd to punish people for seeing the 'wrong' film, but a young man on a film course might properly be made to go and see the right film – because the narrower practice would be utilitarianly useful and the wider one not. But rules come in in a second sense, namely that many social practices only have good effects if they are made the subject of obligatory rules. It is not only that the rule-of-thumb approach tells us that punishing people for killing others is almost always maximally expedient, it is also that the security each of us gets from the rule comes from our knowledge that others adopt it *as a rule* rather than simply as a rule of thumb. If we thought everyone else might ask whether it was a good idea to make an exception of ourselves, we should be paralysed with terror. Not only is there this second kind of rule in play; there is a third kind, which is where we invent artificial practices for utilitarian purposes. The rules governing inheritance in a given society are purely conventional; but it is not a convention but a genuine effect that *having* such conventions promotes utility. Hume was so impressed by the role of convention that he identified justice with the observance of conventional rules, and declared that where there was no property there was no injustice. Mill did not think that, but he was aware of the importance of conventions.

We now have most of what we can get from Mill. Utilitarian morality, narrowly construed, is defined by the answers we get to the question of what rules it would be best to enforce by punishment, punishment here covering physical sanctions, the pressure of public opinion and the reproaches of the agent's own conscience. Utilitarian morality, construed more widely, asks in addition what qualities of character promote general happiness, and what qualities of character promote the higher qualities of happiness we associate with nobility of outlook. Mill's essay on *Liberty* fits into this schema by insisting that the realm of morality, narrowly construed, is 'self-defence' and by giving self-defence a utilitarian gloss, while spelling out the virtues which go to make up the individual excellence which *Utilitarianism* refers to in passing. The reader who understands both essays then sees that utilitarianism is as rigorous as any other creed in insisting on strict devotion to duty, but is more self-conscious than other creeds in its understanding of how to limit the scope of duty's demands.

Does this give a satisfactory rendering of what we ask of a theory of justice, too? There is no decisive answer. On the one hand, it must be true that utilitarianism cannot accept Kant's principle that each man must be treated as an end in himself as a fundamental principle. There can be only one fundamental principle in utilitarianism and that is the greatest happiness principle. On the other hand, the greater part of morality is the drawing of secondary principles, some of which are 'fundamental' in the looser sense that in a society of utilitarians they would never be broken. In that sense, a society which accepted the teaching of *Utilitarianism* and *Liberty* would treat Kant's dictum as a fundamental principle. But, Mill himself argued that it was possible to accept it only at a relatively late stage in history; he thought human development had been rendered possible only by ancient slavery – although slavery today would be *absolutely* wrong.

Finally, we must ask whether Mill's conception of the task of moral theory was correct. Most of Mill's readers are readily persuaded that he is on the side of reason; he wishes to establish the first principle from which all secondary principles are derived, and is that not definitive of ethical rationality? We are all of us acutely conscious that sometimes honesty is irreconcilable with kindness, that strict justice is at odds with mercy, and so on. Rational argument about which must yield to which appears to depend upon being able to see what each contributes to the ultimate end. This is Mill's point, and it is why Mill tries to give a quasi-proof of the ultimate end. Since Mill's time, there has been no consensus on the prospects of achieving what Mill wanted, though there has been a consensus that Mill's account was not wholly successful.

Three critical views are worth distinguishing, of increasing degrees of scepticism about a conception of rationality such as Mill's. The first denies that there is any way of proving an ultimate end to be the only possible end for morality. On this view, however, it may be possible to trade off different values against each other, without doing so by reference to their 'weight' in terms of an ultimate value. Thus, if we value both justice and efficiency, we may be willing to sacrifice some of one in order to obtain more of the other without believing that we are cashing this trade in terms of how much either principle yields of some more ultimate value. The thought is analogous to the economist's idea that we can trade carrots against ball-point pens without having to estimate what 'utility' carrots and ball-point pens yield their consumers. If we have consistent and determinate preferences, we are rational consumers and rational valuers. It is quite clear that Mill would have denied this, but one may think that his difficulties press such a solution upon us.[60]

A second view goes further than this and denies that there is the same precision in ethics as in consumer behaviour. As do all pluralist views in ethics, this holds that there are a multiplicity of values which cannot be reduced to general utility or to anything else. Moreover, they cannot be traded against each other in a determinate fashion. We just do the best we can. If this sounds very feeble and unargued, we can turn the argument against Mill. He, after all, allows that the choice between happiness of a higher and a lower quality can only be made by a person who has experience of both kinds of happiness and has the right tastes. That kind of choice is no better and no worse than all our other moral choices.

But the third view, put forward with great vigour by Bernard Williams.[61] repudiates Mill's conception of ethical rationality altogether. (Williams's target is Henry Sidgwick's *The Methods of Ethics*, with its guiding principle that we ought to adopt 'the standpoint of the universe', but Sidgwick's *magnum opus* was squarely in the tradition created by Bentham and Mill.) On Williams's view, it is a mistake to assimilate rationality in ethics to rationality in science; as we have seen, Mill did precisely that, and understood his task as giving an account of rationality which would apply to science and ethics. It was this that induced him to harry Whewell across the entire intellectual landscape. Williams's riposte to this is that science does indeed aim to adopt the standpoint of the universe, and to explain how the world is in itself, and viewed from no particular standpoint. But evaluative questions must be settled from some point of view; what is good and bad is so for us, and we cannot so to speak leap out of our own, admittedly limited, standpoint into an 'objective' one.

Utilitarianism of the kind Mill defends is particularly vulnerable to this objection, because Mill wants to combine two ethical positions at once. He wants to defend the ethics of individual worth, so that he can promote the pursuit of an ideal goodness of character, and at the same time he wants to show that the principle of utility is the only principle which would commend itself to someone who had no biases in his own favour. But, what of the man who flinches from telling a lie in the public interest? Are we to insist that as a utilitarian he must grit his teeth and tell the lie? What then becomes of the idea that his own character is rightly the subject of overriding concern? Is he to tell the truth, on the grounds that the greatest happiness principle licenses the pursuit of individual excellence of character? What then becomes of the overriding aim of promoting utility? Williams implies that once we see these dilemmas for what they are – tragic and unamenable to rational resolution – we shall see that utilitarianism is wholly unacceptable.[62] Readers more sympathetic to Mill may suspect that, faced with critics as radical and as sophisticated as Williams, he would have turned again to the task to which all his essays in this book were devoted – the task of showing how an adequate utilitarianism would resolve what could be resolved and would illuminate what could not.

Notes

1. John Rawls, *A Theory of Justice*, (Oxford University Press, 1972), pp. 22ff.
2. *Later Letters, Collected Works of John Stuart Mill*, (University of Toronto Press, 1971), p. 190, p. 1740.
3. Two good accounts of Bentham's desire for sound administration and democratic control are L. J. Hume, *Bentham and Bureaucracy*, (Cambridge University Press, 1981) and Frederick Rosen, *Jeremy Bentham and Representative Democracy*, (Oxford University Press, 1983). The

sinister face of the *Panopticon* is explored in Gertrude Himmelfarb's essay 'The Haunted House of Jeremy Bentham', in her collection *Victorian Minds*, (Faber, 1968).

4. E. Halévy, *The Growth of Philosophic Radicalism*, (Allen & Unwin, 1928).

5. J. S. Mill, *Autobiography* in *Collected Works of John Stuart Mill*, vol. I, (University of Toronto Press, 1981), pp. 5–88.

6. Besides Halévy, above, see William Thomas, *The Philosophic Radicals*, (Oxford University Press, 1979).

7. 'Sedgwick's Discourse' in *Essays on Religion, Ethics and Society*, vol. X of *Collected Works*, (University of Toronto Press, 1969), pp, 31–74.

8. 'Bentham' is reprinted here; 'Remarks on Bentham's Philosophy' was an appendix to Edward Bulwer Lytton's *England and the English* and it to be found in *Collected Works*, vol. X, pp. 3–18.

9. 'Of the Definition of Political Economy' in *Essays on Economics and Society*, vol. IV of *Collected Works*, (University of Toronto Press, 1967), pp. 309–39.

10. Alan Ryan, *The Philosophy of John Stuart Mill*, (Macmillan, 1970).

11. Mark Philp, *William Godwin's Political Justice*, (Duckworth, 1986).

12. William Godwin, *An Enquiry Concerning Political Justice*, (ed. Codell Carter, Oxford University Press, 1971), pp. 70–73.

13. Mark Philp, op. cit., ch. IV.

14. David Hume, *A Treatise of Human Nature*, (Oxfoed University Press, 1964), Book III, pt. 1.

15. J. S. Mill, *Collected Works*, vol. X, p. 51.

16. I. Kant, *The Groundwork of the Metaphysics of Morals*, translated by H. J. Paton, (Hutchinson, 1949); below p. 275.

17. R. M. Hare's work has done much to reconcile a Kantian and utilitarian perspective; he starts from just this distinction between universality and generality. See *The Language of Morals*, (Oxford University Press, 1952) and *Freedom and Reason*, (Oxford University Press, 1963).

18. Below, p. 65.

19. Below, p. 67.

20. Below, p. 65.

21. Below, p. 67.

22. J. S. Mill, *Collected Works*, vol. X, pp. 5–6.

23. Below, p. 68.

24. Below, p. 69.

25. Below, pp. 72–3.

26. Below, p. 74.

27. Below, pp. 78–83.

28. J. S. Mill, *Collected Works*, vol. X, p. 7.

29. Below, p. 86.

30. Below, pp. 86–7.

31. Below, p. 170.

32. Below, p. 92.

33. H. L. A. Hart, *Law, Liberty and Morality*, (Oxford University Press, 1963).

34. Gertrude Himmelfarb, op. cit., ch. 1.

35. Ronald Dworkin, *Taking Rights Seriously*, (Duckworth, 1977); John Rawls, *A Theory of Justice*, (Oxford University Press, 1972).

36. J. S. Mill, *Collected Works*, vol. I, pp. 131ff.

37. *ibid.*, vol. I, p. 139.

38. *ibid.*, vol. I, p. 145.

39. Below, pp. 198–200; *Collected Works*, vol. I, pp. 169–71.

40. Below, p. 153.

41. Below, pp. 165–8; *Liberty* in *Essays on Politics and Society, Collected Works*, vol. XVIII, pp. 217–310.

42. pp. 117–9.

43. Below, p. 119; *An Examination of Sir William Hamilton's Philosophy, Collected Works*, vol. XI, (University of Toronto Press, 1971), ch. XXVI.

44. *Collected Works*, vol. XVIII, p. 217.

45. See F. R. Leavis's Introduction to his edition of *Mill on Bentham and Coleridge*, (Cambridge University Press, 1983) and Richard Wollheim, 'John Stuart Mill and Isaiah Berlin: The Ends of Life and the Preliminaries of Morality' in Alan Ryan, ed., *The Idea of Freedom*, (Oxford University Press, 1979), pp. 253–69.

46. J. S. Mill, *Collected Works*, vol. I, p. 233.

47. Below, p. 275.

48. Below, p. 276.

49. Below, p. 279.

50. Below, pp. 129–30.

51. Below, pp. 296–7.

52. Below, p. 307.

53. Below, p. 307.

54. Below, p. 308.

55. *Later Letters of John Stuart Mill, Collected Works*, (University of Toronto Press, 1972), vol. XVI, p. 1414.

56. This was denied in a famous essay: H. A. Prichard, 'Does Moral Philosophy Rest on a Mistake', *Mind*, 1912; but his view is now entirely out of favour.

57. John Rawls's *A Theory of Justice* relies on just this argument.
58. Below, p. 324.
59. Below, p. 336; but see Alan Ryan, op. cit., pp. 228–9.
60. Brian Barry, *Political Argument*, (Routledge and Kegan Paul, 1965), pp. 8–9.
61. Bernard Williams, *Ethics and the Limits of Philosophy*, (Fontana, 1985).
62. See his contribution in J. J. C. Smart and Bernard Williams, *Utilitarianism: Pro and Con*, (Cambridge University Press, 1974).

Editor's Note

The text of Bentham's *Introduction to the Principles of Morals and Legislation* is taken from the 1824 edition, but I have suppressed the footnotes which Bentham liberally added to the text over the years, with the exception of the famous list of 'capricious' principles in Chapter II.

From *An Introduction to the Principles of Morals and Legislation*

BY JEREMY BENTHAM

Chapter I
Of the Principle of Utility

I. *Mankind governed by pain and pleasure*. Nature has placed mankind under the governance of two sovereign masters, *pain* and *pleasure*. It is for them alone to point out what we ought to do, as well as to determine what we shall do. On the one hand the standard of right and wrong, on the other the chain of causes and effects, are fastened to their throne. They govern us in all we do, in all we say, in all we think: every effort we can make to throw off our subjection, will serve but to demonstrate and confirm it. In words a man may pretend to abjure their empire: but in reality he will remain subject to it all the while. The *principle of utility* recognizes this subjection, and assumes it for the foundation of that system, the object of which is to rear the fabric of felicity by the hands of reason and of law. Systems which attempt to question it deal in sounds instead of sense, in caprice instead of reason, in darkness instead of light.

But enough of metaphor and declamation: it is not by such means that moral science is to be improved.

II. *Principle of utility, what*. The principle of utility is the foundation of the present work: it will be proper therefore at the outset to give an explicit and determinate account of what is meant by it. By the principle of utility is meant that principle which approves or disapproves of every action whatsoever, according to the tendency which it appears to have to augment or diminish the happiness of the party whose interest is in question: or, what is the same thing in other words, to promote or to oppose that happiness. I say of every action whatsoever; and therefore not only of every action of a private individual, but of every measure of government.

III. *Utility, what.* By utility is meant that property in any object, whereby it tends to produce benefit, advantage, pleasure, good, or happiness (all this in the present case comes to the same thing) or (what comes again to the same thing) to prevent the happening of mischief, pain, evil, or unhappiness to the party whose interest is considered; if that party be the community in general, then the happiness of the community; if a particular individual, then the happiness of that individual.

IV. *Interest of the community, what.* The interest of the community is one of the most general expressions that can occur in the phraseology of morals: no wonder that the meaning of it is often lost. When it has a meaning, it is this. The community is a fictitious *body*, composed of the individual persons who are considered as constituting as it were its *members.* The interest of the community then is, what? – the sum of the interests of the several members who compose it.

V. It is in vain to talk of the interest of the community, without understanding what is the interest of the individual. A thing is said to promote the interest, or to be *for* the interest, of an individual, when it tends to add to the sum total of his pleasures: or, what comes to the same thing, to diminish the sum total of his pains.

VI. *An action conformable to the principle of utility, what.* An action then may be said to be conformable to the principle of utility, or, for shortness' sake, to utility, (meaning with respect to the community at large) when the tendency it has to augment the happiness of the community is greater than any it has to diminish it.

VII. *A measure of government conformable to the principle of utility, what.* A measure of government (which is but a particular kind of action, performed by a particular person or persons) may be said to be conformable to or dictated by the principle of utility, when in like manner the tendency which it has to augment the happiness of the community is greater than any which it has to diminish it.

VIII. *Laws or dictates of utility, what.* When an action, or in particular a measure of government, is supposed by a man to be conformable to the principle of utility, it may be convenient, for the purposes of discourse, to imagine a kind of law or dictate, called a law or dictate of utility: and to speak of the action in question, as being conformable to such law or dictate.

IX. *A partisan of the principle of utility, who.* A man may be said to be a partisan of the principle of utility, when the approbation or disapprobation he annexes to any action, or to any measure, is determined by and proportioned to the tendency which he conceives it to have to augment or to diminish the happiness of the community: or in other words, to its conformity or unconformity to the laws or dictates of utility.

X. *Ought, ought not, right and wrong, etc., how to be understood.* Of an action that is conformable to the principle of utility one may always say either that it is one that ought to be done, or at least that it is not one that ought not to be done. One may say also, that it is right it should be done; at least that it is not wrong it should be done: that it is a right action; at least that it is not a wrong action. When thus interpreted, the words *ought*, and *right* and *wrong*, and others of that stamp, have a meaning: when otherwise, they have none.

XI. *To prove the rectitude of this principle is at once unnecessary and impossible.* Has the rectitude of this principle been ever formally contested? It should seem that it had, by those who have not known what they have been meaning. Is it susceptible of any direct proof? It should seem not: for that which is used to prove every thing else, cannot itself be proved: a chain of proofs must have their commencement somewhere. To give such proof is as impossible as it is needless.

XII. *It has seldom, however, as yet been consistently pursued.* Not that there is or ever has been that human creature breathing, however stupid or perverse, who has not on many, perhaps on most occasions of his life, deferred to it. By the natural constitution of the human frame, on most occasions of their lives men in general embrace this principle, without thinking of it: if not for the ordering of their own actions, yet for the trying of their own actions, as well as of those of other men. There have been, at the same time, not many, perhaps, even of the most intelligent, who have been disposed to embrace it purely and without reserve. There are even few who have not taken some occasion or other to quarrel with it, either on account of their not understanding always how to apply it, or on account of some prejudice or other which they were afraid to examine into, or could not bear to part with. For such is the stuff that man is made of: in principle and in practice, in a right track and in a wrong one, the rarest of all human qualities is consistency.

XIII. *It can never be consistently combated.* When a man attempts to combat the principle of utility, it is with reasons drawn, without his being aware of it, from that very principle itself. His arguments, if they prove anything, prove not that the principle is *wrong*, but that, according to the applications he supposes to be made of it, it is *misapplied*. Is it possible for a man to move the earth? Yes; but he must first find out another earth to stand upon.

XIV. *Course to be taken for surmounting prejudices that may have been entertained against it.* To disprove the propriety of it by arguments is impossible; but, from the causes that have been mentioned, or from some confused or partial view of it, a man may happen to be disposed not to relish it. Where this is the case, if he thinks the settling of his opinions on such a subject worth the trouble, let him take the following steps, and at length, perhaps, he may come to reconcile himself to it.

1. Let him settle with himself, whether he would wish to discard this principle altogether; if so, let him consider what it is that all his reasonings (in matters of politics especially) can amount to?

2. If he would, let him settle with himself, whether he would judge an act without any principle, or whether there is any other he would judge and act by?

3. If there be, let him examine and satisfy himself whether the principle he thinks he has found is really any separate intelligible principle; or whether it be not a mere principle in words, a kind of phrase, which at bottom expresses neither more nor less than the mere averment of his own unfounded sentiments; that is, what in another person he might be apt to call caprice?

4. If he is inclined to think that his own approbation or disapprobation, annexed to the idea of an act, without any regard to

its consequences, is a sufficient foundation for him to judge and act upon, let him ask himself whether his sentiment is to be a standard of right and wrong, with respect to every other man, or whether every man's sentiment has the same privilege of being a standard to itself?

5. In the first case, let him ask himself whether his principle is not despotical, and hostile to all the rest of the human race?

6. In the second case, whether it is not anarchical, and whether at this rate there are not as many different standards of right and wrong as there are men? and whether even to the same man, the same thing, which is right today, may not (without the least change in its nature) be wrong tomorrow? and whether the same thing is not right and wrong in the same place at the same time? and in either case, whether all argument is not at an end? and whether, when two men have said, 'I like this,' and 'I don't like it,' they can (upon such a principle) have any thing more to say?

7. If he should have said to himself, No: for that the sentiment which he proposes as a standard must be grounded on reflection, let him say on what particulars the reflection is to turn? If on particulars having relation to the utility of the act, then let him say whether this is not deserting his own principle, and borrowing assistance from that very one in opposition to which he sets it up: or if not on those particulars, on what other particulars?

8. If he should be for compounding the matter, and adopting his own principle in part, and the principle of utility in part, let him say how far he will adopt it?

9. When he has settled with himself where he will stop, then let him ask himself how he justifies to himself the adopting it so far? and why he will not adopt it any farther?

10. Admitting any other principle than the principle of utility to be a right principle, a principle that it is right for a man to pursue; admitting (what is not true) that the word *right* can have a meaning without reference to utility, let him say whether there is any such thing as a *motive* that a man can have to pursue the dictates of it: if there is, let him say what that motive is, and how it is to be distinguished from those which enforce the dictates of utility: if not, then lastly let him say what it is this other principle can be good for?

Chapter II
Of Principles Adverse to That of Utility

I. *All other principles than that of utility must be wrong.* If the principle of utility be a right principle to be governed by, and that in all cases, it follows from what has been just observed, that whatever principle differs from it in any case must necessarily be a wrong one. To prove any other principle, therefore, to be a wrong one, there needs no more than just to show it to be what it is, a principle of which the dictates are in some point or other different from those of the principle of utility: to state it is to confute it.

II. *Ways in which a principle may be wrong.* A principle may be different from that of utility in two ways: 1. By being constantly opposed to it: this is the case with a principle which may be termed the principle of *asceticism*. 2. By being sometimes opposed to it, and sometimes not, as it may happen: this is the case with another, which may be termed the principle of *sympathy* and *antipathy*.

III. *Principle of asceticism, what.* By the principle of asceticism I mean that principle, which, like the principle of utility, approves or disapproves of any action, according to the tendency which it appears to have to augment or diminish the happiness of the party whose interest is in question; but in an inverse manner: approving of actions in as far as they tend to diminish his happiness; disapproving of them in as far as they tend to augment it.

IV. *A partisan of the principle of asceticism, who.* It is evident that any one who reprobates any the least particle of pleasure, as such, from whatever source derived, is *pro tanto* a partisan of the principle of asceticism. It is only upon that principle, and not from the principle of utility, that the most abominable pleasure which the vilest of malefactors ever reaped from his crime would be to be reprobated, if it stood alone. The case is that it never does stand alone; but is necessarily followed by such a quantity of pain (or, what comes to the same thing, such a chance for a certain quantity of pain) that the pleasure in comparison of it is as nothing: and this is the true and sole, but perfectly sufficient, reason for making it a ground for punishment.

V. *This principle has had in some a philosophical, in others a religious origin*. There are two classes of men of very different complexions, by whom the principle of asceticism appears to have been embraced; the one a set of moralists, the other a set of religionists. Different accordingly have been the motives which appear to have recommended it to the notice of these different parties. Hope, that is the prospect of pleasure, seems to have animated the former: hope, the aliment of philosophic pride: the hope of honour and reputation at the hands of men. Fear, that is the prospect of pain, the latter: fear, the offspring of superstitious fancy: the fear of future punishment at the hands of a splenetic and revengeful Deity. I say in this case fear: for of the invisible future, fear is more powerful than hope. These circumstances characterize the two different parties among the partisans of the principle of asceticism; the parties and their motives different, the principle the same.

VI. *It has been carried farther by the religious party than by the philosophical*. The religious party, however, appear to have carried it farther than the philosophical: they have acted more consistently and less wisely. The philosophical party have scarcely gone farther than to reprobate pleasure: the religious party have frequently gone so far as to make it a matter of merit and of duty to court pain. The philosophical party have hardly gone farther than the making pain a matter of indifference. It is no evil, they have said: they have not said, it is a good. They have not so much as reprobated all pleasure in the lump. They have discarded only what they have called the gross; that is, such as are organical, or of which the origin is easily traced up to such as are organical: they have even cherished and magnified the refined. Yet this, however, not under the name of pleasure: to cleanse itself from the sordes of its impure original, it was necessary it should change its name: the honourable, the glorious, the reputable, the becoming, the *honestum*, the *decorum*, it was to be called: in short, any thing but pleasure.

VII. *The philosophical branch of it has had most influence among persons of education, the religious among the vulgar*. From these two sources have flowed the doctrines from which the sentiments of the bulk of mankind have all along received a tincture of this principle; some from the philosophical, some from the religious, some from both. Men of education more frequently from the philosophical, as more suited to the elevation of their sentiments: the vulgar more frequently from the superstitious, as more suited to the narrowness of their intellect, undilated by knowledge: and to the abjectness of their condition, continually open to the attacks of fear. The tinctures, however, derived from the two sources, would naturally intermingle, insomuch that a man would not always know by which of them he was most influenced: and they would often serve to corroborate and enliven one another. It was this conformity that made a kind of alliance between parties of a complexion otherwise so dissimilar: and disposed them to unite upon various occasions against the common enemy, the partisan of the principle of utility, whom they joined in branding with the odious name of Epicurean.

VIII. *The principle of asceticism has never been steadily applied by either party to the Business of Government.* The principle of asceticism, however, with whatever warmth it may have been embraced by its partisans as a rule of private conduct, seems not to have been carried to any considerable length, when applied to the business of government. In a few instances it has been carried a little way by the philosophical party: witness the Spartan regimen. Though then, perhaps, it may be considered as having been a measure of security: and an application, though a precipitate and perverse application, of the principle of utility. Scarcely in any instances, to any considerable length, by the religious: for the various monastic orders, and the societies of the Quakers, Dumplers, Moravians and other religionists, have been free societies, whose regimen no man has been astricted to without the intervention of his own consent. Whatever merit a man may have thought there would be in making himself miserable, no such notion seems ever to have occurred to any of them, that it may be a merit, much less a duty, to make others miserable: although it should seem, that if a certain quantity of misery were a thing so desirable, it would not matter much whether it were brought by each man upon himself, or by one man upon another. It is true, that from the same source from whence, among the religionists, the attachment to the principle of asceticism took its rise, flowed other doctrines and practices, from which misery in abundance was produced in one man by the instrumentality of another: witness the holy wars, and the persecutions for religion. But the passion for producing misery in these cases proceeded upon some special ground: the exercise of it was confined to persoi.s of particular descriptions: they were tormented, not as men, but as heretics and infidels. To have inflicted the same miseries on their fellow-believers and fellow-sectaries, would have been as blameable in the eyes even of these religionists, as in those of a partisan of the principle of utility. For a man to give himself a certain number of stripes was indeed meritorious: but to give the same number of stripes to another man, not consenting, would have been a sin. We read of saints, who for the good of their souls, and the mortification of their bodies, have voluntarily yielded themselves a prey to vermin: but though many persons of this class have wielded the reins of empire, we read of none who have set themselves to work, and made laws on purpose, with a view of stocking the body politic with the breed of highwaymen, housebreakers, or incendiaries. If at any time they have suffered the nation to be preyed upon by swarms of idle pensioners, or useless placemen, it has rather been from negligence and imbecility, than from any settled plan for oppressing and plundering of the people. If at any time they have sapped the sources of national wealth, by cramping commerce, and driving the inhabitants into emigration, it has been with other views, and in pursuit of other ends. If they have declaimed against the pursuit of pleasure, and the use of wealth, they have commonly stopped at declamation: they have not, like Lycurgus, made express ordinances for the purpose of banishing the precious metals. If they have established idleness by a law, it has been not because idleness, the mother of vice and misery, is itself a virtue, but because idleness (say they) is the road to holiness. If under the notion of fasting, they have joined in the plan of confining their subjects to a diet, thought by some to be of the most nourishing and prolific nature, it has been not for the sake of making them tributaries to the nations by whom that diet was to be supplied, but for the sake of manifesting their own power, and exercising the obedience of the people. If they have established, or suffered to be established, punishments for the breach of celibacy, they have done no more than comply with the petitions of those deluded rigorists, who, dupes to the ambitious and deep-laid policy of their rulers, first laid themselves under that idle obligation by a vow.

IX. *The principle of asceticism, in its origin, was but that of utility misapplied*. The principle of asceticism seems originally to have been the reverie of certain hasty speculators, who having perceived, or fancied, that certain pleasures, when reaped in certain circumstances, have, at the long run, been attended with pains more than equivalent to them, took occasion to quarrel with every thing that offered itself under the name of pleasure. Having then got thus far, and having forgot the point which they set out from, they pushed on, and went so much further as to think it meritorious to fall in love with pain. Even this, we see, is at bottom but the principle of utility misapplied.

X. *It can never be consistently pursued*. The principle of utility is capable of being consistently pursued; and it is but tautology to say, that the more consistently it is pursued, the better it must ever be for humankind. The principle of asceticism never was, nor ever can be, consistently pursued by any living creature. Let but one tenth part of the inhabitants of this earth pursue it consistently, and in a day's time they will have turned it into a hell.

XI. *The principle of sympathy and antipathy, what*. Among principles adverse to that of utility, that which at this day seems to have most influence in matters of government, is what may be called the principle of sympathy and antipathy. By the principle of sympathy and antipathy, I mean that principle which approves or disapproves of certain actions, not on account of their tending to augment the happiness, nor yet on account of their tending to diminish the happiness of the party whose interest is in question, but merely because a man finds himself disposed to approve or disapprove of them: holding up that approbation or disapprobation as a sufficient reason for itself, and disclaiming the necessity of looking out for any extrinsic ground. Thus far in the general department of morals: and in the particular department of politics, measuring out the quantum (as well as determining the ground) of punishment, by the degree of the disapprobation.

XII. *This is rather the negation of all principle, than any thing positive*. It is manifest, that this is rather a principle in name than in reality: it is not a positive principle of itself, so much as a term employed to signify the negation of all principle. What one expects to find in a principle is something that points out some external consideration, as a means of warranting and guiding the internal sentiments of approbation and disapprobation: this expectation is but ill fulfilled by a proposition, which does neither more nor less than hold up each of those sentiments as a ground and standard for itself.

XIII. *Sentiments of a partisan of the principle of antipathy.* In looking over the catalogue of human actions (says a partisan of this principle) in order to determine which of them are to be marked with the seal of disapprobation, you need but to take counsel of your own feelings: whatever you find in yourself a propensity to condemn, is wrong for that very reason. For the same reason it is also meet for punishment: in what proportion it is adverse to utility, or whether it be adverse to utility at all, is a matter that makes no difference. In that same *proportion* also is it meet for punishment: if you hate much, punish much: if you hate little, punish little: punish as you hate. If you hate not at all, punish not at all: the fine feelings of the soul are not to be overborne and tyrannized by the harsh and rugged dictates of political utility.

XIV. *The systems that have been formed concerning the standard of right and wrong, are all reducible to this principle.* The various systems that have been formed concerning the standard of right and wrong, may all be reduced to the principle of sympathy and antipathy. One account may serve for all of them. They consist all of them in so many contrivances for avoiding the obligation of appealing to any external standard, and for prevailing upon the reader to accept of the author's sentiment or opinion as a reason for itself. The phrases different, but the principle the same.*

XV. *This principle will frequently coincide with that of utility.* It is manifest, that the dictates of this principle will frequently coincide with those of utility, though perhaps without intending any such thing. Probably more frequently than not: and hence it is that the business of penal justice is carried on upon that tolerable sort of footing upon which we see it carried on in common at this day. For what more natural or more general ground of hatred to a

* Bentham's list of such phrases is printed at the end of this chapter, p. 78.

practice can there be, than the mischievousness of such practice? What all men are exposed to suffer by, all men will be disposed to hate. It is far yet, however, from being a constant ground: for when a man suffers, it is not always that he knows what it is he suffers by. A man may suffer grievously, for instance, by a new tax, without being able to trace up the cause of his sufferings to the injustice of some neighbour, who has eluded the payment of an old one.

XVI. *This principle is most apt to err on the side of severity.* The principle of sympathy and antipathy is most apt to err on the side of severity. It is for applying punishment in many cases which deserve none: in many cases which deserve some, it is for applying more than they deserve. There is no incident imaginable, be it ever so trivial, and so remote from mischief, from which this principle may not extract a ground of punishment. Any difference in taste: any difference in opinion: upon one subject as well as upon another. No disagreement so trifling which perseverance and altercation will not render serious. Each becomes in the other's eyes an enemy, and, if laws permit, a criminal. This is one of the circumstances by which the human race is distinguished (not much indeed to its advantage) from the brute creation.

XVII. *But errs, in some instances, on the side of lenity.* It is not, however, by any means unexampled for this principle to err on the side of lenity. A near and perceptible mischief moves antipathy. A remote and imperceptible mischief, though not less real, has no effect. Instances in proof of this will occur in numbers in the course of the work. It would be breaking in upon the order of it to give them here.

XVIII. *The theological principle, what – not a separate principle.* It may be wondered, perhaps, that in all this while no mention has been made of the *theological* principle; meaning that principle which professes to recur for the standard of right and wrong to the will of God. But the case is, this is not in fact a distinct principle. It is never any thing more or less than one or other of the three before-mentioned principles presenting itself under another shape. The *will* of God here meant cannot be his revealed will, as contained in the sacred writings: for that is a system which nobody ever thinks of recurring to at this time of day, for the details of political administration: and even before it can be applied to the details of private conduct, it is universally allowed, by the most eminent divines of all persuasions, to stand in need of pretty ample interpretations; else to what use are the works of those divines? And for the guidance of these interpretations, it is also allowed, that some other standard must be assumed. The will then which is meant on this occasion, is that which may be called the *presumptive* will: that is to say, that which is presumed to be his will on account of the conformity of its dictates to those of some other principle. What then may be this other principle? It must be one or other of the three mentioned above: for there cannot, as we have seen, be any more. It is plain, therefore, that, setting revelation out of the question, no light can ever be thrown upon the standard of right and wrong, by any thing that can be said upon the question, what is God's will. We may be perfectly sure, indeed, that whatever is right is conformable to the will of God: but so far is that from answering the purpose of showing us what is right, that it is necessary to know first whether a thing is right, in order to know from thence whether it be conformable to the will of God.

XIX. *Antipathy, let the actions it dictates be ever so right, is never of itself a right ground of action.* There are two things which are very apt to be confounded, but which it imports us carefully to distinguish: – the motive or cause, which, by operating on the mind of an individual, is productive of any act: and the ground or reason which warrants a legislator, or other bystander, in regarding that act with an eye of approbation. When the act happens, in the particular instance in question, to be productive of effects which we approve of, much more if we happen to observe that the same motive may frequently be productive, in other instances, of the like effects, we are apt to transfer our approbation to the motive itself, and to assume, as the just ground for the approbation we bestow on the act, the circumstance of its originating from that motive. It is in this way that the sentiment of antipathy has often been considered as a just ground of action. Antipathy, for instance, in such or such a case, is the cause of an action which is attended with good effects: but this does not make it a right ground of action in that case, any more than in any

77

other. Still farther. Not only the effects are good, but the agent sees beforehand that they will be so. This may make the action indeed a perfectly right action: but it does not make antipathy a right ground of action. For the same sentiment of antipathy, if implicitly deferred to, may be, and very frequently is, productive of the very worst effects. Antipathy, therefore, can never be a right ground of action. No more, therefore, can resentment, which, as will be seen more particularly hereafter, is but a modification of antipathy. The only right ground of action, that can possibly subsist, is, after all the consideration of utility, which, if it is a right principle of action, and of approbation, in any one case, is so in every other. Other principles in abundance, that is, other motives, may be the reasons why such and such an act *has* been done: that is, the reasons or causes of its being done: but it is this alone that can be the reason why it might or ought to have been done. Antipathy or resentment requires always to be regulated, to prevent its doing mischief: to be regulated by what? always by the principle of utility. The principle of utility neither requires nor admits of any other regulator than itself.

* *Various phrases that have served as the characteristic marks of so many pretended systems.* It is curious enough to observe the variety of inventions men have hit upon, and the variety of phrases they have brought forward, in order to conceal from the world, and, if possible, from themselves, this very general and therefore very pardonable self-sufficiency.

1. *Moral Sense.* One man says, he has a thing made on purpose to tell him what is right and what is wrong; and that it is called a *moral sense*: and then he goes to work at his ease, and says, such a thing is right, and such a thing is wrong – why? 'because my moral sense tells me it is.'

2. *Common Sense.* Another man comes and alters the phrase: leaving out *moral*, and putting in *common*, in the room of it. He then tells you, that his common sense teaches him what is right and wrong, as surely as the other's moral sense did: meaning by common sense, a sense of some kind or other, which, he says, is possessed by all mankind: the sense of those, whose sense is not the same as the author's, being struck out of the account as not

worth taking. This contrivance does better than the other; for a moral sense, being a new thing, a man may feel about him a good while without being able to find it out: but common sense is as old as the creation; and there is no man but would be ashamed to be thought not to have as much of it as his neighbours. It has another great advantage: by appearing to share power, it lessens envy: for when a man gets up upon this ground, in order to anathematize those who differ from him, it is not by a *sic volo sic jubeo*, but by a *velitis jubeatis*.

3. *Understanding*. Another man comes, and says, that as to a moral sense indeed, he cannot find that he has any such thing: that however he has an *understanding*, which will do quite as well. This understanding, he says, is the standard of right and wrong: it tells him so and so. All good and wise men understand as he does: if other men's understandings differ in any point from his, so much the worse for them: it is a sure sign they are either defective or corrupt.

4. *Rule of Right*. Another man says, that there is an eternal and immutable Rule of Right: that that rule of right dictates so and so: and then he begins giving you his sentiments upon any thing that comes uppermost: and these sentiments (you are to take for granted) are so many branches of the eternal rule of right.

5. *Fitness of Things*. Another man, or perhaps the same man (it's no matter) says, that there are certain practices conformable, and others repugnant, to the Fitness of Things; and then he tells you, at his leisure, what practices are conformable and what repugnant: just as he happens to like a practice or dislike it.

6. *Law of Nature*. A great multitude of people are continually talking of the Law of Nature; and then they go on giving you their sentiments about what is right and what is wrong: and these sentiments, you are to understand, are so many chapters and sections of the Law of Nature.

7. *Law of Reason, Right Reason, Natural Justice, Natural Equity, Good Order*. Instead of the phrase, Law of Nature, you have sometimes, Law of Reason, Right Reason, Natural Justice, Natural Equity, Good Order. Any of them will do equally well. This latter is most used in politics. The three last are much more tolerable than the others, because they do not very explicitly claim to

be any thing more than phrases: they insist but feebly upon the being looked upon as so many positive standards of themselves, and seem content to be taken, upon occasion, for phrases express-ive of the conformity of the thing in question to the proper stan-dard, whatever that may be. On most occasions, however, it will be better to say *utility*: *utility* is clearer, as referring more explicitly to pain and pleasure.

8. *Truth*. We have one philosopher, who says, there is no harm in any thing in the world but in telling a lie: and that if, for example, you were to murder your own father, this would only be a particular way of saying, he was not your father. Of course, when this philosopher sees any thing that he does not like, he says, it is a particular way of telling a lie. It is saying that the act ought to be done, or may be done, when, *in truth*, it ought not to be done.

9. *Doctrine of Election*. The fairest and openest of them all is that sort of man who speaks out, and says, I am of the number of the Elect: now God himself takes care to inform the Elect what is right: and that with so good effect, and let them strive ever so, they cannot help not only knowing it but practising it. If therefore a man wants to know what is right and what is wrong, he has nothing to do but to come to me.

Repugnancy to Nature. It is upon the principle of antipathy that such and such acts are often reprobated on the score of their being *unnatural*: the practice of exposing children, established among the Greeks and Romans, was an unnatural practice. Unnatural, when it means any thing, means unfrequent: and there it means something; although nothing to the present purpose. But here it means no such thing: for the frequency of such acts is perhaps the great complaint. It therefore means nothing; nothing, I mean, which there is in the act itself. All it can serve to express is, the disposition of the person who is talking of it: the disposition he is in to be angry at the thought of it. Does it merit his anger? Very likely it may: but whether it does or no is a question, which, to be answered rightly, can only be answered upon the principle of utility.

Unnatural, is as good a word as moral sense, or common sense; and would be as good a foundation for a system. Such an act is unnatural; that is, repugnant to nature: for I do not like to practise it: and, consequently, do not practise it. It is therefore repugnant to what ought to be the nature of everybody else.

Mischief they produce. The mischief common to all these ways of thinking and arguing (which, in truth, as we have seen, are but one and the same method, couched in different forms of words) is their serving as a cloak, and pretence, and aliment, to despotism: if not a despotism in practice, a despotism however in disposition: which is but too apt, when pretence and power offer, to show itself in practice. The consequence is, that with intentions very commonly of the purest kind, a man becomes a torment either to himself or his fellow creatures. If he be of the melancholy cast, he sits in silent grief, bewailing their blindness and depravity: if of the irascible, he declaims with fury and virulence against all who differ from him; blowing up the coals of fanaticism, and branding with the charge of corruption and insincerity every man who does not think, or profess to think, as he does.

If such a man happens to possess the advantages of style, his book may do a considerable deal of mischief before the nothingness of it is understood.

These principles, if such they can be called, it is more frequent to see applied to morals than to politics: but their influence extends itself to both. In politics, as well as morals, a man will be at least equally glad of a pretence for deciding any question in the manner that best pleases him, without the trouble of inquiry. If a man is an infallible judge of what is right and wrong in the actions of private individuals, why not in the measures to be observed by public men in the direction of those actions? accordingly (not to mention other chimeras) I have more than once known the pretended law of nature set up in legislative debates, in opposition to arguments derived from the principle of utility.

Whether utility is actually the sole ground of all the approbation we ever bestow, is a different consideration. 'But is it never, then, from any other considerations than those of utility, that we derive our notions of right and wrong?' I do not know: I do not care. Whether a moral sentiment can be originally conceived from any other source than a view of utility, is one question: whether upon examination and reflection it can, in point of fact, be actually persisted in and justified on any other ground, by a person reflecting within himself, is another: whether in point of right it can properly be justified on any other ground, by a person addressing himself to the community, is a third. The two first are questions of speculation: it matters not, comparatively speaking, how they are decided. The last is a question of practice: the decision of it is of as much importance as that of any can be.

'I feel in myself,' (say you) 'a disposition to approve of such or such an action in a moral view: but this is not owing to any notions I have of its being a useful one to the community. I do not pretend to know whether it be a useful one or not: it may be, for aught I know, a mischievous one.' 'But is it then,' (say I) 'a mischievous one? Examine; and if you can make yourself sensible that it is so, then, if duty means any thing, that is, moral duty, it is your *duty* at least to abstain from it: and more than that, if it is what lies in your power, and can be done without too great a sacrifice, to endeavour to prevent it. It is not your cherishing the notion of it in your bosom, and giving it the name of virtue, that will excuse you.'

'I feel in myself,' (say you again) 'a disposition to detest such or such an action in a moral view; but this is not owing to any notions I have of its being a mischievous one to the community. I do not pretend to know whether it be a mischievous one or not: it may not be a mischievous one: it may be, for aught I know, a useful one.' – 'May it indeed,' (say I) 'be a useful one? but let me tell you then, that unless duty, and right and wrong, be just what you please to make them, if it really be not a mischievous one, and anybody has a mind to do it, it is no duty of yours, but, on the contrary, it would be very wrong in you, to take upon you to prevent him: detest it within yourself as much as you please; that may be a very good reason (unless it be also a useful one) for your not doing it yourself: but if you go about, by word or deed, to do any thing to hinder him, or make him suffer for it, it is you, and not he, that have done wrong: it is not your setting yourself to blame his conduct, or branding it with the name of vice, that will make him culpable, or you blameless. Therefore, if you can make yourself content that he shall be of one mind, and you of another, about that matter, and so continue, it is well: but if nothing will serve you, but that you and he must needs be of the same mind, I'll tell you what you have to do: it is for you to get the better of your antipathy, not for him to truckle to it.'

Chapter III
Of the Four Sanctions or Sources of Pain and Pleasure

I. *Connection of this chapter with preceding.* It has been shown that happiness of the individuals, of whom a community is composed, that is their pleasures and their security, is the end and the sole end which the legislator ought to have in view: the sole standard, in conformity to which each individual ought, as far as depends upon the legislator, to be *made* to fashion his behaviour. But whether it be this or anything else that is to be *done*, there is nothing by which a man can ultimately be *made* to do it, but either pain or pleasure. Having taken a general view of these two grand objects (*viz.* pleasure, and what comes to the same thing, immunity from pain) in the character of *final* causes; it will be necessary to take a view of pleasure and pain itself, in the character of *efficient* causes or means.

II. *Four sanctions or sources of pleasure and pain.* There are four distinguishable sources from which pleasure and pain are in use to flow: considered separately, they may be termed the *physical*, the *political*, the *moral*, and the *religious*: and inasmuch as the pleasures and pains belonging to each of them are capable of giving a binding force to any law or rule of conduct, they may all of them be termed *sanctions*.

III. *The physical sanction.* If it be in the present life, and from the ordinary course of nature, not purposely modified by the interposition of the will of any human being, nor by any extra-ordinary interposition of any superior invisible being, that the pleasure or the pain takes place or is expected, it may be said to issue from or to belong to the *physical sanction*.

IV. *The political.* If at the hands of a *particular* person or set of persons in the community, who under names correspondent to that of *judge*, are chosen for the particular purpose of dispensing it, according to the will of the sovereign or supreme ruling power in the state, it may be said to issue from the *political sanction*.

V. *The moral or popular*. If at the hands of such *chance* persons in the community, as the party in question may happen in the course of his life to have concerns with, according to each man's spontaneous disposition, and not according to any settled or concerted rule, it may be said to issue from the *moral* or *popular sanction*.

VI. *The religious*. If from the immediate hand of a superior invisible being, either in the present life, or in a future, it may be said to issue from the *religious sanction*.

VII. *The pleasures and pains which belong to the religious sanction, may regard either the present life or a future*. Pleasures or pains which may be expected to issue from the *physical*, *political*, or *moral* sanctions, must all of them be expected to be experienced, if ever, in the *present* life: those which may be expected to issue from the *religious* sanction, may be expected to be experienced either in the *present* life or in a *future*.

VIII. *Those which regard the present life, from whichsoever source they flow, differ only in the circumstances of their production*. Those which can be experienced in the present life, can of course, be no others than such as human nature in the course of the present life is susceptible of: and from each of these sources may flow all the pleasures or pains of which, in the course of the present life, human nature is susceptible. With regard to these then (with which alone we have in this place any concern) those of them which belong to any one of those sanctions, differ not ultimately in kind from those which belong to any one of the other three: the only difference there is among them lies in the circumstances that accompany their production. A suffering which befalls a man in the natural and spontaneous course of things, shall be styled, for instance, a *calamity*; in which case, if it be supposed to befall him through any imprudence of his, it may be styled a punishment issuing from the physical sanction. Now this same suffering, if inflicted by the law, will be what is commonly called a *punishment*; if incurred for want of any friendly assistance, which the misconduct, or supposed misconduct, of the sufferer has occasioned to be withholden, a punishment issuing from the *moral* sanction; if through the immediate interposition of a particular providence, a punishment issuing from the *religious* sanction.

IX. *Example*. A man's goods, or his person are consumed by fire. If this happened to him by what is called an accident, it was a calamity: if by reason of his own imprudence (for instance, from his neglecting to put his candle out) it may be styled a punishment of the physical sanction: if it happened to him by the sentence of the political magistrate, a punishment belonging to the political sanction; that is, what is commonly called a punishment: if for want of any assistance which his *neighbour* withheld from him out of some dislike to his *moral* character, a punishment of the *moral* sanction: if by an immediate act of *God's* displeasure, manifested on account of some *sin* committed by him, or through any distraction of mind, occasioned by the dread of such displeasure, a punishment of the *religious* sanction.

X. *Those which regard a future life are not specifically known.* As to such of the pleasures and pains belonging to the religious sanction, as regard a future life, of what kind these may be we cannot know. These lie not open to our observation. During the present life they are matter only of expectation: and, whether that expectation be derived from natural or revealed religion, the particular kind of pleasure or pain, if it be different from all those which lie open to our observation, is what we can have no idea of. The best ideas we can obtain of such pains and pleasures are altogether unliquidated in point of quality. In what other respects our ideas of them *may* be liquidated will be considered in another place.

XI. *The physical sanction included in each of the other three.* Of these four sanctions the physical is altogether, we may observe, the groundwork of the political and the moral: so is it also of the religious, in as far as the latter bears relation to the present life. It is included in each of those other three. This may operate in any case, (that is, any of the pains or pleasures belonging to it may operate) independently of *them*: none of *them* can operate but by means of this. In a word, the powers of nature may operate of themselves; but neither the magistrate, nor men at large, *can* operate, nor is God in the case in question *supposed* to operate, but through the powers of nature.

XII. *Use of this chapter.* For these four objects, which in their nature have so much in common, it seemed of use to find a common name. It seemed of use, in the first place, for the convenience of giving a name to certain pleasures and pains, for which a name equally characteristic could hardly otherwise have been found: in the second place, for the sake of holding up the efficacy of certain moral forces, the influence of which is apt not to be sufficiently attended to. Does the political sanction exert an influence over the conduct of mankind? The moral, the religious sanctions do so too. In every inch of his career are the operations of the political magistrate liable to be aided or impeded by these two foreign powers: who, one or other of them, or both, are sure to be either his rivals or his allies. Does it happen to him to leave them out in his calculations? He will be sure almost to find himself mistaken in the result. Of all this we shall find abundant proofs in the sequel of this work. It behoves him, therefore, to have them continually before his eyes; and that under such a name as exhibits the relation they bear to his own purposes and designs.

Chapter IV
Value of a Lot of Pleasure or Pain,
How to be Measured

I. *Use of this chapter.* Pleasures then, and the avoidance of pains, are the *ends* which the legislator has in view: it behoves him therefore to understand their *value*. Pleasures and pains are the *instruments* he has to work with: it behoves him therefore to understand their force, which is again, in other words, their value.

II. *Circumstances to be taken into the account in estimating the value of a pleasure or pain considered with reference to a single person, and by itself.* To a person considered *by himself*, the value of a pleasure or pain considered *by itself*, will be greater or less, according to the four following circumstances:

1. Its *intensity*.
2. Its *duration*.
3. Its *certainty* or *uncertainty*.

4. Its *propinquity* or *remoteness*.

III. – *considered as connected with other pleasures or pains*. These are the circumstances which are to be considered in estimating a pleasure or a pain considered each of them by itself. But when the value of any pleasure or pain is considered for the purpose of estimating the tendency of any *act* by which it is produced, there are two other circumstances to be taken into the account; these are:

5. Its *fecundity*, or the chance it has of being followed by sensations of the *same* kind: that is, pleasures, if it be a pleasure: pains, if it be a pain.

6. Its *purity*, or the chance it has of *not* being followed by sensations of the *opposite* kind: that is, pains, if it be a pleasure: pleasures, if it be a pain.

These two last, however, are in strictness scarcely to be deemed properties of the pleasure or the pain itself; they are not, therefore, in strictness to be taken into the account of the value of that pleasure or that pain. They are in strictness to be deemed properties only of the act, or other event, by which such pleasure or pain has been produced; and accordingly are only to be taken into the account of the tendency of such act or such event.

IV. – *considered with reference to a number of persons*. To a *number* of persons, with reference to each of whom the value of a pleasure or a pain is considered, it will be greater or less, according to seven circumstances: to wit, the six preceding ones; *viz.*

1. Its *intensity*.

2. Its *duration*.

3. Its *certainty* or *uncertainty*.

4. Its *propinquity* or *remoteness*.

5. Its *fecundity*.

6. Its *purity*.

And one other; to wit:

7. Its *extent*; that is, the number of persons to whom it *extends*; or (in other words) who are affected by it.

V. *Process for estimating the tendency of any act or event*. To take an exact account then of the general tendency of any act, by which the interests of a community are affected, proceed as follows.

Begin with any one person of those whose interests seem most immediately to be affected by it: and take an account,

1. Of the value of each distinguishable *pleasure* which appears to be produced by it in the *first* instance.

2. Of the value of each *pain* which appears to be produced by it in the *first* instance.

3. Of the value of each pleasure which appears to be produced by it *after* the first. This constitutes the *fecundity* of the first *pleasure* and the *impurity* of the first *pain*.

4. Of the value of each *pain* which appears to be produced by it *after* the first. This constitutes the *fecundity* of the first *pain*, and the *impurity* of the first *pleasure*.

5. Sum up all the values of all the *pleasures* on the one side, and those of all the pains on the other. The balance, if it be on the side of pleasure, will give the *good* tendency of the act upon the whole, with respect to the interests of that *individual* person; if on the side of pain, the *bad* tendency of it upon the whole.

6. Take an account of the *number* of persons whose interests appear to be concerned; and repeat the above process with respect to each. *Sum up* the numbers expressive of the degrees of *good* tendency, which the act has, with respect to each individual, in regard to whom the tendency of it is *good* upon the whole: do this again with respect to each individual, in regard to whom the tendency of it is *bad* upon the whole. Take the *balance*; which, if on the side of *pleasure*, will give the general *good tendency* of the act, with respect to the total number or community of individuals concerned; if on the side of pain, the general *evil tendency*, with respect to the same community.

VI. *Use of the foregoing process.* It is not to be expected that this process should be strictly pursued previously to every moral judgement, or to every legislative or judicial operation. It may, however, be always kept in view: and as near as the process actually pursued on these occasions approaches to it, so near will such process approach to the character of an exact one.

VII. *The same process applicable to good and evil, profit and mischief, and all other modifications of pleasure and pain.* The same process is alike applicable to pleasure and pain, in whatever shape they appear: and by whatever denomination they are distinguished: to pleasure, whether it be called *good* (which is properly the cause or instrument of pleasure) or *profit* (which is distant pleasure, or the cause or instrument of distant pleasure,) or *convenience*, or *advantage*, *benefit*, *emolument*, *happiness*, and so forth: to pain, whether it be called *evil*, (which corresponds to *good*) or *mischief*, or *inconvenience*, or *disadvantage*, or *loss*, or *unhappiness*, and so forth.

VIII. *Conformity of men's practice to this theory*. Nor is this a novel and unwarranted, any more than it is a useless, theory. In all this there is nothing but what the practice of mankind, wheresoever they have a clear view of their own interest, is perfectly conformable to. An article of property, an estate in land, for instance, is valuable, on what account? On account of the pleasures of all kinds which it enables a man to produce, and what comes to the same thing the pains of all kinds which it enables him to avert. But the value of such an article of property is universally understood to rise or fall according to the length or shortness of the time which a man has in it: the certainty or uncertainty of its coming into possession: and the nearness or remoteness of the time at which, if at all, it is to come into possession. As to the *intensity* of the pleasures which a man may derive from it, this is never thought of, because it depends upon the use which each particular person may come to make of it; which cannot be estimated till the particular pleasures he may come to derive from it, or the particular pains he may come to exclude by means of it, are brought to view. For the same reason, neither does he think of the *fecundity* or *purity* of those pleasures.

Thus much for pleasure and pain, happiness and unhappiness, in *general*. We come now to consider the several particular kinds of pain and pleasure.

Chapter V
Pleasures and Pains, Their Kinds

I. *Pleasures and pains are either 1. Simple: or, 2. Complex*. Having represented what belongs to all sorts of pleasures and pains alike, we come now to exhibit, each by itself, the several sorts of pains and pleasures. Pains and pleasures may be called by one general word, interesting perceptions. Interesting perceptions are either simple or complex. The simple ones are those which cannot any one of them be resolved into more: complex are those which are resolvable into divers simple ones. A complex interesting perception may accordingly be composed either, 1. Of pleasures alone: 2. Of pains alone: or, 3. Of a pleasure or pleasures, and a pain or pains together. What determines a lot of pleasure, for example, to be regarded as one complex pleasure, rather than as divers simple ones, is the nature of the exciting cause. Whatever pleasures are excited all at once by the action of the same cause, are apt to be looked upon as constituting all together but one pleasure.

II. *The simple pleasures enumerated.* The several simple pleasures of which human nature is susceptible, seem to be as follows: 1. The pleasures of sense. 2. The pleasures of wealth. 3. The pleasures of skill. 4. The pleasures of amity. 5. The pleasures of a good name. 6. The pleasures of power. 7. The pleasures of piety. 8. The pleasures of benevolence. 9. The pleasures of malevolence. 10. The pleasures of memory. 11. The pleasures of imagination. 12. The pleasures of expectation. 13. The pleasures dependent on association. 14. The pleasures of relief.

III. *The simple pains enumerated.* The several simple pains seem to be as follows: 1. The pains of privation. 2. The pains of the senses. 3. The pains of awkwardness. 4. The pains of enmity. 5. The pains of an ill name. 6. The pains of piety. 7. The pains of benevolence. 8. The pains of malevolence. 9. The pains of the memory. 10. The pains of the imagination. 11. The pains of expectation. 12. The pains dependent on association.

IV. 1. *Pleasures of sense enumerated.* The pleasures of sense seem to be as follows: 1. The pleasures of the taste or palate; including whatever pleasures are experienced in satisfying the appetites of hunger and thirst. 2. The pleasure of intoxication. 3. The pleasures of the organ of smelling. 4. The pleasures of the touch. 5. The simple pleasures of the ear; independent of association. 6. The simple pleasures of the eye; independent of association. 7. The pleasure of the sexual sense. 8. The pleasure of health: or, the internal pleasurable feeling or flow of spirits (as it is called), which accompanies a state of full health and vigour; especially at times of moderate bodily exertion. 9. The pleasures of novelty: or, the pleasures derived from the gratification of the appetite of curiosity, by the application of new objects to any of the senses.

V. 2. *Pleasures of wealth, which are either of acquisition or of possession.* By the pleasures of wealth may be meant those pleasures which a man is apt to derive from the consciousness of possessing any article or articles which stand in the list of instruments of enjoyment or security, and more particularly at the time of his first acquiring them; at which time the pleasure may be styled a pleasure of gain or a pleasure of acquisition: at other times a pleasure of possession.

3. *Pleasures of skill.* The pleasures of skill, as exercised upon particular objects, are those which accompany the application of such particular instruments of enjoyment to their uses, as cannot be so applied without a greater or less share of difficulty or exertion.

VI. 4. *Pleasures of amity.* The pleasures of amity, or self-recommendation, are the pleasures that may accompany the persuasion of a man's being in the acquisition or the possession of the goodwill of such or such assignable person or persons in particular: or, as the phrase is, of being upon good terms with him or them: and as a fruit of it, of his being in a way to have the benefit of their spontaneous and gratuitous services.

VII. 5. *Pleasures of a good name.* The pleasures of a good name are the pleasures that accompany the persuasion of a man's being in the acquisition or the possession of the goodwill of the world about him; that is, of such members of society as he is likely to have concerns with; and as a means of it, either their love or their esteem, or both: and as a fruit of it, of his being in the way to have the benefit of their spontaneous and gratuitous services. These may likewise be called the pleasure of good repute, the pleasures of honour, or the pleasures of the moral sanction.

VIII. 6. *Pleasures of power.* The pleasures of power are the pleasures that accompany the persuasion of a man's being in a condition to dispose people, by means of their hopes and fears, to give him the benefit of their services: that is, by the hope of some service, or by the fear of some disservice, that he may be in the way to render them.

IX. 7. *Pleasures of piety*. The pleasures of piety are the pleasures that accompany the belief of a man's being in the acquisition or in possession of the goodwill or favour of the Supreme Being: and as a fruit of it, of his being in a way of enjoying pleasures to be received by God's special appointment, either in this life, or in a life to come. These may also be called the pleasures of religion, the pleasures of a religious disposition, or the pleasures of the religious sanction.

X. 8. *Pleasures of benevolence or goodwill*. The pleasures of benevolence are the pleasures resulting from the view of any pleasures supposed to be possessed by the beings who may be the objects of benevolence; to wit, the sensitive beings we are acquainted with; under which are commonly included, 1. The Supreme Being. 2. Human beings. 3. Other animals. These may also be called the pleasures of goodwill, the pleasures of sympathy, or the pleasures of the benevolent or social affections.

XI. 9. *Pleasures of malevolence or ill will*. The pleasures of malevolence are the pleasures resulting from the view of any pain supposed to be suffered by the beings who may become the objects of malevolence; to wit, 1. Human beings. 2. Other animals. These may also be styled the pleasures of ill will, the pleasures of the irascible appetite, the pleasures of antipathy, or the pleasures of the malevolent or dissocial affections.

XII. 10. *Pleasures of the memory*. The pleasures of the memory are the pleasures which, after having enjoyed such and such pleasures, or even in some case after having suffered such and such pains, a man will now and then experience, at recollecting them exactly in the order and in the circumstances in which they were actually enjoyed or suffered. These derivative pleasures may of course be distinguished into as many species as there are of original perceptions, from whence they may be copied. They may also be styled pleasures of simple recollection.

XIII. 11. *Pleasures of the imagination*. The pleasures of the imagination are the pleasures which may be derived from the contemplation of any such pleasures as may happen to be suggested by the memory, but in a different order, and accompanied be different groups of circumstances. These may accordingly be referred to any one of the three cardinal points of time, present, past, or future. It is evident they may admit of as many distinctions as those of the former class.

XIV. 12. *Pleasures of expectation.* The pleasures of expectation are the pleasures that result from the contemplation of any sort of pleasure, referred to time *future*, and accompanied with the sentiment of *belief.* These also may admit of the same distinctions.

XV. 13. *Pleasures depending on association.* The pleasures of association are the pleasures which certain objects or incidents may happen to afford, not of themselves, but merely in virtue of some association they have contracted in the mind with certain objects or incidents which are in themselves pleasurable. Such is the case, for instance, with the pleasure of skill, when afforded by such a set of incidents as compose a game of chess. This derives its pleasurable quality from its association partly with the pleasures of skill, as exercised in the production of incidents pleasurable of themselves: partly from its association with the pleasures of power. Such is the case also with the pleasure of good luck, when afforded by such incidents as compose the game of hazard, or any other game of chance, when played at for nothing. This derives its pleasurable quality from its association with one of the pleasures of wealth; to wit, with the pleasure of acquiring it.

XVI. 14. *Pleasures of relief.* Farther on we shall see pains grounded upon pleasures; in like manner may we now see pleasures grounded upon pains. To the catalogue of pleasures may accordingly be added the pleasures of *relief*: or, the pleasures which a man experiences when, after he has been enduring a pain of any kind for a certain time, it comes to cease, or to abate. These may of course be distinguished into as many species as there are of pains: and may give rise to so many pleasures of memory, of imagination, and of expectation.

XVII. 1. *Pains of privation.* Pains of privation are the pains that may result from the thought of not possessing in the time present any of the several kinds of pleasures. Pains of privation may accordingly be resolved into as many kinds as there are of pleasures to which they may correspond, and from the absence whereof they may be derived.

XVIII. *These include,* 1. *Pains of desire.* There are three sorts of pains which are only so many modifications of the several pains of privation. When the enjoyment of any particular pleasure happens to be particularly desired, but without any expectation approaching to assurance, the pain of privation which thereupon results takes a particular name, and is called the pain of *desire,* or of unsatisfied desire.

XIX. 2. *Pains of disappointment.* Where the enjoyment happens to have been looked for with a degree of expectation approaching to assurance, and that expectation is made suddenly to cease, it is called a pain of disappointment.

XX. 3. *Pains of regret.* A pain of privation takes the name of a pain of regret in two cases: 1. Where it is grounded on the memory of a pleasure, which having been once enjoyed, appears not likely to be enjoyed again: 2. Where it is grounded on the idea of a pleasure, which was never actually enjoyed, nor perhaps so much as expected, but which might have been enjoyed (it is supposed,) had such or such a contingency happened, which, in fact, did not happen.

XXI. 2. *Pains of the senses.* The several pains of the senses seem to be as follows: 1. The pains of hunger and thirst: or the disagreeable sensations produced by the want of suitable substances which need at times to be applied to the alimentary canal. 2. The pains of the taste: or the disagreeable sensations produced by the application of various substances to the palate, and other superior parts of the same canal. 3. The pains of the organ of smell: or the disagreeable sensations produced by the effluvia of various substances when applied to that organ. 4. The pains of the touch: or the disagreeable sensations produced by the application of various substances to the skin. 5. The simple pains of the hearing: or the disagreeable sensations excited in the organ of that sense by various kinds of sounds: independently (as before,) of association. 6. The simple pains of the sight: or the disagreeable sensations if any such there be, that may be excited in the organ of that sense by visible images, independent of the principle of association. 7. The pains resulting from excessive heat or cold, unless these be referable to the touch. 8. The pains of disease: or the acute and uneasy sensations resulting from the several diseases and indispositions to which human nature is liable. 9. The pain of exertion, whether bodily or mental: or the uneasy sensation which is apt to accompany any intense effort, whether of mind or body.

XXII. 3. *Pains of awkwardness*. The pains of awkwardness are the pains which sometimes result from the unsuccessful endeavour to apply any particular instruments of enjoyment or security to their uses, or from the difficulty a man experiences in applying them.

XXIII. 4. *Pains of enmity*. The pains of enmity are the pains that may accompany the persuasion of a man's being obnoxious to the ill will of such or such an assignable person or persons in particular: or, as the phrase is, of being upon ill terms with him or them: and, in consequence, of being obnoxious to certain pains of some sort or other, of which he may be the cause.

XXIV. 5. *Pains of an ill name*. The pains of an ill name are the pains that accompany the persuasion of a man's being obnoxious, or in a way to be obnoxious to the ill will of the world about him. These may likewise be called the pains of ill repute, the pains of dishonour, or the pains of the moral sanction.

XXV. 6. *Pains of piety*. The pains of piety are the pains that accompany the belief of a man's being obnoxious to the displeasure of the Supreme Being: and in consequence to certain pains to be inflicted by his especial appointment, either in this life or in a life to come. These may also be called the pains of religion; the pains of a religious disposition; or the pains of the religious sanction. When the belief is looked upon as well grounded, these pains are commonly called religious terrors; when looked upon as ill grounded, superstitious terrors.

XXVI. 7. *Pains of benevolence*. The pains of benevolence are the pains resulting from the view of any pains supposed to be endured by other beings. These may also be called the pains of goodwill, of sympathy, or the pains of the benevolent or social affections.

XXVII. 8. *Pains of malevolence*. The pains of malevolence are the pains resulting from the view of any pleasures supposed to be enjoyed by any beings who happen to be the objects of a man's displeasure. These may also be styled the pains of ill will, of antipathy, or the pains of the malevolent or dissocial affections.

XXVIII. 9. *Pains of the memory*. The pains of the memory may be grounded on every one of the above kinds, as well of pains of privation as of positive pains. These correspond exactly to the pleasures of the memory.

XXIX. 10. *Pains of the imagination*. The pains of the imagination may also be grounded on any one of the above kinds, as well of pains of privation as of positive pains: in other respects they correspond exactly to the pleasures of the imagination.

XXX. 11. *Pains of expectation*. The pains of expectation may be grounded on each one of the above kinds, as well of pains of privation as of positive pains. These may be also termed pains of apprehension.

XXXI. 12. *Pains of association*. The pains of association correspond exactly to the pleasures of association.

XXXII. *Pleasures and pains are either self-regarding or extra-regarding*. Of the above list there are certain pleasures and pains which suppose the existence of some pleasure or pain of some other person, to which the pleasure or pain of the person in question has regard: such pleasures and pains may be termed *extra-regarding*. Others do not suppose any such thing: these may be termed *self-regarding*. The only pleasures and pains of the extra-regarding class are those of benevolence and those of malevolence: all the rest are self-regarding.

XXXIII. *In what ways the law is concerned with the above pains and pleasures*. Of all these several sorts of pleasures and pains, there is scarce any one which is not liable, on more accounts than one, to come under the consideration of the law. Is an offence committed? It is the tendency which it has to destroy, in such or such persons, some of these pleasures, or to produce some of these pains, that constitutes the mischief of it, and the ground for punishing it. It is the prospect of some of these pleasures, or of security from some of these pains, that constitutes the motive or temptation, it is the attainment of them that constitutes the profit of the offence. Is the offender to be punished? It can be only by the production of one or more of these pains, that the punishment can be inflicted.

Editor's Note

Chapters VI–XII of *Introduction to the Principles of Morals and Legislation* discuss the aspects of motivation and intention which Bentham believes the legislator must take into account when framing laws and allocating punishments for their infraction. They go into baroque detail. Something of their flavour persists into Bentham's discussion of situations where punishment would be entirely inappropriate and of the factors which ought to influence the legislator's decision on the severity of penal sanctions.

Chapter XIII
Cases Unmeet for Punishment

1. *General view of cases unmeet for punishment.*

I. *The end of law is, to augment happiness.* The general object which all laws have, or ought to have, in common, is to augment the total happiness of the community; and therefore, in the first place, to exclude, as far as may be, every thing that tends to subtract from that happiness: in other words, to exclude mischief.

II. *But punishment is an evil.* But all punishment is mischief: all punishment in itself is evil. Upon the principle of utility, if it ought at all to be admitted, it ought only to be admitted in as far as it promises to exclude some greater evil.

III. *Therefore ought not to be admitted.* It is plain, therefore, that in the following cases punishment ought not to be inflicted.

1. *Where groundless.* Where it is *groundless*: where there is no mischief for it to prevent; the act not being mischievous upon the whole.

2. *Inefficacious.* Where it must be *inefficacious*: where it cannot act so as to prevent the mischief.

3. *Unprofitable.* Where it is *unprofitable*, or too *expensive*: where

the mischief it would produce would be greater than what it prevented.

4. *Or needless*. Where it is *needless*: where the mischief may be prevented, or cease of itself, without it: that is, at a cheaper rate.

2. *Cases in which punishment is groundless.*

These are,

IV. 1. *Where there has never been any mischief: as in the case of consent*. Where there has never been any mischief: where no mischief has been produced to anybody by the act in question. Of this number are those in which the act was such as might, on some occasions, be mischievous or disagreeable, but the person whose interest it concerns gave his *consent* to the performance of it. This consent, provided it be free, and fairly obtained, is the best proof that can be produced, that, to the person who gives it, no mischief, at least no immediate mischief, upon the whole, is done. For no man can be so good a judge as the man himself, what it is gives him pleasure or displeasure.

V. 2. *Where the mischief was outweighed: as in precaution against calamity, and the exercise of powers*. Where the mischief was *outweighed*: although a mischief was produced by that act, yet the same act was necessary to the production of a benefit which was of greater value than the mischief. This may be the case with any thing that is done in the way of precaution against instant calamity, as also with any thing that is done in the exercise of the several sorts of powers necessary to be established in every community, to wit, domestic, judicial, military, and supreme.

VI. 3. – *or will, for a certainty be cured by compensation*. Where there is a certainty of an adequate compensation: and that in all cases where the offence can be committed. This supposes two things: 1. That the offence is such as admits of an adequate compensation: 2. That such a compensation is sure to be forthcoming. Of these suppositions, the latter will be found to be a merely ideal one: a supposition that cannot, in the universality here given to it, be verified by fact. It cannot, therefore, in practice, be numbered amongst the grounds of absolute impunity. It may, however, be admitted as a ground for an abatement of that punishment, which other considerations, standing by themselves, would seem to dictate.

3. Cases in which punishment must be inefficacious.

These are,

VII. 1. *Where the penal provision comes too late: as in, 1. An ex-post-facto law, 2. An ultra-legal sentence.* Where the penal provision is *not established* until after the act is done. Such are the cases, 1. Of an *ex-post-facto* law; where the legislator himself appoints not a punishment till after the act is done. 2. Of a sentence beyond the law; where the judge, of his own authority, appoints a punishment which the legislator had not appointed.

VIII. 2. *Or is not made known: as in a law not sufficiently promulgated.* Where the penal provision, though established, is *not conveyed* to the notice of the person on whom it seems intended that it should operate. Such is the case where the law has omitted to employ any of the expedients which are necessary, to make sure that every person whatsoever, who is within the reach of the law, be apprised of all the cases whatsoever, in which (being in the station of life he is in) he can be subjected to the penalties of the law.

IX. 3. *Where the will cannot be deterred from any act: as in,* Where the penal provision, though it were conveyed to a man's notice, *could produce no effect* on him, with respect to the preventing him from engaging in any act of the *sort* in question. Such is the case, 1. In extreme *infancy*; where a man has not yet attained that state or disposition of mind in which the prospect of evils so distant as those which are held forth by the law, has the effect of influencing his conduct. 2. In *insanity*; where the person, if he has attained to that disposition, has since been deprived of it through the influence of some permanent though unseen cause. 3. In *intoxication*; where he has been deprived of it by the transient influence of a visible cause: such as the use of wine, or opium, or other drugs, that act in this manner on the nervous system: which condition is indeed neither more nor less than a temporary insanity produced by an assignable cause.

X. 4. *Or not from the individual act in question, as in*, Where the penal provision (although, being conveyed to the party's notice, it might very well prevent his engaging in acts of the sort in question, provided he knew that it related to those acts) could not have this effect, with regard to the *individual* act he is about to engage in: to wit, because he knows not that it is of the number of those to which the penal provision relates. This may happen, 1. In the case of *unintentionality*; where he intends not to engage, and thereby knows not that he is about to engage, in the *act* in which eventually he is about to engage. 2. In the case of *unconsciousness*; where, although he may know that he is about to engage in the *act* itself, yet, from not knowing all the material *circumstances* attending it, he knows not of the *tendency* it has to produce that mischief, in contemplation of which it has been made penal in most instances. 3. In the case of *mis-supposal*; where, although he may know of the tendency the act has to produce that degree of mischief, he supposes it, though mistakenly, to be attended with some circumstance, or set of circumstances, which, if it had been attended with, it would either not have been productive of that mischief, or have been productive of such a greater degree of good, as has determined the legislator in such a case not to make it penal.

XI. 5. *Or is acted on by an opposite superior force: as by*, Where, though the penal clause might exercise a full and prevailing influence, were it to act alone, yet by the *predominant* influence of some opposite cause upon the will, it must necessarily be ineffectual; because the evil which he sets himself about to undergo, in the case of his *not* engaging in the act, is so great, that the evil denounced by the penal clause, in case of his engaging in it, cannot appear greater. This may happen, 1. In the case of *physical danger*; where the evil is such as appears likely to be brought about by the unassisted powers of *nature*. 2. In the case of a *threatened mischief*; where it is such as appears likely to be brought about through the intentional and conscious agency of *man*.

XII. 6. – *or the bodily organs cannot follow its determination: as under*, Where (though the penal clause may exert a full and prevailing influence over the *will* of the party) yet his *physical faculties* (owing to the predominant influence of some physical cause) are not in a condition to follow the determination of the will: insomuch that the act is absolutely *involuntary*. Such is the case of physical *compulsion* or *restraint*, by whatever means brought about; where the man's hand, for instance, is pushed against some object which his will disposes him *not* to touch; or tied down from touching some object which his will disposes him to touch.

4. *Cases where punishment is unprofitable.*

These are,

XIII. 1. *Where, in the* sort *of case in question, the punishment would produce more evil than the offence would.* Where, on the one hand, the nature of the offence, on the other hand, that of the punishment, are, *in the ordinary state of things*, such, that when compared together, the evil of the latter will turn out to be greater than that of the former.

XIV. *Evil producible by a punishment – its four branches – viz.* Now the evil of the punishment divides itself into four branches, by which so many different sets of persons are affected. 1. The evil of *coercion* or *restraint*: or the pain which it gives a man not to be able to do the act, whatever it be, which by the apprehension of the punishment he is deterred from doing. This is felt by those by whom the law is *observed*. 2. The evil of *apprehension*: or the pain which a man, who has exposed himself to punishment, feels at the thoughts of undergoing it. This is felt by those by whom the law has been *broken*, and who feel themselves in *danger* of its being executed upon them. 3. The evil of *sufferance*: or the pain which a man feels, in virtue of the punishment itself, from the time when he begins to undergo it. This is felt by those by whom the law is broken, and upon whom it comes actually to be executed. 4. The pain of sympathy, and the other *derivative* evils resulting to the persons who are in *connection* with the several classes of original sufferers just mentioned. Now of these four lots of evil, the first will be greater or less, according to the nature of the act from which the party is restrained: the second and third according to the nature of the punishment which stands annexed to that offence.

XV. (*The evil of the offence being different, according to the nature of the offence, cannot be represented here.*) On the other hand, as to the evil of the offence, this will also, of course, be greater or less, according to the nature of each offence. The proportion between the one evil and the other will therefore be different in the case of each particular offence. The cases, therefore, where punishment is unprofitable on this ground, can by no other means be discovered, than by an examination of each particular offence; which is what will be the business of the body of the work.

XVI. 2. – *or in the* individual *case in question: by reason of,* Where, although in the *ordinary state* of things, the evil resulting from the punishment is not greater than the benefit which is likely to result from the force with which it operates, during the same space of time, towards the excluding the evil of the offences, yet it may have been rendered so by the influence of some *occasional circumstances*. In the number of these circumstances may be, 1. *The multitude of delinquents*. The multitude of delinquents at a particular juncture; being such as would increase, beyond the ordinary measure, the *quantum* of the second and third lots, and thereby also of a part of the fourth lot, in the evil of the punishment. 2. *The value of a delinquent's service*. The extraordinary value of the services of some one delinquent; in the case where the effect of the punishment would be to deprive the community of the benefit of those services. 3. *The displeasure of the people*. The displeasure of the *people*; that is, of an indefinite number of the members of the *same* community, in cases where (owing to the influence of some occasional incident) they happen to conceive, that the offence or the offender ought not to be punished at all, or at least ought not to be punished in the way in question. 4. *The displeasure of foreign powers*. The displeasure of *foreign powers*; that is, of the governing body, or a considerable number of the members of some *foreign* community or communities, with which the community in question is connected.

5. *Cases where punishment is needless.*

These are,

XVII. 1. *Where the mischief is to be prevented at a cheaper rate; as,* Where the purpose of putting an end to the practice may be attained as effectually at a cheaper rate: by instruction, for instance, as well as by terror: by informing the understanding; as well as by exercising an immediate influence on the will. *By instruction*. This seems to be the case with respect to all those offences which consist in the disseminating pernicious principles in matters of *duty*; of whatever kind the duty be; whether political, or moral, or religious. And this, whether such principles be disseminated *under*, or even *without*, a sincere persuasion of their being beneficial. I say, even *without*: for though in such a case it is not instruction that can prevent the writer from endeavouring to inculcate his principles, yet it may the readers from adopting them: without which, his endeavouring to inculcate them will do no harm. In such a case, the sovereign will commonly have little need to take an active part: if it be the interest of *one* individual to inculcate principles that are pernicious, it will as surely be the interest of *other* individuals to expose them. But if the sovereign must needs take a part in the controversy, the pen is the proper weapon to combat error with, not the sword.

Chapter XIV
Of the Proportion Between Punishments and Offences

I. *Recapitulation*. We have seen that the general object of all laws is to prevent mischief; that is to say, when it is worth while; but that, where there are no other means of doing this than punishment, there are four cases in which it is *not* worth while.

II. *Four objects of punishment*. When it *is* worth while, there are four subordinate designs or objects, which, in the course of his endeavours to compass, as far as may be, that one general object, a legislator, whose views are governed by the principle of utility, comes naturally to propose to himself.

III. 1. *1st Object – to prevent all offences*. His first, most extensive, and most eligible object, is to prevent, in as far as it is possible, and worth while, all sorts of offences whatsoever: in other words, so to manage, that no offence whatsoever may be committed.

IV. 2. *2nd Object – to prevent the worst.* But if a man must needs commit an offence of some kind or other, the next object is to induce him to commit an offence *less* mischievous, *rather* than one *more* mischievous: in other words, to choose always the *least* mischievous, of two offences that will either of them suit his purpose.

V. 3. *3rd Object – to keep down the mischief.* When a man has resolved upon a particular offence, the next object is to dispose him to do *no more* mischief than is *necessary* to his purpose: in other words, to do as little mischief as is consistent with the benefit he has in view.

VI. 4. *4th Object – to act at the least expense.* The last object is, whatever the mischief be, which it is proposed to prevent, to prevent it at as *cheap* a rate as possible.

VII. *Rules of proportion between punishments and offences.* Subservient to these four objects, or purposes, must be the rules or canons by which the proportion of punishments to offences is to be governed.

VIII. Rule 1. *Outweigh the profit of the offence.* The first object, it has been seen, is to prevent, in as far as it is worth while, all sorts of offences; therefore,

The value of the punishment must not be less in any case than what is sufficient to outweigh that of the profit of the offence.

If it be, the offence (unless some other considerations, independent of the punishment, should intervene and operate efficaciously in the character of tutelary motives) will be sure to be committed notwithstanding: the whole lot of punishment will be thrown away: it will be altogether *inefficacious.*

IX. *The propriety of taking the strength of the temptation for a ground of abatement, no objection to this rule.* The above rule has been often objected to, on account of its seeming harshness: but this can only have happened for want of its being properly understood. The strength of the temptation, *ceteris paribus*, is as the profit of the offence: the quantum of the punishment must rise with the profit of the offence: *ceteris paribus*, it must therefore rise with the strength of the temptation. This there is no disputing. True it is, that the stronger the temptation, the less conclusive is the indication which the act of delinquency affords of the depravity of the offender's disposition. So far then as the absence of any aggravation, arising from extraordinary depravity of disposition, may operate, or at the utmost, so far as the presence of a ground of extenuation, resulting from the innocence or beneficence of the offender's disposition, can operate, the strength of the temptation may operate in abatement of the demand for punishment. But it can never operate so far as to indicate the propriety of making the punishment ineffectual, which it is sure to be when brought below the level of the apparent profit of the offence.

The partial benevolence which should prevail for the reduction of it below this level, would counteract as well those purposes which such a motive would actually have in view, as those more extensive purposes which benevolence ought to have in view: it would be cruelty not only to the public, but to the very persons in whose behalf it pleads: in its effects, I mean, however opposite in its intention. Cruelty to the public, that is cruelty to the innocent, by suffering them, for want of an adequate protection, to lie exposed to the mischief of the offence: cruelty even to the offender himself, by punishing him to no purpose, and without the chance of compassing that beneficial end, by which alone the introduction of the evil of punishment is to be justified.

X. Rule 2. *Venture more against a great offence than a small one.* But whether a given offence shall be prevented in a given degree by a given quantity of punishment, is never any thing better than a chance; for the purchasing of which, whatever punishment is employed, is so much expended in advance. However, for the sake of giving it the better chance of outweighing the profit of the offence.

The greater the mischief of the offence, the greater is the expense, which it may be worth while to be at, in the way of punishment.

XI. Rule 3. *Cause the least of two offences to be preferred.* The next object is, to induce a man to choose always the least mischievous of two offences; therefore

Where two offences come in competition, the punishment for the greater offence must be sufficient to induce a man to prefer the less.

XII. Rule 4. *Punish for each particle of the mischief.* When a man has resolved upon a particular offence, the next object is, to induce him to do no more mischief than what is necessary for his purpose: therefore

The punishment should be adjusted in such manner to each particular offence, that for every part of the mischief there may be a motive to restrain the offender from giving birth to it.

XIII. Rule 5. *Punish in no degree without special reason.* The last object is, whatever mischief is guarded against, to guard against it at as cheap a rate as possible: therefore

The punishment ought in no case to be more than what is necessary to bring it into conformity with the rules here given.

XIV. Rule 6. *Attend to circumstances influencing sensibility.* It is further to be observed, that owing to the different manners and degrees in which persons under different circumstances are affected by the same exciting cause, a punishment which is the same in name will not always either really produce, or even so much as appear to others to produce, in two different persons the same degree of pain: therefore

That the quantity actually inflicted on each individual offender may correspond to the quantity intended for similar offenders in general, the several circumstances influencing sensibility ought always to be taken into account.

XV. *Comparative view of the above rules.* Of the above rules of proportion, the four first, we may perceive, serve to mark out the limits on the side of diminution; the limits *below* which a punishment ought not to be *diminished*: the fifth, the limits on the side of increase; the limits *above* which it ought not to be *increased*. The five first are calculated to serve as guides to the legislator: the sixth is calculated, in some measure, indeed, for the same purpose; but principally for guiding the judge in his endeavours to conform, on both sides, to the intentions of the legislator.

XVI. *Into the account of the* value *of a punishment must be taken its deficiency in point of certainty and proximity.* Let us look back a little. The first rule, in order to render it more conveniently applicable to practice, may need perhaps to be a little more particularly unfolded. It is to be observed, then, that for the sake of accuracy, it was necessary, instead of the word *quantity* to make use of the less perspicuous term *value*. For the word *quantity* will not properly include the circumstances either of certainty or proximity: circumstances which, in estimating the value of a lot of pain or pleasure, must always be taken into the account. Now, on the one hand, a lot of punishment is a lot of pain; on the other hand, the profit of an offence is a lot of pleasure, or what is equivalent to it. But the profit of the offence *is* commonly more *certain* than the punishment, or, what comes to the same thing, *appears* so at least to the offender. It is at any rate commonly more *immediate*. It follows, therefore, that, in order to maintain its superioity over the profit of the offence, the punishment must have its value made up in some other way, in proportion to that whereby it falls short in the two points of *certainty* and *proximity*. Now there is no other way in which it can receive any addition to its *value*, but by receiving an addition in point of *magnitude*. Wherever then the value of the punishment falls short, either in point of *certainty*, or of *proximity*, of that of the profit of the offence, it must receive a proportionable addition in point of *magnitude*.

XVII. *Also into the account of the mischief and profit of the offence, the mischief and profit of other offences of the same* habit. Yet farther. To make sure of giving the value of the punishment the superiority over that of the offence, it may be necessary, in some cases, to take into the account the profit not only of the *individual* offence to which the punishment is to be annexed, but also of such *other* offences of the *same sort* as the offender is likely to have already committed without detection. This random mode of calculation, severe as it is, it will be impossible to avoid having recourse to, in certain cases: in such, to wit, in which the profit is pecuniary, the chance of detection very small, and the obnoxious act of such a nature as indicates a habit: for example, in the case of frauds against the coin. If it be *not* recurred to, the practice of committing the offence will be sure to be, upon the balance of the account, a gainful practice. That being the case, the legislator will be absolutely sure of *not* being able to suppress it, and the whole punishment that is bestowed upon it will be thrown away. In a word (to keep to the same expressions we set out with) that whole quantity of punishment will be *inefficacious*.

XVIII. Rule 7. *Want of certainty must be made up in magnitude.* These things being considered, the three following rules may be laid down by way of supplement and explanation to Rule 1.

To enable the value of the punishment to outweigh that of the profit of the offence, it must be increased, in point of magnitude, in proportion as it falls short in point of certainty.

XIX. Rule 8. (*So also want of proximity.*) *Punishment must be further increased in point of magnitude, in proportion as it falls short in point of proximity.*

XX. Rule 9. (*For acts indicative of a habit punish as for the habit.*) *Where the act is conclusively indicative of a habit, such an increase must be given to the punishment as may enable it to outweigh the profit not only of the individual offence, but of such other like offences as are likely to have been committed with impunity by the same offender.*

XXI. *The remaining rules are of less importance.* There may be a few other circumstances or considerations which may influence, in some small degree, the demand for punishment: but as the propriety of these is either not so demonstrable, or not so constant, or the application of them not so determinate, as that of the foregoing, it may be doubted whether they be worth putting on a level with the others.

XXII. Rule 10. (*For the sake of quality, increase in quantity.*) *When a punishment, which in point of quality is particularly well calculated to answer its intention, cannot exist in less than a certain quantity, it may sometimes be of use, for the sake of employing it, to stretch a little beyond that quantity which, on other accounts, would be strictly necessary.*

XXIII. Rule 11. (*Particularly for a moral lesson.*) *In particular, this may sometimes be the case, where the punishment proposed is of such a nature as to be particularly well calculated to answer the purpose of a moral lesson.*

XXIV. Rule 12. *Attend to circumstances which may render punishment unprofitable.* The tendency of the above considerations is to dictate an augmentation in the punishment: the following rule operates in the way of diminution. There are certain cases (it has been seen) in which, by the influence of accidental circumstances, punishment may be rendered unprofitable in the whole: in the same cases it may chance to be rendered unprofitable as to a part only. Accordingly,

In adjusting the quantum of punishment, the circumstances, by which all punishment may be rendered unprofitable, ought to be attended to.

XXV. Rule 13. *For simplicity's sake, small disproportions may be neglected*. It is to be observed, that the more various and minute any set of provisions are, the greater the chance is that any given article in them will not be borne in mind: without which, no benefit can ensue from it. Distinctions, which are more complex than what the conceptions of those whose conduct it is designed to influence can take in, will even be worse than useless. The whole system will present a confused appearance: and thus the effect, not only of the proportions established by the articles in question, but of whatever is connected with them, will be destroyed. To draw a precise line of direction in such case seems impossible. However, by way of memento, it may be of some use to subjoin the following rule.

Among provisions designed to perfect the proportion between punishments and offences, if any occur, which, by their own particular good effects, would not make up for the harm they would do by adding to the intricacy of the Code, they should be omitted.

XXVI. *Auxiliary force of the physical, moral, and religious sanction, not here allowed for – why.* It may be remembered, that the political sanction, being that to which the sort of punishment belongs, which in this chapter is all along in view, is but one of four sanctions, which may all of them contribute their share towards producing the same effects. It may be expected, therefore, that in adjusting the quantity of political punishment, allowance should be made for the assistance it may meet with from those other controlling powers. True it is, that from each of these several sources a very powerful assistance may sometimes be derived. But the case is, that (setting aside the moral sanction, in the case where the force of it is expressly adopted into and modified by the political) the force of those other powers is never determinate enough to be depended upon. It can never be reduced, like political punishment, into exact lots, nor meted out in number, quantity, and value. The legislator is therefore obliged to provide the full complement of punishment, as if he were sure of not receiving any assistance whatever from any of those quarters. If he does, so much the better: but lest he should not, it is necessary he should, at all events, make that provision which depends upon himself.

XXVII. *Recapitulation.* It may be of use, in this place, to recapitulate the several circumstances, which, in establishing the proportion betwixt punishments and offences, are to be attended to. These seem to be as follows:

I. *On the part of the offence:*

1. The profit of the offence;
2. The mischief of the offence;
3. The profit and mischief of other greater or lesser offences, of different sorts, which the offender may have to choose out of;
4. The profit and mischief of other offences, of the same sort, which the same offender may probably have been guilty of already.

II. *On the part of the punishment:*

5. The magnitude of the punishment: composed of its intensity and duration;
6. The deficiency of the punishment in point of certainty;
7. The deficiency of the punishment in point of proximity;
8. The quality of the punishment;
9. The accidental advantage in point of quality of a punishment, not strictly needed in point of quantity;
10. The use of a punishment of a particular quality, in the character of a moral lesson.

III. *On the part of the offender:*

11. The responsibility of the class of persons in a way to offend;
12. The sensibility of each particular offender;
13. The particular merits or useful qualities of any particular offender, in case of a punishment which might deprive the community of the benefit of them;
14. The multitude of offenders on any particular occasion.

IV. *On the part of the public*, at any particular conjuncture:

15. The inclinations of the people, for or against any quantity or mode of punishment;
16. The inclinations of foreign powers.

V. *On the part of the law:* that is, of the public for a continuance:

17. The necessity of making small sacrifices, in point of proportionality, for the sake of simplicity.

XXVIII. *The nicety here observed vindicated from the charge of inutility*. There are some, perhaps, who, at first sight, may look upon the nicety employed in the adjustment of such rules, as so much labour lost: for gross ignorance, they will say, never troubles itself about laws, and passion does not calculate. But the evil of ignorance admits of cure: and as to the proposition that passion does not calculate, this, like most of these very general and oracular propositions, is not true. When matters of such importance as pain and pleasure are at stake, and these in the highest degree (the only matters, in short, that can be of importance) who is there that does not calculate? Men calculate, some with less exactness, indeed, some with more: but all men calculate. I would not say that even a madman does not calculate. Passion calculates, more or less, in every man: in different men, according to the warmth or coolness of their dispositions: according to the firmness or irritability of their minds: according to the nature of the motives by which they are acted upon. Happily, of all passions, that is the most given to calculation, from the excesses of which, by reason of its strength, constancy, and universality, society has most to apprehend: I mean that which corresponds to the motive of pecuniary interest: so that these niceties, if such they are to be called, have the best chance of being efficacious, where efficacy is of the most importance.

Editor's Note

The text of these two chapters from Book VI of *A System of Logic* comes from the last edition printed in Mill's lifetime; I have omitted the very last section of Chapter XII, which is a short conclusion to the whole Book and unrelated to the rest of the chapter.

From *A System of Logic*

BY J. S. MILL

Of Liberty and Necessity*

1. *Are human actions subject to the law of causality?* The question, whether the law of causality applies in the same strict sense to human actions as to other phenomena, is the celebrated controversy concerning the freedom of the will: which, from at least as far back as the time of Pelagius, has divided both the philosophical and the religious world. The affirmative opinion is commonly called the doctrine of Necessity, as asserting human volitions and actions to be necessary and inevitable. The negative maintains that the will is not determined, like other phenomena, by antecedents, but determines itself; that our volitions are not, properly speaking, the effects of causes, or at least have no causes which they uniformly and implicitly obey.

I have already made it sufficiently apparent that the former of these opinions is that which I consider the true one; but the misleading terms in which it is often expressed, and the indistinct manner in which it is usually apprehended, have both obstructed its reception, and perverted its influence when received. The metaphysical theory of free will, as held by philosophers (for the practical feeling of it, common in a greater or less degree to all mankind, is in no way inconsistent with the contrary theory), was invented because the supposed alternative of admitting human actions to be *necessary*, was deemed inconsistent with every one's instinctive consciousness, as well as humiliating to the pride and even degrading to the moral nature of man. Nor do I deny that the doctrine, as sometimes held, is open to these imputations; for the misapprehension in which I shall be able to show that they originate, unfortunately is not confined to the opponents of the

*Originally Chapter II of Book VI.

doctrine, but is participated in by many, perhaps we might say by most, of its supporters.

2. *The doctrine commonly called Philosophical Necessity, in what sense true?* Correctly conceived, the doctrine called Philosophical Necessity is simply this: that, given the motives which are present to an individual's mind, and given likewise the character and disposition of the individual, the manner in which he will act might be unerringly inferred: that if we knew the person thoroughly, and knew all the inducements which are acting upon him, we could foretell his conduct with as much certainty as we can predict any physical event. This proposition I take to be a mere interpretation of universal experience, a statement in words of what every one is internally convinced of. No one who believed that he knew thoroughly the circumstances of any case, and the characters of the different persons concerned, would hesitate to foretell how all of them would act. Whatever degree of doubt he may in fact feel, arises from the uncertainty whether he really knows the circumstances, or the character of some one or other of the persons, with the degree of accuracy required: but by no means from thinking that if he did know these things, there could be any uncertainty what the conduct would be. Nor does this full assurance conflict in the smallest degree with what is called our feeling of freedom. We do not feel ourselves the less free, because those to whom we are intimately known are well assured how we shall will to act in a particular case. We often, on the contrary, regard the doubt of what our conduct will be as a mark of ignorance of our character, and sometimes even resent it as an imputation. The religious metaphysicians who have asserted the freedom of the will, have always maintained it to be consistent with divine foreknowledge of our actions: and if with divine, then with any other foreknowledge. We may be free, and yet another may have reason to be perfectly certain what use we shall make of our freedom. It is not, therefore, the doctrine that our volitions and actions are invariable consequents of our antecedent states of mind, that is either contradicted by our consciousness, or felt to be degrading.

But the doctrine of causation, when considered as obtaining between our volitions and their antecedents, is almost universally conceived as involving more than this. Many do not believe, and very few practically feel, that there is nothing in causation but invariable, certain and unconditional sequence. There are few to whom mere constancy of succession appears a sufficiently stringent bond of union for so peculiar a relation as that of cause and effect. Even if the reason repudiates, the imagination retains the feeling of some more intimate connection, of some peculiar tie, or mysterious constraint exercised by the antecedent over the consequent. Now this it is which, considered as applying to the human will, conflicts with our consciousness, and revolts our feelings. We are certain that, in the case of our volitions, there is not this mysterious constraint. We know that we are not compelled, as by a magical spell, to obey any particular motive. We feel, that if we wished to prove that we have the power of resisting the motive, we could do so (that wish being, it needs scarcely be observed, a *new antecedent*), and it would be humiliating to our pride, and (what is of more importance) paralysing to our desire of excellence, if we thought otherwise. But neither is any such mysterious compulsion now supposed, by the best philosophical authorities, to be exercised by any other cause over its effect. Those who think that causes draw their effects after them by a mystical tie, are right in believing that the relation between volitions and their antecedents is of another nature. But they should go farther, and admit that this is also true of all other effects and their antecedents. If such a tie is considered to be involved in the word necessity, the doctrine is not true of human actions; but neither is it then true of inanimate objects. It would be more correct to say that matter is not bound by necessity, than that mind is so.

That the free-will metaphysicians, being mostly of the school which rejects Hume's and Brown's analysis of Cause and Effect, should miss their way for want of the light which that analysis affords, cannot surprise us. The wonder is, that the necessitarians, who usually admit that philosophical theory, should in practice equally lose sight of it. The very same misconception of the doctrine called Philosophical Necessity, which prevents the opposite party from recognizing its truth, I believe to exist more or less obscurely in the minds of most necessitarians, however they may in words disavow it. I am much mistaken if they habitually feel that the necessity which they recognize in actions is but uniformity of order, and capability of being predicted. They have a feeling as if there were at bottom a stronger tie between the volitions and their causes: as if, when they asserted that the will is governed by the balance of motives, they meant something more cogent than if they had only said that whoever knew the motives, and our habitual susceptibilities to them, could predict how we should will to act. They commit, in opposition to their own scientific system, the very same mistake which their adversaries commit in obedience to theirs; and in consequence do really in some instances suffer those depressing consequences, which their opponents erroneously impute to the doctrine itself.

3. *Inappropriateness and pernicious effect of the term Necessity*. I am inclined to think that this error is almost wholly an effect of the associations with a word; and that it would be prevented, by forbearing to employ, for the expression of the simple fact of causation, so extremely inappropriate a term as Necessity. That word, in its other acceptations, involves much more than mere uniformity of sequence: it implies irresistibleness. Applied to the will, it only means that the given cause will be followed by the effect, subject to all possibilities of counteraction by other causes: but in common use it stands for the operation of those causes exclusively, which are supposed too powerful to be counteracted at all. When we say that all human actions take place of necessity, we only mean that they will certainly happen if nothing prevents: – when we say that dying of want, to those who cannot get food, is a necessity, we mean that it will certainly happen whatever may be done to prevent it. The application of the same term to the agencies on which human actions depend, as is used to express those agencies of nature which are really uncontrollable, cannot fail, when habitual, to create a feeling of uncontrollableness in the former also. This however is a mere illusion. There are physical sequences which we call necessary, as death for want of food or air; there are others which, though as much cases of causation as the former, are not said to be necessary, as death from poison, which an antidote, or the use of the stomach-pump, will sometimes avert. It is apt to be forgotten by people's feelings, even if

remembered by their understandings, that human actions are in this last predicament: they are never (except in some cases of mania) ruled by any one motive with such absolute sway, that there is no room for the influence of any other. The causes, therefore, on which action depends, are never uncontrollable; and any given effect is only necessary provided that the causes tending to produce it are not controlled. That whatever happens, could not have happened otherwise unless something had taken place which was capable of preventing it, no one surely needs hesitate to admit. But to call this by the name necessity is to use the term in a sense so different from its primitive and familiar meaning, from that which it bears in the common occasions of life, as to amount almost to a play upon words. The associations derived from the ordinary sense of the term will adhere to it in spite of all we can do: and though the doctrine of Necessity, as stated by most who hold it, is very remote from fatalism, it is probable that most necessitarians are fatalists, more or less, in their feelings.

A fatalist believes, or half believes (for nobody is a consistent fatalist), not only that whatever is about to happen will be the infallible result of the causes which produce it (which is the true necessitarian doctrine), but moreover that there is no use in struggling against it; that it will happen however we may strive to prevent it. Now, a necessitarian, believing that our actions follow from our characters, and that our characters follow from our organization, our education, and our circumstances, is apt to be, with more or less of consciousness on his part, a fatalist as to his own actions, and to believe that his nature is such, or that his education and circumstances have so moulded his character, that nothing can now prevent him from feeling and acting in a particular way, or at least that no effort of his own can hinder it. In the words of the sect which in our own day has most perseveringly inculcated and most perversely misunderstood this great doctrine, his character is formed *for* him, and not *by* him; therefore his wishing that it had been formed differently is of no use; he has no power to alter it. But this is a grand error. He has, to a certain extent, a power to alter his character. It being, in the ultimate resort, formed for him, is not inconsistent with its being, in part, formed *by* him as one of the intermediate agents. His character is formed by his circumstances (including among these his particular organization); but his own desire to mould it in a particular way is one of those circumstances, and by no means one of the least influential. We cannot, indeed, directly will to be different from what we are. But neither did those who are supposed to have formed our characters, directly will that we should be what we are. Their will had no direct power except over their own actions. They made us what they did make us, by willing, not the end, but the requisite means; and we, when our habits are not too inveterate, can, by similarly willing the requisite means, make ourselves different. If they could place us under the influence of certain circumstances, we, in like manner, can place ourselves under the influence of other circumstances. We are exactly as capable of making our own character, *if we will*, as others are of making it for us.

Yes (answers the Owenite), but these words, 'if we will', surrender the whole point: since the will to alter our own character is given us, not by any efforts of ours, but by circumstances which we cannot help; it comes to us either from external causes, or not at all. Most true: if the Owenite stops here, he is in a position from which nothing can expel him. Our character is formed by us as well as for us; but the wish which induces us to attempt to form it is formed for us; and how? Not, in general, by our organization, nor wholly by our education, but by our experience; experience of the painful consequences of the character we previously had: or by some strong feeling of admiration or aspiration, accidentally aroused. But to think that we have no power of altering our character, and to think that we shall not use our power unless we desire to use it, are very different things, and have a very different effect on the mind. A person who does not wish to alter his character, cannot be the person who is supposed to feel discouraged or paralysed by thinking himself unable to do it. The depressing effect of the fatalist doctrine can only be felt where there *is* a wish to do what that doctrine represents as impossible. It is of no consequence what we think forms our character, when we have no desire of our own about forming it; but it is of great consequence that we should not be prevented from forming such a desire by thinking the attainment impracticable, and that if we have the desire, we should know that the work is not so irrevocably done as to be incapable of being altered.

And indeed, if we examine closely, we shall find that this feeling, of our being able to modify our own character *if we wish*, is itself the feeling of moral freedom which we are conscious of. A person feels morally free who feels that his habits or his temptations are not his masters, but he theirs: who even in yielding to them knows that he could resist; that were he desirous of altogether throwing them off, there would not be required for that purpose a stronger desire than he knows himself to be capable of feeling. It is of course necessary, to render our consciousness of freedom complete, that we should have succeeded in making our character all we have hitherto attempted to make it; for if we have wished and not attained, we have, to that extent, not power over our own character, we are not free. Or at least, we must feel that our wish, if not strong enough to alter our character, is strong enough to conquer our character when the two are brought into conflict in any particular case of conduct. And hence it is said with truth, that none but a person of confirmed virtue is completely free.

The application of so improper a term as Necessity to the doctrine of cause and effect in the matter of human character, seems to me one of the most signal instances in philosophy of the abuse of terms, and its practical consequences one of the most striking examples of the power of language over our associations. The subject will never be generally understood, until that objectionable term is dropped. The free-will doctrine, by keeping in view precisely that portion of the truth which the word Necessity puts out of sight, namely the power of the mind to co-operate in the formation of its own character, has given to its adherents a practical feeling much nearer to the truth than has generally (I believe) existed in the minds of necessitarians. The latter may have had a stronger sense of the importance of what human beings can do to shape the characters of one another; but the free-will doctrine has, I believe, fostered in its supporters a much stronger spirit of self-culture.

4. *A motive not always the anticipation of a pleasure or pain.* There is still one fact which requires to be noticed (in addition to the

existence of a power of self-formation) before the doctrine of the causation of human actions can be freed from the confusion and misapprehensions which surround it in many minds. When the will is said to be determined by motives, a motive does not mean always or solely, the anticipation of a pleasure or of a pain. I shall not here inquire whether it be true that, in the commencement, all our voluntary actions are mere means consciously employed to obtain some pleasure, or avoid some pain. It is at least certain that we gradually, through the influence of association, come to desire the means without thinking of the end: the action itself becomes an object of desire, and is performed without reference to any motive beyond itself. Thus far, it may still be objected, that, the action having through association become pleasurable, we are, as much as before, moved to act by the anticipation of a pleasure, namely, the pleasure of the action itself. But granting this, the matter does not end here. As we proceed in the formation of habits, and become accustomed to will a particular act or a particular course of conduct because it is pleasurable, we at last continue to will it without any reference to its being pleasurable. Although, from some change in us or in our circumstances, we have ceased to find any pleasure in the action, or perhaps to antici- pate any pleasure as the consequence of it, we still continue to desire the action, and consequently to do it. In this manner it is that habits of hurtful excess continue to be practised although they have ceased to be pleasurable; and in this manner also it is that the habit of willing to persevere in the course which he has chosen, does not desert the moral hero, even when the reward, however real, which he doubtless receives from the consciousness of well-doing, is anything but an equivalent for the sufferings he undergoes, or the wishes which he may have to renounce.

A habit of willing is commonly called a purpose; and among the causes of our volitions, and of the actions which flow from them, must be reckoned not only likings and aversions, but also purposes. It is only when our purposes have become independent of the feelings of pain or pleasure from which they originally took their rise, that we are said to have a confirmed character. A character, says Novalis, is a completely fashioned will: and the will, once so fashioned, may be steady and constant, when the passive susceptibilities of pleasure and pain are greatly weakened, or materially changed.

With the corrections and explanations now given, the doctrine of the causation of our volitions by motives, and of motives by the desirable objects offered to us, combined with our particular susceptibilities of desire, may be considered, I hope, as sufficiently established for the purposes of this treatise.

Of the Logic of Practice, or Art; Including Morality and Policy*

1. *Morality not a Science, but an Art.* In the preceding chapters we have endeavoured to characterize the present state of those among the branches of knowledge called Moral, which are sciences in the only proper sense of the term, that is, inquiries into the course of nature. It is customary, however, to include under the term moral knowledge, and even (though improperly) under that of moral science, an inquiry the results of which do not express themselves in the indicative, but in the imperative mood, or in periphrases equivalent to it; what is called the knowledge of duties; practical ethics or morality.

Now, the imperative mood is the characteristic of art, as distinguished from science. Whatever speaks in rules, or precepts, not in assertions respecting matters of fact, is art: and ethics, or morality, is properly a portion of the art corresponding to the sciences of human nature and society.

The Method, therefore, of Ethics, can be no other than that of Art, or Practice, in general: and the portion yet uncompleted, of the task which we proposed to ourselves in the concluding Book, is to characterize the general Method of Art, as distinguished from Science.

2. *Relation between rules of art and the theorems of the corresponding science.* In all branches of practical business, there are cases in which individuals are bound to conform their practice to a pre-established rule, while there are others in which it is part of their

*Originally Chapter XII of Book VI.

task to find or construct the rule by which they are to govern their conduct. The first, for example, is the case of a judge, under a definite written code. The judge is not called upon to determine what course would be intrinsically the most advisable in the particular case in hand, but only within what rule of law it falls; what the legislature has ordained to be done in the kind of case, and must therefore be presumed to have intended in the individual case. The method must here be wholly and exclusively one of ratiocination, or syllogism; and the process is obviously, what in our analysis of the syllogism we showed that all ratiocination is, namely the interpretation of a formula.

In order that our illustration of the opposite case may be taken from the same class of subjects as the former, we will suppose, in contrast with the situation of the judge, the position of the legislator. As the judge has laws for his guidance, so the legislator has rules, and maxims of policy; but it would be a manifest error to suppose that the legislator is bound by these maxims in the same manner as the judge is bound by the laws, and that all he has to do is to argue down from them to the particular case, as the judge does from the laws. The legislator is bound to take into consideration the reasons or grounds of the maxim; the judge has nothing to do with those of the law, except so far as a consideration of them may throw light upon the intention of the lawmaker, where his words have left it doubtful. To the judge, the rule, once positively ascertained, is final; but the legislator, or other practitioner, who goes by rules rather than by their reasons, like the old-fashioned German tacticians who were vanquished by Napoleon, or the physician who preferred that his patients should die by rule rather than recover contrary to it, is rightly judged to be a mere pedant, and the slave of his formulas.

Now, the reasons of a maxim of policy, or of any other rule of art, can be no other than the theorems of the corresponding science.

The relation in which rules of art stand to doctrines of science may be thus characterized. The art proposes to itself an end to be attained, defines the end, and hands it over to the science. The science receives it, considers it as a phenomenon or effect to be studied, and having investigated its causes and conditions, sends it back to art with a theorem of the combinations of circumstances by which it could be produced. Art then examines these combinations of circumstances, and according as any of them are or are not in human power, pronounces the end attainable or not. The only one of the premises, therefore, which Art supplies, is the original major premise, which asserts that the attainment of the given end is desirable. Science then lends to Art the proposition (obtained by a series of inductions or of deductions) that the performance of certain actions will attain the end. From these premises Art concludes that the performance of these actions is desirable, and finding it also practicable, converts the theorem into a rule or precept.

3. *What is the proper function of rules of art?* It deserves particular notice, that the theorem or speculative truth is not ripe for being turned into a precept, until the whole, and not a part merely, of the operation which belongs to science, has been performed. Suppose that we have completed the scientific process only up to a certain point; have discovered that a particular cause will produce the desired effect, but have not ascertained all the negative conditions which are necessary, that is, all the circumstances which, if present, would prevent its production. If, in this imperfect state of the scientific theory, we attempt to frame a rule of art, we perform that operation prematurely. Whenever any counteracting cause, overlooked by the theorem, takes place, the rule will be at fault: we shall employ the means and the end will not follow. No arguing from or about the rule itself will then help us through the difficulty: there is nothing for it but to turn back and finish the scientific process which should have preceded the formation of the rule. We must re-open the investigation, to inquire into the remainder of the conditions on which the effect depends; and only after we have ascertained the whole of these, are we prepared to transform the completed law of the effect into a precept, in which those circumstances or combinations of circumstances which the science exhibits as conditions, are prescribed as means.

It is true that, for the sake of convenience, rules must be formed from something less than this ideally perfect theory; in the first place, because the theory can seldom be made ideally perfect; and next, because, if all the counteracting contingencies, whether of frequent or of rare occurrence, were included, the rules would be too cumbrous to be apprehended and remembered by ordinary capacities, on the common occasions of life. The rules of art do not attempt to comprise more conditions than require to be atte: ded to in ordinary cases; and are therefore always imperfect. In the manual arts, where the requisite conditions are not numerous, and where those which the rules do not specify are generally either plain to common observation or speedily learnt from practice, rules may often be safely acted on by persons who know nothing more than the rule. But in the complicated affairs of life, and still more in those of states and societies, rules cannot be relied on, without constantly referring back to the scientific laws on which they are founded. To know what are the practical contingencies which require a modification of the rule, or which are altogether exceptions to it, is to know what combinations of circumstances would interfere with, or entirely counteract, the consequences of those laws: and this can only be learnt by a reference to the theoretic grounds of the rule.

By a wise practitioner, therefore, rules of conduct will only be considered as provisional. Being made for the most numerous cases, or for those of most ordinary occurrence, they point out the manner in which it will be least perilous to act, where time or means do not exist for analysing the actual circumstances of the case, or where we cannot trust our judgement in estimating them. But they do not at all supersede the propriety of going through (when circumstances permit) the scientific process requisite for framing a rule from the data of the particular case before us. At the same time, the common rule may very properly serve as an admonition that a certain mode of action has been found by ourselves and others to be well adapted to the cases of most common occurrence; so that if it be unsuitable to the case in hand, the reason of its being so will be likely to arise from some unusual circumstance.

4. *Art cannot be deductive*. The error is therefore apparent, of those who would deduce the line of conduct proper to particular cases, from supposed universal practical maxims; overlooking the necessity of constantly referring back to the principles of the

speculative science, in order to be sure of attaining even the specific end which the rules have in view. How much greater still, then, must the error be, of setting up such unbending principles, not merely as universal rules for attaining a given end, but as rules of conduct generally; without regard to the possibility, not only that some modifying cause may prevent the attainment of the given end by the means which the rule prescribes, but that success itself may conflict with some other end, which may possibly chance to be more desirable.

This is the habitual error of many of the political speculators whom I have characterized as the geometrical school; especially in France, where ratiocination from rules of practice forms the staple commodity of journalism and political oratory; a misapprehension of the functions of Deduction which has brought much discredit, in the estimation of other countries, upon the spirit of generalization so honourably characteristic of the French mind. The commonplaces of politics, in France, are large and sweeping practical maxims, from which, as ultimate premises, men reason downwards to particular applications, and this they call being logical and consistent. For instance, they are perpetually arguing that such and such a measure ought to be adopted, because it is a consequence of the principle on which the form of government is founded; of the principle of legitimacy, or the principle of the sovereignty of the people. To which it may be answered, that if these be really practical principles, they must rest on speculative grounds; the sovereignty of the people (for example) must be a right foundation for government, because a government thus constituted tends to produce certain beneficial effects. Inasmuch, however, as no government produces all possible beneficial effects, but all are attended with more or fewer inconveniences; and since these cannot usually be combated by means drawn from the very causes which produce them; it would be often a much stronger recommendation of some practical arrangement, that it does not follow from what is called the general principle of the government, than that it does. Under a government of legitimacy, the presumption is far rather in favour of institutions of popular origin; and in a democracy, in favour of arrangements tending to check the impetus of popular will. The line of argumentation so commonly mistaken in France for political philosophy, tends to the practical conclusion that we should exert our utmost efforts to aggravate, instead of alleviating, whatever are the characteristic imperfections of the system of institutions which we prefer, or under which we happen to live.

5. *Every Art consists of truths of Science, arranged in the order suitable for some practical use.* The grounds, then, of every rule of art, are to be found in the theorems of science. An art, or a body of art, consists of the rules, together with as much of the speculative propositions as comprises the justification of those rules. The complete art of any matter, includes a selection of such a portion from the science, as is necessary to show on what conditions the effects, which the art aims at producing, depend. And Art in general, consists of the truths of Science, arranged in the most convenient order for practice, instead of the order which is the most convenient for thought. Science groups and arranges its truths, so as to enable us to take in at one view as much as possible of the general order of the universe. Art, though it must assume the same general laws, follows them only into such of their detailed consequences as have led to the formation of rules of conduct; and brings together from parts of the field of science most remote from one another, the truths relating to the production of the different and heterogeneous conditions necessary to each effect which the exigencies of practical life require to be produced.

Science, therefore, following one cause to its various effects, while art traces one effect to its multiplied and diversified causes and conditions; there is need of a set of intermediate scientific truths, derived from the higher generalities of science, and destined to serve as the generalia or first principles of the various arts. The scientific operation of framing these intermediate principles, M. Comte characterizes as one of those results of philosophy which are reserved for futurity. The only complete example which he points out as actually realized, and which can be held up as a type to be imitated in more important matters, is the general theory of the art of Descriptive Geometry, as conceived by M. Monge. It is not, however, difficult to understand what the nature of these intermediate principles must generally be.

After framing the most comprehensive possible conception of the end to be aimed at, that is, of the effect to be produced, and determining in the same comprehensive manner the set of conditions on which that effect depends; there remains to be taken, a general survey of the resources which can be commanded for realizing this set of conditions; and when the result of this survey has been embodied in the fewest and most extensive propositions possible, those propositions will express the general relation between the available means and the end, and will constitute the general scientific theory of the art; from which its practical methods will follow as corollaries.

6. *Teleology, or the Doctrine of Ends.* But though the reasonings which connect the end or purpose of every art with its means, belong to the domain of Science, the definition of the end itself belongs exclusively to Art, and forms its peculiar province. Every art has one first principle, or general major premise, not borrowed from science; that which enunciates the object aimed at, and affirms it to be a desirable object. The builder's art assumes that it is desirable to have buildings; architecture (as one of the fine arts), that it is desirable to have them beautiful or imposing. The hygienic and medical arts assume, the one that the preservation of health, the other that the cure of disease, are fitting and desirable ends. These are not propositions of science. Propositions of science assert a matter of fact: an existence, a coexistence, a succession, or a resemblance. The propositions now spoken of do not assert that anything is, but enjoin or recommend that something should be. They are a class by themselves. A proposition of which the predicate is expressed by the words *ought* or *should be*, is generically different from one which is expressed by *is*, or *will be*. It is true, that in the largest sense of the words, even these propositions assert something as a matter of fact. The fact affirmed in them is, that the conduct recommended excites in the speaker's mind the feeling of approbation. This, however, does not go to the bottom of the matter; for the speaker's approbation is no sufficient reason why other people should approve; nor ought it to be a conclusive reason even with himself. For the purposes of practice, every one must be required to justify his approbation: and for this there is need of general premises,

determining what are the proper objects of approbation, and what the proper order of precedence among those objects.

These general premises, together with the principal conclusions which may be deduced from them, form (or rather might form) a body of doctrine, which is properly the Art of Life, in its three departments, Morality, Prudence or Policy, and Aesthetics; the Right, the Expedient, and the Beautiful or Noble, in human conduct and works. To this art (which, in the main, is unfortunately still to be created), all other arts are subordinate; since its principles are those which must determine whether the special aim of any particular art is worthy and desirable, and what is its place in the scale of desirable things. Every art is thus a joint result of laws of nature disclosed by science, and of the general principles of what has been called Teleology, or the Doctrine of Ends; which, borrowing the language of the German metaphysicians, may also be termed, not improperly, the principles of Practical Reason.

A scientific observer or reasoner, merely as such, is not an adviser for practice. His part is only to show that certain consequences follow from certain causes, and that to obtain certain ends, certain means are the most effectual. Whether the ends themselves are such as ought to be pursued, and if so, in what cases and to how great a length, it is no part of his business as a cultivator of science to decide, and science alone will never qualify him for the decision. In purely physical science, there is not much temptation to assume this ulterior office; but those who treat of human nature and society invariably claim it; they always undertake to say, not merely what is, but what ought to be. To entitle them to do this, a complete doctrine of Teleology is indispensable. A scientific theory, however perfect, of the subject matter, considered merely as part of the order of nature, can in no degree serve as a substitute. In this respect the various subordinate arts afford a misleading analogy. In them there is seldom any visible necessity for justifying the end, since in general its desirableness is denied by nobody, and it is only when the question of precedence is to be decided between that end and some other, that the general principles of Teleology have to be called in: but a writer on Morals and Politics requires those principles at every step.

The most elaborate and well-digested exposition of the laws of succession and coexistence among mental or social phenomena, and of their relation to one another as causes and effects, will be of no avail towards the art of Life or of Society, if the ends to be aimed at by that art are left to the vague suggestions of the *intellectus sibi permissus*, or are taken for granted without analysis or questioning.

7. *Necessity of an ultimate standard, or first principle of Teleology.*
There is, then, a Philosophia Prima peculiar to Art, as there is one which belongs to Science. There are not only first principles of Knowledge, but first principles of Conduct. There must be some standard by which to determine the goodness or badness, absolute and comparative, of ends, or objects of desire. And whatever that standard is, there can be but one: for if there were several ultimate principles of conduct, the same conduct might be approved by one of those principles and condemned by another; and there would be needed some more general principle, as umpire between them.

Accordingly, writers on moral philosophy have mostly felt the necessity not only of referring all rules of conduct, and all judgements of praise and blame, to principles, but of referring them to some one principle; some rule, or standard, with which all other rules of conduct were required to be consistent, and from which by ultimate consequence they could all be deduced. Those who have dispensed with the assumption of such an universal standard, have only been enabled to do so by supposing that a moral sense, or instinct, inherent in our constitution, informs us, both what principles of conduct we are bound to observe, and also in what order these should be subordinated to one another.

The theory of the foundations of morality is a subject which it would be out of place, in a work like this, to discuss at large, and which could not to any useful purpose be treated incidentally. I shall content myself therefore with saying, that the doctrine of intuitive moral principles, even if true, would provide only for that portion of the field of conduct which is properly called moral. For the remainder of the practice of life some general principle, or standard, must still be sought; and if that principle be rightly chosen, it will be found, I apprehend, to serve quite as well for the ultimate principle of Morality, as for that of Prudence, Policy or Taste.

Without attempting in this place to justify my opinion, or even to define the kind of justification which it admits of, I merely declare my conviction, that the general principle to which all rules of practice ought to conform, and the test by which they should be tried, is that of conduciveness to the happiness of mankind, or rather, of all sentient beings: in other words, that the promotion of happiness is the ultimate principle of Teleology.

I do not mean to assert that the promotion of happiness should be itself the end of all actions, or even of all rules of action. It is the justification, and ought to be the controller, of all ends, but is not itself the sole end. There are many virtuous actions, and even virtuous modes of action (though the cases are, I think, less frequent than is often supposed) by which happiness in the particular instance is sacrificed, more pain being produced than pleasure. But conduct of which this can be truly asserted, admits of justification only because it can be shown that on the whole more happiness will exist in the world, if feelings are cultivated which will make people, in certain cases, regardless of happiness. I fully admit that this is true: that the cultivation of an ideal nobleness of will and conduct, should be to individual human beings an end, to which the specific pursuit either of their own happiness or of that of others (except so far as included in that idea) should, in any case of conflict, give way. But I hold that the very question, what constitutes this elevation of character, is itself to be decided by a reference to happiness as the standard. The character itself should be, to the individual, a paramount end, simply because the existence of this ideal nobleness of character, or of a near approach to it, in any abundance, would go further than all things else towards making human life happy; both in the comparatively humble sense, of pleasure and freedom from pain, and in the higher meaning, of rendering life, not what it now is almost universally, puerile and insignificant – but such as human beings with highly developed faculties can care to have.

Editor's Note

'Bentham' was first published in the *London and Westminster Review*, August 1838; the text printed here is taken from Mill's collected essays, *Dissertations and Discussions*, the edition of 1867, the last of Mill's lifetime.

'Bentham'

BY J. S. MILL

There are two men, recently deceased, to whom their country is indebted not only for the greater part of the important ideas which have been thrown into circulation among its thinking men in their time, but for a revolution in its general modes of thought and investigation. These men, dissimilar in almost all else, agreed in being closet-students – secluded in a peculiar degree, by circumstances and character, from the business and intercourse of the world: and both were, through a large portion of their lives, regarded by those who took the lead in opinion (when they happened to hear of them) with feelings akin to contempt. But they were destined to renew a lesson given to mankind by every age, and always disregarded – to show that speculative philosophy, which to the superficial appears a thing so remote from the business of life and the outward interests of men, is in reality the thing on earth which most influences them, and in the long run overbears every other influence save those which it must itself obey. The writers of whom we speak have never been read by the multitude; except for the more slight of their works, their readers have been few: but they have been the teachers of the teachers; there is hardly to be found in England an individual of any importance in the world of mind, who (whatever opinions he may have afterwards adopted) did not first learn to think from one of these two; and though their influences have but begun to diffuse themselves through these intermediate channels over society at large, there is already scarcely a publication of any consequence addressed to the educated classes, which, if these persons had not existed, would not have been different from what it is. These men are, Jeremy Bentham and Samuel Taylor Coleridge – the two great seminal minds of England in their age.

No comparison is intended here between the minds or

influences of these remarkable men: this were impossible unless there were first formed a complete judgement of each, considered apart. It is our intention to attempt, on the present occasion, an estimate of one of them; the only one, a complete edition of whose works is yet in progress, and who, in the classification which may be made of all writers into Progressive and Conservative, belongs to the same division with ourselves. For although they were far too great men to be correctly designated by either appellation exclusively, yet in the main, Bentham was a Progressive philosopher, Coleridge a Conservative one. The influence of the former has made itself felt chiefly on minds of the Progressive class, of the latter, on those of the Conservative: and the two systems of concentric circles which the shock given by them is spreading over the ocean of mind, have only just begun to meet and intersect. The writings of both contain severe lessons to their own side, on many of the errors and faults they are addicted to: but to Bentham it was given to discern more particularly those truths with which existing doctrines and institutions were at variance; to Coleridge, the neglected truths which lay *in* them.

A man of great knowledge of the world, and of the highest reputation for practical talent and sagacity among the official men of his time (himself no follower of Bentham, nor of any partial or exclusive school whatever) once said to us, as the result of his observation, that to Bentham more than to any other source might be traced the questioning spirit, the disposition to demand the *why* of everything, which had gained so much ground and was producing such important consequences in these times. The more this assertion is examined, the more true it will be found. Bentham has been in this age and country the great questioner of things established. It is by the influence of the modes of thought with which his writings inoculated a considerable number of thinking men, that the yoke of authority has been broken, and innumerable opinions, formerly received on tradition as incontestable, are put upon their defence, and required to give an account of themselves. Who, before Bentham, (whatever controversies might exist on points of detail) dared to speak disrespectfully, in express terms, of the British Constitution, or the English Law? He did so; and his arguments and his example together encouraged others. We do not mean that his writings caused the Reform Bill, or that the Appropriation Clause owns him as its parent: the changes which have been made, and the greater changes which will be made, in our institutions, are not the work of philosophers, but of the interests and instincts of large portions of society recently grown into strength. But Bentham gave voice to those interests and instincts: until he spoke out, those who found our institutions unsuited to them did not dare to say so, did not dare consciously to think so; they had never heard the excellence of those institutions questioned by cultivated men, by men of acknowledged intellect; and it is not in the nature of uninstructed minds to resist the united authority of the instructed. Bentham broke the spell. It was not Bentham by his own writings; it was Bentham through the minds and pens which those writings fed – through the men in more direct contact with the world, into whom his spirit passed. If the superstition about ancestorial wisdom has fallen into decay; if the public are grown familiar with the idea that their laws and institutions are in great part not the product of intellect and virtue, but of modern corruption grafted upon ancient barbarism; if the hardiest innovation is no longer scouted because it is an innovation – establishments no longer considered sacred because they are establishments – it will be found that those who have accustomed the public mind to these ideas have learnt them in Bentham's school, and that the assault on ancient institutions has been, and is, carried on for the most part with his weapons. It matters not although these thinkers, or indeed thinkers of any description, have been but scantily found among the persons prominently and ostensibly at the head of the Reform movement. All movements, except directly revolutionary ones, are headed, not by those who originate them, but by those who know best how to compromise between the old opinions and the new. The father of English innovation, both in doctrines and in institutions, is Bentham: he is the great *subversive* or, in the language of continental philosophers, the great *critical* thinker of his age and country.

We consider this, however, to be not his highest title to fame. Were this all, he were only to be ranked among the lowest order of the potentates of mind – the negative, or destructive philosophers; those who can perceive what is false, but not what is true; who awaken the human mind to the inconsistencies and absurdities of time-sanctioned opinions and institutions, but substitute nothing in the place of what they take away. We have no desire to undervalue the services of such persons: mankind have been deeply indebted to them; nor will there ever be a lack of work for them, in a world in which so many false things are believed, in which so many which have been true, are believed long after they have ceased to be true. The qualities, however, which fit men for perceiving anomalies, without perceiving the truths which would rectify them, are not among the rarest of endowments. Courage, verbal acuteness, command over the forms of argumentation, and a popular style, will make, out of the shallowest man, with a sufficient lack of reverence, a considerable negative philosopher. Such men have never been wanting in periods of culture; and the period in which Bentham formed his early impressions was emphatically their reign, in proportion to its barrenness in the more noble products of the human mind. An age of formalism in the Church and corruption in the State, when the most valuable part of the meaning of traditional doctrines had faded from the minds even of those who retained from habit a mechanical belief in them, was the time to raise up all kinds of sceptical philosophy. Accordingly, France had Voltaire, and his school of negative thinkers, and England (or rather Scotland) had the profoundest negative thinker on record, David Hume: a man, the peculiarities of whose mind qualified him to detect failure of proof, and want of logical consistency, at a depth which French sceptics, with their comparatively feeble powers of analysis and abstraction, stopped far short of, and which German subtlety alone could thoroughly appreciate, or hope to rival.

If Bentham had merely continued the work of Hume, he would scarcely have been heard of in philosophy; for he was far inferior to Hume in Hume's qualities, and was in no respect fitted to excel as a metaphysician. We must not look for subtlety, or the power of recondite analysis, among his intellectual characteristics. In the former quality, few great thinkers have ever been so deficient; and to find the latter, in any considerable measure, in a mind acknowledging any kindred with his, we must have recourse to the late Mr Mill – a man who united the great qualities of the metaphysicians of the eighteenth century, with others of a different complexion, admirably qualifying him to complete and correct their work. Bentham had not these peculiar gifts; but he possessed others, not inferior, which were not possessed by any of his precursors; which have made him a source of light to a generation which has far outgrown their influence and, as we called him, the chief subversive thinker of an age which has long lost all that they could subvert.

To speak of him first as a merely negative philosopher – as one who refutes illogical arguments, exposes sophistry, detects contradiction and absurdity; even in that capacity there was a wide field left vacant for him by Hume, and which he has occupied to an unprecedented extent; the field of practical abuses. This was Bentham's peculiar province: to this he was called by the whole bent of his disposition: to carry the warfare against absurdity into things practical. His was an essentially practical mind. It was by practical abuses that his mind was first turned to speculation – by the abuses of the profession which was chosen for him, that of the law. He has himself stated what particular abuse first gave that shock to his mind, the recoil of which has made the whole mountain of abuse totter; it was the custom of making the client pay for three attendances in the office of a Master in Chancery, when only one was given. The law, he found, on examination, was full of such things. But were these discoveries of his? No; they were known to every lawyer who practised, to every judge who sat on the bench, and neither before nor for long after did they cause any apparent uneasiness to the consciences of these learned persons, nor hinder them from asserting, whenever occasion offered, in books, in Parliament, or on the bench, that the law was the perfection of reason. During so many generations, in each of which thousands of educated young men were successively placed in Bentham's position and with Bentham's opportunities, he alone was found with sufficient moral sensibility and self-reliance to say to himself that these things, however profitable they might be, were frauds, and that between them and himself there should be a gulf fixed. To this rare union of self-reliance and moral sensibility we are indebted for all that

Bentham has done. Sent to Oxford by his father at the unusually early age of fifteen – required, on admission, to declare his belief in the Thirty-nine Articles – he felt it necessary to examine them; and the examination suggested scruples, which he sought to get removed, but instead of the satisfaction he expected, was told that it was not for boys like him to set up their judgement against the great men of the Church. After a struggle, he signed; but the impression that he had done an immoral act never left him; he considered himself to have committed a falsehood, and throughout life he never relaxed in his indignant denunciations of all laws which command such falsehoods, all institutions which attach rewards to them.

By thus carrying the war of criticism and refutation, the conflict with falsehood and absurdity, into the field of practical evils, Bentham, even if he had done nothing else, would have earned an important place in the history of intellect. He carried on the warfare without intermission. To this, not only many of his most piquant chapters, but some of the most finished of his entire works, are entirely devoted: the *Defence of Usury*; the *Book of Fallacies*; and the onslaught upon Blackstone, published anonymously under the title of *A Fragment on Government*, which, though a first production, and of a writer afterwards so much ridiculed for his style, excited the highest admiration no less for its composition than for its thoughts, and was attributed by turns to Lord Mansfield, to Lord Camden, and (by Dr Johnson) to Dunning, one of the greatest masters of style among the lawyers of his day. These writings are altogether original; though of the negative school, they resemble nothing previously produced by negative philosophers; and would have sufficed to create for Bentham, among the subversive thinkers of modern Europe, a place peculiarly his own. But it is not these writings that constitute the real distinction between him and them. There was a deeper difference. It was that they were purely negative thinkers, he was positive: they only assailed error, he made it a point of conscience not to do so until he thought he could plant instead the corresponding truth. Their character was exclusively analytic, his was synthetic. They took for their starting point the received opinion on any subject, dug round it with their logical implements, pronounced its foundations defective, and condemned it: he began *de novo*, laid his own foundations deeply and firmly, built up his own structure, and bade mankind compare the two; it was when he had solved the problem himself, or thought he had done so, that he declared all other solutions to be erroneous. Hence, what they produced will not last; it must perish, much of it has already perished, with the errors which it exploded: what he did has its own value, by which it must outlast all errors to which it is opposed. Though we may reject, as we often must, his practical conclusions, yet his premises, the collections of facts and observations from which his conclusions were drawn, remain for ever, a part of the materials of philosophy.

A place, therefore, must be assigned to Bentham among the masters of wisdom, the great teachers and permanent intellectual ornaments of the human race. He is among those who have enriched mankind with imperishable gifts; and although these do not transcend all other gifts, nor entitle him to those honours 'above all Greek, above all Roman fame', which by a natural reaction against the neglect and contempt of the ignorant, many of his admirers were once disposed to accumulate upon him, yet to refuse an admiring recognition of what he was, on account of what he was not, is a much worse error, and one which, pardonable in the vulgar, is no longer permitted to any cultivated and instructed mind.

If we were asked to say, in the fewest possible words, what we conceive to be Bentham's place among these great intellectual benefactors of humanity; what he was, and what he was not; what kind of service he did and did not render to truth; we should say – he was not a great philosopher, but he was a great reformer in philosophy. He brought into philosophy something which it greatly needed, and for want of which it was at a stand. It was not his doctrines which did this, it was his mode of arriving at them. He introduced into morals and politics those habits of thought and modes of investigation, which are essential to the idea of science; and the absence of which made those departments of inquiry, as physics had been before Bacon, a field of interminable discussion, leading to no result. It was not his opinions, in short, but his method, that constituted the novelty and the value of what he did; a value beyond all price, even though we should reject the whole, as we unquestionably must a large part, of the opinions themselves.

Bentham's method may be shortly described as the method of detail; of treating wholes by separating them into their parts, abstractions by resolving them into Things, – classes and generalities by distinguishing them into the individuals of which they are made up; and breaking every question into pieces before attempting to solve it. The precise amount of originality of this process, considered as a logical conception – its degree of connection with the methods of physical science, or with the previous labours of Bacon, Hobbes or Locke – is not an essential consideration in this place. Whatever originality there was in the method – in the subjects he applied it to, and in the rigidity with which he adhered to it, there was the greatest. Hence his interminable classifications. Hence his elaborate demonstrations of the most acknowledged truths. That murder, incendiarism, robbery, are mischievous actions, he will not take for granted without proof; let the thing appear ever so self-evident, he will know the why and the how of it with the last degree of precision; he will distinguish all the different mischiefs of a crime, whether of the *first*, the *second*, or the *third* order, namely 1. the evil to the sufferer, and to his personal connections; 2. the *danger* from example, and the *alarm* or painful feeling of insecurity; and 3. the discouragement to industry and useful pursuits arising from the *alarm*, and the trouble and resources which must be expended in warding off the *danger*. After this enumeration, he will prove from the laws of human feeling, that even the first of these evils, the sufferings of the immediate victim, will on the average greatly outweigh the pleasure reaped by the offender; much more when all the other evils are taken into account. Unless this could be proved, he would account the infliction of punishment unwarrantable; and for taking the trouble to prove it formally, his defence is, 'there are truths which it is necessary to prove, not for their own sakes, because they are acknowledged, but that an opening may be made for the reception of other truths which depend upon them. It is in this manner we provide for the reception of first principles, which, once received, prepare the way for admission of all other truths.' To which may be added, that in this manner also we discipline the mind for practising the same sort of dissection upon questions more complicated and of more doubtful issue.

It is a sound maxim, and one which all close thinkers have felt, but which no one before Bentham ever so consistently applied, that error lurks in generalities: that the human mind is not capable of embracing a complex whole, until it has surveyed and catalogued the parts of which that whole is made up; that abstractions are not realities *per se*, but an abridged mode of expressing facts, and that the only practical mode of dealing with them is to trace them back to the facts (whether of experience or of consciousness) of which they are the expression. Proceeding on this principle, Bentham makes short work with the ordinary modes of moral and political reasoning. These, it appeared to him, when hunted to their source, for the most part terminated in *phrases*. In politics, liberty, social order, constitution, law of nature, social compact, etc., were the catchwords: ethics had its analogous ones. Such were the arguments on which the gravest questions of morality and policy were made to turn; not reasons, but allusions to reasons; sacramental expressions, by which a summary appeal was made to some general sentiment of mankind, or to some maxim in familiar use, which might be true or not, but the limitations of which no one had ever critically examined. And this satisfied other people; but not Bentham. He required something more than opinion as a reason for opinion. Whenever he found a *phrase* used as an argument for or against anything, he insisted upon knowing what it meant; whether it appealed to any standard, or gave intimation of any matter of fact relevant to the question; and if he could not find that it did either, he treated it as an attempt on the part of the disputant to impose his own individual sentiment on other people, without giving them a reason for it; a 'contrivance for avoiding the obligation of appealing to any external standard, and for prevailing upon the reader to accept of the author's sentiment and opinion as a reason, and that a sufficient one, for itself'. Bentham shall speak for himself on this subject: the passage is from his first systematic work, *Introduction to the Principles of Morals and Legislation*, and we could scarcely quote anything more strongly exemplifying both the strength and weakness of his mode of philosophizing.

It is curious enough to observe the variety of inventions men have hit upon, and the variety of phrases they have brought forward, in order to conceal from the world, and, if possible, from themselves, this very general and therefore very pardonable self-sufficiency.

1. One man says, he has a thing made on purpose to tell him what is right and what is wrong; and that is called a 'moral sense': and then he goes to work at his ease, and says, such a thing is right, and such a thing is wrong – why? 'Because my moral sense tells me it is.'

2. Another man comes and alters the phrase: leaving out *moral*, and putting in *common* in the room of it. He then tells you that his common sense tells him what is right and wrong, as surely as the other's moral sense did: meaning by common sense, a sense of some kind or other, which, he says, is possessed by all mankind: the sense of those whose sense is not the same as the author's being struck out as not worth taking. This contrivance does better than the other; for a moral sense being a new thing, a man may feel about him a good while without being able to find it out: but common sense is as old as the creation; and there is no man but would be ashamed to be thought not to have as much of it as his neighbours. It has another great advantage: by appearing to share power, it lessens envy; for when a man gets up upon this ground, in order to anathematize those who differ from him, it is not by a *sic volo sic jubeo*, but by a *velitis jubeatis*.

3. Another man comes, and says, that as to a moral sense indeed, he cannot find that he has any such thing: that, however, he has an *understanding*, which will do quite as well. This understanding, he says, is the standard of right and wrong: it tells him so and so. All good and wise men understand as he does: if other men's understandings differ in any part from his, so much the worse for them: it is a sure sign they are either defective or corrupt.

4. Another man says, that there is an eternal and immutable Rule of Right: that that rule of right dictates so and so: and then he begins giving you his sentiments upon anything that comes uppermost: and these sentiments (you are to take for granted) are so many branches of the eternal rule of right.

5. Another man, or perhaps the same man (it is no matter), says that there are certain practices conformable, and others repugnant, to the Fitness of Things; and then he tells you, at his leisure, what practices are

conformable, and what repugnant: just as he happens to like a practice or dislike it.

6. A great multitude of people are continually talking of the Law of Nature; and then they go on giving you their sentiments about what is right and what is wrong: and these sentiments, you are to understand, are so many chapters and sections of the Law of Nature.

7. Instead of the phrase, Law of Nature, you have sometimes Law of Reason, Right Reason, Natural Justice, Natural Equity, Good Order. Any of them will do equally well. This latter is most used in politics. The three last are much more tolerable than the others, because they do not very explicitly claim to be anything more than phrases: they insist but feebly upon the being looked upon as so many positive standards of themselves, and seem content to be taken, upon occasion, for phrases expressive of the conformity of the thing in question to the proper standard, whatever that may be. On most occasions, however, it will be better to say *utility*: *utility* is clearer, as referring more explicitly to pain and pleasure.

8. We have one philosopher, who says, there is no harm in anything in the world but in telling a lie; and that if, for example, you were to murder your own father, this would only be a particular way of saying, he was not your father. Of course when this philosopher sees anything that he does not like, he says, it is a particular way of telling a lie. It is saying, that the act ought to be done, or may be done, when, *in truth*, it ought not to be done.

9. The fairest and openest of them all is that sort of man who speaks out, and says, I am of the number of the Elect: now God himself takes care to inform the Elect what is right: and that with so good effect, that let them strive ever so, they cannot help not only knowing it but practising it. If therefore a man wants to know what is right and what is wrong, he has nothing to do but to come to me.

Few will contend that this is a perfectly fair representation of the *animus* of those who employ the various phrases so amusingly animadverted on; but that the phrases contain no argument, save what is grounded on the very feelings they are adduced to justify, is a truth which Bentham had the eminent merit of first pointing out.

It is the introduction into the philosophy of human conduct, of this method of detail – of this practice of never reasoning about wholes until they have been resolved into their parts, nor about abstractions until they have been translated into realities – that constitutes the originality of Bentham in philosophy, and makes him the great reformer of the moral and political branch of it. To what he terms the 'exhaustive method of classification', which is but one branch of this more general method, he himself ascribes everything original in the systematic and elaborate work from which we have quoted. The generalities of his philosophy itself have little or no novelty: to ascribe any to the doctrine that general utility is the foundation of morality, would imply great ignorance of the history of philosophy, of general literature, and of Bentham's own writings. He derived the idea, as he says himself, from Helvetius; and it was the doctrine, no less, of the religious philosophers of that age, prior to Reid and Beattie. We never saw an abler defence of the doctrine of utility than in a book written in refutation of Shaftesbury, and now little read – Brown's *Essays on the Characteristics*; and in Johnson's celebrated review of Soame Jenyns, the same doctrine is set forth as that both of the author and of the reviewer. In all ages of philosophy one of its schools has been utilitarian – not only from the time of Epicurus, but long before. It was by mere accident that this opinion became connected in Bentham with his peculiar method. The utilitarian philosophers antecedent to him had no more claims to the method than their antagonists. To refer, for instance, to the Epicurean philosophy, according to the most complete view we have of the moral part of it, by the most accomplished scholar of antiquity, Cicero; we ask any one who has read his philosophical writings, the *De Finibus*, for instance, whether the arguments of the Epicureans do not, just as much as those of the Stoics or Platonists, consist of mere rhetorical appeals to common notions, to εἰκότα and σημεῖα instead of τεκμήρια, notions picked up as it were casually, and when true at all, never so narrowly looked into as to ascertain in what sense and under what limitations they are true. The application of a real inductive philosophy to the problems of ethics, is as unknown to the Epicurean moralists as to any of the other schools; they never take a question to pieces, and join issue on a definite point. Bentham certainly did not learn his sifting and anatomizing method from them.

This method Bentham has finally installed in philosophy; has made it henceforth imperative on philosophers of all schools. By it he has formed the intellects of many thinkers, who either never adopted, or have abandoned, many of his peculiar opinions. He has taught the method to men of the most opposite schools to his; he has made them perceive that if they do not test their doctrines by the method of detail, their adversaries will. He has thus, it is not too much to say, for the first time introduced precision of thought into moral and political philosophy. Instead of taking up their opinions by intuition, or by ratiocination from premises adopted on a mere rough view, and couched in language so vague that it is impossible to say exactly whether they are true or false, philosophers are now forced to understand one another, to break down the generality of their propositions, and join a precise issue in every dispute. This is nothing less than a revolution in philosophy. Its effect is gradually becoming evident in the writings of English thinkers of every variety of opinion, and will be felt more and more in proportion as Bentham's writings are diffused, and as the number of minds to whose formation they contribute is multiplied.

It will naturally be presumed that of the fruits of this great philosophical improvement some portion at least will have been reaped by its author. Armed with such a potent instrument, and wielding it with such singleness of aim; cultivating the field of practical philosophy with such unwearied and such consistent use of a method right in itself, and not adopted by his predecessors; it cannot be but that Bentham by his own inquiries must have accomplished something considerable. And so, it will be found, he has; something not only considerable, but extraordinary; though but little compared with what he has left undone, and far short of what his sanguine and almost boyish fancy made him flatter himself that he had accomplished. His peculiar method, admirably calculated to make clear thinkers, and sure ones to the extent of their materials, has not equal efficacy for making those materials complete. It is a security for accuracy, but not for comprehensiveness; or rather, it is a security for one sort of comprehensiveness, but not for another.

Bentham's method of laying out his subject is admirable as a preservative against one kind of narrow and partial views. He begins by placing before himself the whole of the field of inquiry to which the particular question belongs, and divides down till he arrives at the thing he is in search of; and thus by successively rejecting all which is not the thing, he gradually works out a definition of what it is. This, which he calls the exhaustive method, is as old as philosophy itself. Plato owes everything to it, and does everything by it; and the use made of it by that great man in his Dialogues, Bacon, in one of those pregnant logical hints scattered through his writings, and so much neglected by most of his pretended followers, pronounces to be the nearest approach to a true inductive method in the ancient philosophy. Bentham was probably not aware that Plato had anticipated him in the process to which he too declared that he owed everything. By the practice of it, his speculations are rendered eminently systematic and consistent; no question, with him, is ever an insulated one; he sees every subject in connection with all the other subjects with which in his view it is related, and from which it requires to be distinguished; and as all that he knows, in the least degree allied to the subject, has been marshalled in an orderly manner before him, he does not, like people who use a looser method, forget and overlook a thing on one occasion to remember it on another. Hence there is probably no philosopher of so wide a range, in whom there are so few inconsistencies. If any of the truths which he did not see, had come to be seen by him, he would have remembered it everywhere and at all times, and would have adjusted his whole system to it. And this is another admirable quality which he has impressed upon the best of the minds trained in his habits of thought: when those minds open to admit new truths, they digest them as fast as they receive them.

But this system, excellent for keeping before the mind of the thinker all that he knows, does not make him know enough; it does not make a knowledge of some of the properties of a thing suffice for the whole of it, nor render a rooted habit of surveying a complex object (though ever so carefully) in only one of its aspects, tantamount to the power of contemplating it in all. To give this last power, other qualities are required: whether Bentham possessed those other qualities we now have to see.

Bentham's mind, as we have already said, was eminently synthetical. He begins all his inquiries by supposing nothing to be known on the subject, and reconstructs all philosophy *ab initio*, without reference to the opinions of his predecessors. But to build either a philosophy or anything else, there must be materials. For the philosophy of matter, the materials are the properties of matter; for moral and political philosophy, the properties of man, and of man's position in the world. The knowledge which any inquirer possesses of these properties, constitutes a limit beyond which, as a moralist or a political philosopher, whatever be his powers of mind, he cannot reach. Nobody's synthesis can be more complete than his analysis. If in his survey of human nature and life he has left any element out, then, wheresoever that element exerts any influence, his conclusions will fail, more or less, in their application. If he has left out many elements, and those very important, his labours may be highly valuable; he may have largely contributed to that body of partial truths which, when completed and corrected by one another, constitute practical truth; but the applicability of his system to practice in its own proper shape will be of an exceedingly limited range.

Human nature and human life are wide subjects, and whoever would embark in an enterprise requiring a thorough knowledge of them, has need both of large stores of his own, and of all aids and appliances from elsewhere. His qualifications for success will be proportional to two things: the degree in which his own nature and circumstances furnish him with a correct and complete picture of man's nature and circumstances; and his capacity of deriving light from other minds.

Bentham failed in deriving light from other minds. His writings contain few traces of the accurate knowledge of any schools of thinking but his own; and many proofs of his entire conviction that they could teach him nothing worth knowing. For some of the most illustrious of previous thinkers, his contempt was unmeasured. In almost the only passage of the *Deontology* which, for its style, and from its having before appeared in print, may be known to be Bentham's, Socrates, and Plato are spoken of in terms distressing to his greatest admirers, and the incapacity to appreciate such men, is a fact perfectly in unison with the general habits of Bentham's mind. He had a phrase, expressive of the view he took of all moral speculations to which his method had not been applied, or (which he considered as the same thing) not founded on a recognition of utility as the moral standard; this phrase was 'vague generalities'. Whatever presented itself to him in such a shape, he dismissed as unworthy of notice, or dwelt upon only to denounce as absurd. He did not heed, or rather the nature of his mind prevented it from occurring to him, that these generalities contained the whole unanalysed experience of the human race.

Unless it can be asserted that mankind did not know anything until logicians taught it to them – that until the last hand has been put to a moral truth by giving it a metaphysically precise expression, all the previous rough-hewing which it has undergone by the common intellect at the suggestion of common wants and common experience is to go for nothing; it must be allowed, that even the originality which can, and the courage which dares, think for itself, is not a more necessary part of the philosophical character than a thoughtful regard for previous thinkers, and for the collective mind of the human race. What has been the opinion of mankind, has been the opinion of persons of all tempers and dispositions, of all partialities and prepossessions, of all varieties in position, in education, in opportunities of observation and inquiry. No one inquirer is all this; every inquirer is either young or old, rich or poor, sickly or healthy, married or unmarried, meditative or active, a poet or a logician, an ancient or a modern, a man or a woman; and if a thinking person, has, in addition, the accidental peculiarities of his individual modes of thought. Every circumstance which gives a character to the life of a human being, carries with it its peculiar biases; its peculiar facilities for perceiving some things, and for missing or forgetting others. But, from points of view different from his, different things are perceptible; and none are more likely to have seen what he does not see, than those who do not see what he sees. The general opinion of mankind is the average of the conclusions of all minds, stripped indeed of their choicest and most recondite thoughts, but freed from their twists and partialities: a net result, in which everybody's particular point of view is represented, nobody's predominant. The collective mind does not penetrate below the surface, but it sees all the surface; which profound thinkers, even by reason of their profundity, often fail to do: their intenser view of a thing in some of its aspects diverting their attention from others.

The hardiest assertor, therefore, of the freedom of private judgement – the keenest detector of the errors of his predecessors, and of the inaccuracies of current modes of thought – is the very person who most needs to fortify the weak side of his own intellect, by study of the opinions of mankind in all ages and nations, and of the speculations of philosophers of the modes of thought most opposite to his own. It is there that he will find the experiences denied to himself – the remainder of the truth of which he sees but half – the truths, of which the errors he detects are commonly but the exaggerations. If, like Bentham, he brings with him an improved instrument of investigation, the greater is the probability that he will find ready prepared a rich abundance of rough ore, which was merely waiting for that instrument. A man of clear ideas errs grievously if he imagines that whatever is seen confusedly does not exist: it belongs to him, when he meets with such a thing, to dispel the mist, and fix the outlines of the vague form which is looming through it.

Bentham's contempt, then, of all other schools of thinkers; his determination to create a philosophy wholly out of the materials furnished by his own mind, and by minds like his own, was his first disqualification as a philosopher. His second, was the incompleteness of his own mind as a representative of universal human nature. In many of the most natural and strongest feelings of human nature he had no sympathy; from many of its graver experiences he was altogether cut off; and the faculty by which one mind understands a mind different from itself, and throws itself into the feelings of that other mind, was denied him by his deficiency of Imagination.

With Imagination in the popular sense, command of imagery and metaphorical expression, Bentham was, to a certain degree, endowed. For want, indeed, of poetical culture, the images with which his fancy supplied him were seldom beautiful, but they were quaint and humorous, or bold, forcible, and intense: passages might be quoted from him both of playful irony, and of declamatory eloquence, seldom surpassed in the writings of philosophers. The Imagination which he had not, was that to which the name is generally appropriated by the best writers of the present day; that which enables us, by a voluntary effort, to conceive the absent as if it were present, the imaginary as if it were real, and to clothe it in the feelings which, if it were indeed real, it would bring along with it. This is the power by which one human being enters into the mind and circumstances of another. This power constitutes the poet, in so far as he does anything but melodiously utter his own actual feelings. It constitutes the dramatist entirely. It is one of the constituents of the historian; by it we understand other times; by it Guizot interprets to us the middle ages; Nisard, in his beautiful Studies on the later Latin poets, places us in the Rome of the Caesars; Michelet disengages the distinctive characters of the different races and generations of mankind from the facts of their history. Without it nobody knows even his own nature, further than circumstances have actually tried it and called it out; nor the nature of his fellow creatures, beyond such generalizations as he may have been enabled to make from his observation of their outward conduct.

By these limits, accordingly, Bentham's knowledge of human nature is bounded. It is wholly empirical; and the empiricism of one who has had little experience. He had neither internal experience nor external; the quiet, even tenor of his life, and his healthiness of mind, conspired to exclude him from both. He never knew prosperity and adversity, passion nor satiety: he never had even the experiences which sickness gives; he lived from childhood to the age of eighty-five in boyish health. He knew no dejection, no heaviness of heart. He never felt life a sore and a weary burthen. He was a boy to the last. Self-consciousness, that demon of the men of genius of our time, from Wordsworth to Byron, from Goethe to Chateaubriand, and to which this age owes so much both of its cheerful and its mournful wisdom, never was awakened in him. How much of human nature slumbered in him he knew not, neither can we know. He had never been made alive to the unseen influences which were acting on himself, nor consequently on his fellow creatures. Other ages and other nations were a blank to him for purposes of instruction. He measured them but by one standard; their knowledge of facts, and their capability to take correct views of utility, and merge all other objects in it. His own lot was cast in a generation of the leanest and barrenest men whom England had yet produced, and he was an old man when a better race came in with the present century. He saw accordingly in man little but what the vulgarest eye can see; recognized no diversities of character but such as he who runs may read. Knowing so little of human feelings, he knew still less of the influences by which those feelings are formed: all the more subtle workings both of the mind upon itself, and of external things upon the mind, escaped him; and no one, probably, who, in a highly instructed age, ever attempted to give a rule to all human conduct, set out with a more limited conception either of the agencies by which human conduct *is*, or of those by which it *should* be, influenced.

This, then, is our idea of Bentham. He was a man both of remarkable endowments for philosophy, and of remarkable deficiencies for it: fitted, beyond almost any man, for drawing from his premises, conclusions not only correct, but sufficiently precise and specific to be practical: but whose general conception of human nature and life, furnished him with an unusually slender stock of premises. It is obvious what would be likely to be achieved by such a man; what a thinker, thus gifted and thus disqualified, could do in philosophy. He could, with close and accurate logic, hunt half-truths to their consequences and practical applications, on a scale both of greatness and of minuteness not previously exemplified; and this is the character which posterity will probably assign to Bentham.

We express our sincere and well-considered conviction when we say, that there is hardly anything positive in Bentham's philosophy which is not true: that when his practical conclusions are erroneous, which in our opinion they are very often, it is not because the considerations which he urges are not rational and valid in themselves, but because some more important principle, which he did not perceive, supersedes those considerations, and turns the scale. The bad part of his writings is his resolute denial of all that he does not see, of all truths but those which he recognizes. By that alone has he exercised any bad influence upon his age; by that he has, not created a school of deniers, for this is an ignorant prejudice, but put himself at the head of the school which exists always, though it does not always find a great man to give it the sanction of philosophy: thrown the mantle of intellect over the natural tendency of men in all ages to deny or disparage all feelings and mental states of which they have no consciousness in themselves.

The truths which are not Bentham's, which his philosophy takes no account of, are many and important; but his non-recognition of them does not put them out of existence; they are still with us, and it is a comparatively easy task that is reserved for us, to harmonize those truths with his. To reject his half of the truth because he overlooked the other half, would be to fall into his error without having his excuse. For our own part, we have a large tolerance for one-eyed men, provided their one eye is a penetrating one: if they saw more, they probably would not see so keenly, nor so eagerly pursue one course of inquiry. Almost all rich veins of original and striking speculation have been opened by systematic half-thinkers: though whether these new thoughts drive out others as good, or are peacefully superadded to them, depends on whether these half-thinkers are or are not followed in the same track by complete thinkers. The field of man's nature and life cannot be too much worked, or in too many directions; until every clod is turned up the work is imperfect; no whole truth is possible but by combining the points of view of all the fractional truths, nor, therefore, until it has been fully seen what each fractional truth can do by itself.

What Bentham's fractional truths could do, there is no such good means of showing as by a review of his philosophy: and such a review, though inevitably a most brief and general one, it is now necessary to attempt.

The first question in regard to any man of speculation is, what is his theory of human life? In the minds of many philosophers, whatever theory they have of this sort is latent, and it would be a revelation to themselves to have it pointed out to them in their writings as others can see it, unconsciously moulding everything to its own likeness. But Bentham always knew his own premises, and made his reader know them: it was not his custom to leave the theoretic grounds of his practical conclusions to conjecture. Few great thinkers have afforded the means of assigning with so much certainty the exact conception which they had formed of a man and of man's life.

Man is conceived by Bentham as a being susceptible of pleasures and pains, and governed in all his conduct partly by the different modifications of self-interest, and the passions commonly classed as selfish, partly by sympathies, or occasionally antipathies, towards other beings. And here Bentham's conception of human nature stops. He does not exclude religion; the prospect of divine rewards and punishments he includes under the head of 'self-regarding interest', and the devotional feeling under that of sympathy with God. But the whole of the impelling or restraining principles, whether of this or of another world, which he recognizes, are either self-love, or love or hatred towards other sentient beings. That there might be no doubt of what he thought on the subject, he has not left us to the general evidence of his writings, but has drawn out a *Table of the Springs of Action*, an express enumeration and classification of human motives, with their various names, laudatory, vituperative and neutral: and this table, to be found in Part I of his collected works, we recommend to the study of those who would understand his philosophy.

Man is never recognized by him as a being capable of pursuing spiritual perfection as an end; of desiring, for its own sake, the conformity of his own character to his standard of excellence, without hope of good or fear of evil from other source than his own inward consciousness. Even in the more limited form of Conscience, this great fact in human nature escapes him. Nothing is more curious than the absence of recognition in any of his writings of the existence of conscience, as a thing distinct from philanthropy, from affection for God or man, and from self-interest in this world or in the next. There is a studied abstinence from any of the phrases which, in the mouths of others, import the acknowledgement of such a fact. If we find the words 'Conscience', 'Principle', 'Moral Rectitude', 'Moral Duty' in his *Table of the Springs of Action*, it is among the synonyms of the 'love of reputation', with an intimation as to the two former phrases, that they are also sometimes synonymous with the *religious* motive, or the motive of *sympathy*. The feeling of moral approbation or disapprobation properly so called, either towards ourselves or our fellow creatures, he seems unaware of the existence of; and neither the word *self-respect*, nor the idea to which that word is appropriated, occurs even once, so far as our recollection serves us, in his whole writings.

Nor is it only the moral part of man's nature, in the strict sense of the term – the desire of perfection, or the feeling of an approving or of an accusing conscience – that he overlooks; he but faintly recognizes, as a fact in human nature, the pursuit of any other ideal end for its own sake. The sense of *honour* and personal dignity – that feeling of personal exaltation and degradation which acts independently of other people's opinion, or even in defiance of it; the love of *beauty*, the passion of the artist; the love of *order*, of congruity, of consistency in all things, and conformity to their end; the love of *power*, not in the limited form of power over other human beings, but abstract power, the power of making our volitions effectual; the love of *action*, the thirst for movement and activity, a principle scarcely of less influence in human life than its opposite, the love of ease: – none of these powerful constituents of human nature are thought worthy of a place among the 'Springs of Action'; and though there is possibly no one of them of the existence of which an acknowledgement might not be found in some corner of Bentham's writings, no conclusions are ever founded on the acknowledgement. Man, that most complex being, is a very simple one in his eyes. Even under the head of *sympathy*, his recognition does not extend to the more complex forms of the feeling – the love of *loving*, the need of a sympathizing support, or of objects of admiration and reverence. If he thought at all of any of the deeper feelings of human nature, it was but as idiosyncrasies of taste, with which the moralist no more than the legislator had any concern, further than to prohibit such as were mischievous among the actions to which they might chance to lead. To say either that man should, or that he should not, take pleasure in one thing, displeasure in another, appeared to him as much an act of despotism in the moralist as in the political ruler.

It would be most unjust to Bentham to surmise (as narrow-minded and passionate adversaries are apt in such cases to do) that this picture of human nature was copied from himself; that all those constituents of humanity which he rejected from his table of motives, were wanting in his own breast. The unusual strength of his early feelings of virtue, was, as we have seen, the original cause of all his speculations; and a noble sense of morality, and especially of justice, guides and pervades them all. But having been early accustomed to keep before his mind's eye the happiness of mankind (or rather of the whole sentient world), as the only thing desirable in itself, or which rendered anything else desirable, he confounded all disinterested feelings which he found in himself, with the desire of general happiness: just as some religious writers, who loved virtue for its own sake as much perhaps as men could do, habitually confounded their love of virtue with their fear of hell. It would have required greater subtlety than Bentham possessed to distinguish from each other feelings which, from long habit, always acted in the same direction; and his want of imagination prevented him from reading the distinction, where it is legible enough, in the hearts of others.

Accordingly, he has not been followed in this grand oversight by any of the able men who, from the extent of their intellectual obligations to him, have been regarded as his disciples. They may have followed him in his doctrine of utility, and in his rejection of a moral sense as the test of right and wrong: but while repudiating it as such, they have, with Hartley, acknowledged it as a fact in human nature; they have endeavoured to account for it, to assign its laws: nor are they justly chargeable either with undervaluing this part of our nature, or with any disposition to throw it into the background of their speculations. If any part of the influence of this cardinal error has extended itself to them, it is circuitously, and through the effect on their minds of other parts of Bentham's doctrines.

Sympathy, the only disinterested motive which Bentham recognized, he felt the inadequacy of, except in certain limited cases, as a security for virtuous action. Personal affection, he well knew, is as liable to operate to the injury of third parties, and requires as much to be kept under government as any other feeling whatever: and general philanthropy, considered as a motive influencing mankind in general, he estimated at its true value when divorced from the feeling of duty – as the very weakest and most unsteady of all feelings. There remained, as a motive by which mankind are influenced, and by which they may be guided to their good, only personal interest. Accordingly, Bentham's idea of the world is that of a collection of persons pursuing each his separate interest or pleasure, and the prevention of whom from jostling one another more than is unavoidable may be attempted by hopes and fears derived from three sources – the law, religion, and public opinion. To these three powers, considered as binding human conduct, he gave the name of *sanctions*: the *political* sanction, operating by the rewards and penalties of the law; the *religious* sanction, by those expected from the Ruler of the Universe; and the *popular*, which he characteristically calls also the *moral* sanction, operating through the pains and pleasures arising from the favour or disfavour of our fellow creatures.

Such is Bentham's theory of the world. And now, in a spirit neither of apology nor of censure, but of calm appreciation, we are to inquire how far this view of human nature and life will carry any one: – how much it will accomplish in morals, and how much in political and social philosophy: what it will do for the individual and what for society.

It will do nothing for the conduct of the individual, beyond prescribing some of the more obvious dictates of worldly prudence, and outward probity and beneficence. There is no need to expatiate on the deficiencies of a system of ethics which does not pretend to aid individuals in the formation of their own character; which recognizes no such wish as that of self-culture, we may even say no such power, as existing in human nature; and if it did recognize, could furnish little assistance to that great duty, because it overlooks the existence of about half of the whole number of mental feelings which human beings are capable of, including all those of which the direct objects are states of their own mind.

Morality consists of two parts. One of these is self-education; the training, by the human being himself, of his affections and will. That department is a blank in Bentham's system. The other and co-equal part, the regulation of his outward actions, must be altogether halting and imperfect without the first; for how can we judge in what manner many an action will affect even the worldly interests of ourselves or others, unless we take in, as part of the question, its influence on the regulation of our, or their, affections and desires? A moralist on Bentham's principles may get as far as this, that he ought not to slay, burn or steal; but what will be his qualifications for regulating the nicer shades of human behaviour, or for laying down even the greater moralities as to those facts in human life which tend to influence the depths of the character quite independently of any influence on worldly circumstances – such, for instance, as the sexual relations, or those of family in general, or any other social and sympathetic connections of an intimate kind? The moralities of these questions depend essentially on considerations which Bentham never so much as took into the account; and when he happened to be in the right, it was always, and necessarily, on wrong or insufficient grounds.

It is fortunate for the world that Bentham's taste lay rather in the direction of jurisprudential than of properly ethical inquiry. Nothing expressly of the latter kind has been published under his name, except the *Deontology* – a book scarcely ever, in our experience, alluded to by any admirer of Bentham without deep regret that it ever saw the light. We did not expect from Bentham correct systematic views of ethics, or a sound treatment of any question the moralities of which require a profound knowledge of the human heart; but we did anticipate that the greater moral questions would have been boldly plunged into, and at least a searching criticism produced of the received opinions; we did not expect that the *petite morale* almost alone would have been treated, and that with the most pedantic minuteness, and on the *quid pro quo* principles which regulate trade. The book has not even the value which would belong to an authentic exhibition of the legitimate consequences of an erroneous line of thought; for the style proves it to have been so entirely rewritten, that it is impossible to tell how much or how little of it is Bentham's. The collected edition, now in progress, will not, it is said, include Bentham's religious writings; these, although we think most of them of exceedingly small value, are at least his, and the world has a right to whatever light they throw upon the constitution of his mind.

But the omission of the *Deontology* would be an act of editorial discretion which we should deem entirely justifiable.

If Bentham's theory of life can do so little for the individual, what can it do for society?

It will enable a society which has attained a certain state of spiritual development, and the maintenance of which in that state is otherwise provided for, to prescribe the rules by which it may protect its material interests. It will do nothing (except sometimes as an instrument in the hands of a higher doctrine) for the spiritual interests of society; nor does it suffice of itself even for the material interests. That which alone causes any material interests to exist, which alone enables any body of human beings to exist as a society, is national character: *that* it is, which causes one nation to succeed in what it attempts, another to fail; one nation to understand and aspire to elevated things, another to grovel in mean ones; which makes the greatness of one nation lasting, and dooms another to early and rapid decay. The true teacher of the fitting social arrangements for England, France or America, is the one who can point out how the English, French or American character can be improved, and how it has been made what it is. A philosophy of laws and institutions, not founded on a philosophy of national character, is an absurdity. But what could Bentham's opinion be worth on national character? How could he, whose mind contained so few and so poor types of individual character, rise to that higher generalization? All he can do is but to indicate means by which, in any given state of the national mind, the material interests of society can be protected; saving the question, of which others must judge, whether the use of those means would have, on the national character, any injurious influence.

We have arrived, then, at a sort of estimate of what a philosophy like Bentham's can do. It can teach the means of organizing and regulating the merely *business* part of the social arrangements. Whatever can be understood or whatever done without reference to moral influences, his philosophy is equal to; where those influences require to be taken into account, it is at fault. He committed the mistake of supposing that the business part of human affairs was the whole of them; all at least that the legislator and the moralist had to do with. Not that he disregarded moral influences when he perceived them; but his want of imagination, small experience of human feelings, and ignorance of the filiation and connection of feelings with one another, made this rarely the case.

The business part is accordingly the only province of human affairs which Bentham has cultivated with any success; into which he has introduced any considerable number of comprehensive and luminous practical principles. That is the field of his greatness; and there he is indeed great. He has swept away the accumulated cobwebs of centuries – he has untied knots which the efforts of the ablest thinkers, age after age, had only drawn tighter; and it is no exaggeration to say of him that over a great part of the field he was the first to shed the light of reason.

We turn with pleasure from what Bentham could not do, to what he did. It is an ungracious task to call a great benefactor of mankind to account for not being a greater – to insist upon the errors of a man who has originated more new truths, has given to the world more sound practical lessons, than it ever received, except in a few glorious instances, from any other individual. The unpleasing part of our work is ended. We are now to show the greatness of the man; the grasp which his intellect took of the subjects with which it was fitted to deal; the giant's task which was before him, and the hero's courage and strength with which he achieved it. Nor let that which he did be deemed of small account because its province was limited: man has but the choice to go a little way in many paths, or a great way in only one. The field of Bentham's labours was like the space between two parallel lines; narrow to excess in one direction, in another it reached to infinity.

Bentham's speculations, as we are already aware, began with law; and in that department he accomplished his greatest triumphs. He found the philosophy of law a chaos, he left it a science: he found the practice of the law an Augean stable, he turned the river into it which is mining and sweeping away mound after mound of its rubbish.

Without joining in the exaggerated invectives against lawyers, which Bentham sometimes permitted to himself, or making one portion of society alone accountable for the fault of all, we may say that circumstances had made English lawyers in a peculiar degree liable to the reproach of Voltaire, who defines lawyers the 'conservators of ancient barbarous usages'. The basis of the English law was, and still is, the feudal system. That system, like all those which existed as custom before they were established as law, possessed a certain degree of suitableness to the wants of the society among whom it grew up – that is to say, of a tribe of rude soldiers, holding a conquered people in subjection, and dividing its spoils among themselves. Advancing civilization had, however, converted this armed encampment of barbarous warriors in the midst of enemies reduced to slavery, into an industrious, commercial, rich and free people. The laws which were suitable to the first of these states of society, could have no manner of relation to the circumstances of the second; which could not even have come into existence unless something had been done to adapt those laws to it. But the adaptation was not the result of thought and design; it arose not from any comprehensive consideration of the new state of society and its exigencies. What was done, was done by a struggle of centuries between the old barbarism and the new civilization; between the feudal aristocracy of conquerors, holding fast to the rude system they had established, and the conquered effecting their emancipation. The last was the growing power, but was never strong enough to break its bonds, though ever and anon some weak point gave way. Hence the law came to be like the costume of a full-grown man who had never put off the clothes made for him when he first went to school. Band after band had burst, and, as the rent widened, then, without removing anything except what might drop off of itself, the hole was darned, or patches of fresh law were brought from the nearest shop and stuck on. Hence all ages of English history have given one another rendezvous in English law; their several products may be seen all together, not interfused, but heaped one upon another, as many different ages of the earth may be read in some perpendicular section of its surface – the deposits of each successive period not substituted but superimposed on those of the preceding. And in the world of law no less than in the physical world, every commotion and conflict of the elements has left its mark behind in some break or irregularity of the strata: every struggle which ever rent the bosom of society is apparent in the disjointed condition of the part of the field of law which covers the spot: nay, the very traps and pitfalls which one contending party set for another are still standing, and the teeth not of hyenas only, but of foxes and all cunning animals, are imprinted on the curious remains found in these antediluvian caves.

In the English law, as in the Roman before it, the adaptations of barbarous laws to the growth of civilized society were made chiefly by stealth. They were generally made by the courts of justice, who could not help reading the new wants of mankind in the cases between man and man which came before them; but who, having no authority to make new laws for those new wants, were obliged to do the work covertly, and evade the jealousy and opposition of an ignorant, prejudiced, and for the most part brutal and tyrannical legislature. Some of the most necessary of these improvements, such as the giving force of law to trusts, and the breaking up of entails, were effected in actual opposition to the strongly declared will of Parliament, whose clumsy hands, no match for the astuteness of judges, could not, after repeated trials, manage to make any law which the judges could not find a trick for rendering inoperative. The whole history of the contest about trusts may still be read in the words of a conveyance, as could the contest about entails, till the abolition of fine and recovery by a bill of the present Attorney-General, but dearly did the client pay for the cabinet of historical curiosities which he was obliged to purchase every time that he made a settlement of his estate. The result of this mode of improving social institutions was, that whatever new things were done had to be done in consistency with old forms and names; and the laws were improved with much the same effect as if, in the improvement of agriculture, the plough could only have been introduced by making it look like a spade; or as if, when the primeval practice of ploughing by the horse's tail gave way to the innovation of harness, the tail, for form's sake, had still remained attached to the plough.

When the conflicts were over, and the mixed mass settled down into something like a fixed state, and that state a very profitable and therefore a very agreeable one to lawyers, they, following the natural tendency of the human mind, began to theorize upon it, and, in obedience to necessity, had to digest it and give it a systematic form. It was from this thing of shreds and patches in which the only part that approached to order or system was the early barbarous part, already more than half superseded, that English lawyers had to construct, by induction and abstraction, their philosophy of law; and without the logical habits and general intellectual cultivation which the lawyers of the Roman empire brought to a similar task. Bentham found the philosophy of law what English practising lawyers had made it; a jumble, in which *real* and *personal* property, *law* and *equity*, *felony*, *praemunire*, *misprision* and *misdemeanour*, words without a vestige of meaning when detached from the history of English institutions – mere tide-marks to point out the line which the sea and the shore, in their secular struggles, had adjusted as their mutual boundary – all passed for distinctions inherent in the nature of things; in which every absurdity, every lucrative abuse, had a reason found for it – a reason which only now and then ever pretended to be drawn from expediency; most commonly a technical reason, one of mere form, derived from the old barbarous system. While the theory of the law was in this state, to describe what the practice of it was would require the pen of a Swift, or of Bentham himself. The whole progress of a suit at law seemed like a series of contrivances for lawyers' profit, in which the suitors were regarded as the prey; and if the poor were not the helpless victims of every Sir Giles Overreach who could pay the price, they might thank opinion and manners for it, not the law.

It may be fancied by some people that Bentham did an easy thing in merely calling all this absurd, and proving it to be so. But he began the contest a young man, and he had grown old before he had any followers. History will one day refuse to give credit to the intensity of the superstition which, till very lately, protected this mischievous mess from examination or doubt – passed off the charming representations of Blackstone for a just estimate of the English law, and proclaimed the shame of human reason to be the perfection of it. Glory to Bentham that he has dealt to this superstition its deathblow – that he has been the Hercules of this hydra, the St George of this pestilent dragon!

The honour is all his – nothing but his peculiar qualities could have done it. There were wanted his indefatigable perseverance, his firm self-reliance, needing no support from other men's opinion; his intensely practical turn of mind, his synthetical habits – about all, his peculiar method. Metaphysicians, armed with vague generalities, had often tried their hands at the subject, and left it no more advanced than they found it. Law is a matter of business; means and ends are the things to be considered in it, not abstractions: vagueness was not to be met by vagueness, but by definiteness and precision: details were not to be encountered with generalities, but with details. Nor could any progress be made, on such a subject, by merely showing that existing things were bad; it was necessary also to show how they might be made better. No great man whom we read of was qualified to do this thing except Bentham. He has done it, once and for ever.

Into the particulars of what Bentham has done we cannot enter: many hundred pages would be required to give a tolerable abstract of it. To sum up our estimate under a few heads. First: he has expelled mysticism from the philosophy of law, and set the example of viewing laws in a practical light, as means to certain definite and precise ends. Secondly: he has cleared up the confusion and vagueness attaching to the idea of law in general, to the idea of a body of laws, and the various general ideas therein involved. Thirdly: he demonstrated the necessity and practicability of *codification*, or the conversion of all law into a written and systematically arranged code: not like the Code Napoleon, a code without a single definition, requiring a constant reference to anterior precedent for the meaning of its technical terms; but one containing within itself all that is necessary for its own interpretation, together with a perpetual provision for its own emendation and improvement. He has shown of what parts such a code would consist; the relation of those parts to one another; and by his distinctions and classifications has done very much towards showing what should be, or might be, its nomenclature and arrangement. What he has left undone, he has made it comparatively easy for others to do. Fourthly: he has taken a systematic view of the exigencies of society for which the civil code is intended to provide, and of the principles of human nature by which its provisions are to be tested: and this view, defective (as we have already intimated) wherever spiritual interests require to be taken into account, is excellent for that large portion of the laws of any country which are designed for the protection of material interests. Fifthly: (to say nothing of the subject of punishment, for which something considerable had been done before) he found the philosophy of judicial procedure, including that of judicial establishments and of evidence, in a more wretched state than even any other part of the philosophy of law; he carried it at once almost to perfection. He left it with every one of its principles established, and little remaining to be done even in the suggestion of practical arrangements.

These assertions in behalf of Bentham may be left, without fear for the result, in the hands of those who are competent to judge of them. There are now even in the highest seats of justice, men to whom the claims made for him will not appear extravagant. Principle after principle of those propounded by him is moreover making its way by infiltration into the understandings most shut against his influence, and driving nonsense and prejudice from one corner of them to another. The reform of the laws of any country according to his principles, can only be gradual, and may be long ere it is accomplished; but the work is in progress, and both Parliament and the judges are every year doing something, and often something not inconsiderable, towards the forwarding of it.

It seems proper here to take notice of an accusation sometimes made both against Bentham and against the principle of codification – as if they required one uniform suit of ready-made laws for all times and all states of society. The doctrine of codification, as the word imports, relates to the form only of the laws, not their substance; it does not concern itself with what the laws should be, but declares that whatever they are, they ought to be systematically arranged, and fixed down to a determinate form of words. To the accusation, so far as it affects Bentham, one of the essays in the collection of his works (then for the first time published in English) is a complete answer: that 'On the Influence of Time and Place in Matters of Legislation'. It may there be seen that the different exigencies of different nations with respect to law, occupied his attention as systematically as any other portion of the wants which render laws necessary: with the limitations, it is true, which were set to all his speculations by the imperfections of his theory of human nature. For, taking, as we have seen, next to no account of national character and the causes which form and maintain it, he was precluded from considering, except to a very limited extent, the laws of a country as an instrument of national culture: one of their most important aspects, and in which they must of course vary according to the degree and kind of culture already attained; as a tutor gives his pupil different lessons according to the progress already made in his education. The same laws would not have suited our wild ancestors, accustomed to rude independence, and a people of Asiatics bowed down by military despotism: the slave needs to be trained to govern himself, the savage to submit to the government of others. The same laws will not suit the English, who distrust everything which emanates from general principles, and the French, who distrust whatever does not so emanate. Very different institutions are needed to train to the perfection of their nature, or to constitute into a united nation and social polity, an essentially *subjective* people like the Germans, and an essentially *objective* people like those of Northern and Central Italy; the one affectionate and dreamy, the other passionate and worldly; the one trustful and loyal, the other calculating and suspicious; the one not practical enough, the other overmuch; the one wanting individuality, the other fellow-feeling; the one failing for want of exacting enough for itself, the other for want of conceding enough to others. Bentham was little accustomed to look at institutions in their relation to these topics. The effects of this oversight must of course be perceptible throughout his speculations, but we do not think the errors into which it led him very material in the greater part of civil and penal law: it is in the department of constitutional legislation that they were fundamental.

The Benthamic theory of government has made so much noise in the world of late years; it has held such a conspicuous place among Radical philosophies, and Radical modes of thinking have participated so much more largely than any others in its spirit, that many worthy persons imagine there is no other Radical philosophy extant. Leaving such people to discover their mistake as they may, we shall expend a few words in attempting to discriminate between the truth and error of this celebrated theory.

There are three great questions in government. First, to what authority is it for the good of the people that they should be subject? Secondly, how are they to be induced to obey that authority? The answers to these two questions vary indefinitely, according to the degree and kind of civilization and cultivation already attained by a people, and their peculiar aptitudes for receiving more. Comes next a third question, not liable to so much variation, namely, by what means are the abuses of this authority to be checked? This third question is the only one of the three to which Bentham seriously applies himself, and he gives it the only answer it admits of – Responsibility: responsibility to persons whose interest, whose obvious and recognizable interest, accords with the end in view – good government. This being granted, it is next to be asked, in what body of persons this identity of interest with good government, that is, with the interest of the whole community, is to be found? In nothing less, says Bentham, than the numerical majority: nor, say we, even in the numerical majority itself; of no portion of the community less than all, will the interest coincide, at all times and in all respects, with the interest of all. But, since power given to all, by a representative government, is in fact given to a majority; we are obliged to fall back upon the first of our three questions, namely, under what authority is it for the good of the people that they be placed? And if to this the answer be, under that of a majority among themselves, Bentham's system cannot be questioned. This one assumption being made, his *Constitutional Code* is admirable. That extraordinary power which he possessed, of at once seizing comprehensive principles, and scheming out minute details, is brought into play with surpassing vigour in devising means for preventing rulers from escaping from the control of the majority; for enabling and inducing the majority to exercise that control unremittingly; and for providing them with servants of every desirable endowment, moral and intellectual, compatible with entire subservience to their will.

But *is* this fundamental doctrine of Bentham's political philosophy a universal truth? Is it, at all times and places, good for mankind to be under the absolute authority of the majority of themselves? We say the authority, not the political authority merely, because it is chimerical to suppose that whatever has absolute power over men's bodies will not arrogate it over their minds – will not seek to control (not perhaps by legal penalties, but by the persecutions of society) opinions and feelings which depart from its standard; will not attempt to shape the education of the young by its model, and to extinguish all books, all schools, all combinations of individuals for joint action upon society, which may be attempted for the purpose of keeping alive a spirit at variance with its own. Is it, we say, the proper condition of man, in all ages and nations, to be under the despotism of Public Opinion?

It is very conceivable that such a doctrine should find acceptance from some of the noblest spirits, in a time of reaction against the aristocratic governments of modern Europe; governments founded on the entire sacrifice (except so far as prudence, and sometimes humane feeling interfere) of the community generally, to the self-interest and ease of a few. European reformers have been accustomed to see the numerical majority everywhere unjustly depressed, everywhere trampled upon, or at the best overlooked, by governments; nowhere possessing power enough to extort redress of their most positive grievances, provision for their mental culture, or even to prevent themselves from being taxed avowedly for the pecuniary profit of the ruling classes. To see these things, and to seek to put an end to them, by means (among other things) of giving more political power to the majority, constitutes Radicalism; and it is because so many in this age have felt this wish, and have felt that the realization of it was an object worthy of men's devoting their lives to it, that such a theory of government as Bentham's has found favour with them. But, though to pass from one form of bad government to another be the ordinary fate of mankind, philosophers ought not to make themselves parties to it, by sacrificing one portion of important truth to another.

The numerical majority of any society whatever, must consist of persons all standing in the same social position, and having, in the main, the same pursuits, namely, unskilled manual labourers; and we mean no disparagement to them: whatever we say to their disadvantage, we say equally of a numerical majority of shopkeepers, or of squires. Where there is identity of position and pursuits, there also will be identity of partialities, passions and prejudices; and to give to any one set of partialities, passions and prejudices, absolute power, without counter-balance from partialities, passions and prejudices of a different sort, is the way to render the correction of any of those imperfections hopeless; to make one narrow, mean type of human nature universal and perpetual, and to crush every influence which tends to the further improvement of man's intellectual and moral nature. There must, we know, be some paramount power in society; and that the majority should be that power, is on the whole right, not as being just in itself, but as being less unjust than any other footing on which the matter can be placed. But it is necessary that institutions of society should make provision for keeping up, in some form or other, as a corrective to partial views, and a shelter for freedom of thought and individuality of character, a perpetual and stand- ing opposition to the will of the majority. All countries which have long continued progressive, or been durably great, have been so because there has been an organized opposition to the ruling power, of whatever kind that power was: plebeians to patricians, clergy to kings, freethinkers to clergy, kings to barons, commons to king and aristocracy. Almost all the greatest men who ever lived have formed part of such an Opposition. Wherever some such quarrel has not been going on – wherever it has been termin- ated by the complete victory of one of the contending principles, and no new contest has taken the place of the old – society has either hardened into Chinese stationariness, or fallen into dissol- ution. A centre of resistance, round which all the moral and social elements which the ruling power views with disfavour may clus- ter themselves, and behind whose bulwarks they may find shelter from the attempts of that power to hunt them out of existence, is as necessary where the opinion of the majority is sovereign, as where the ruling power is a hierarchy or an aristocracy. Where no such *point d'appui* exists, there the human race will inevitably degenerate; and the question, whether the United States, for instance, will in time sink into another China (also a most commercial and industrious nation), resolves itself, to us, into the question, whether such a centre of resistance will gradually evolve itself or not.

These things being considered, we cannot think that Bentham made the most useful employment which might have been made of his great powers, when, not content with enthroning the majority as sovereign, by means of universal suffrage without king or house of lords, he exhausted all the resources of ingenuity in devising means for riveting the yoke of public opinion closer and closer round the necks of all public functionaries, and excluding every possibility of the exercise of the slightest or most temporary influence either by a minority, or by the functionary's own notions of right. Surely when any power has been made the strongest power, enough has been done for it, care is thenceforth wanted rather to prevent that strongest power from swallowing up all others. Wherever all the forces of society act in one single direction, the just claims of the individual human being are in extreme peril. The power of the majority is salutary so far as it is used defensively, not offensively – as its exertion is tempered by respect for the personality of the individual, and deference to superiority of cultivated intelligence. If Bentham had employed himself in pointing out the means by which institutions fundamentally democratic might be best adapted to the preservation and strengthening of those two sentiments, he would have done something more permanently valuable, and more worthy of his great intellect. Montesquieu, with the lights of the present age, would have done it; and we are possibly destined to receive this benefit from the Montesquieu of our own times, M. de Tocqueville.

Do we then consider Bentham's political speculations useless? Far from it. We consider them only one-sided. He has brought out into a strong light, has cleared from a thousand confusions and misconceptions, and pointed out with admirable skill the best means of promoting, one of the ideal qualities of a perfect government – identity of interest between the trustees and the community for whom they hold their power in trust. This quality is not attainable in its ideal perfection, and must moreover be striven for with a perpetual eye to all other requisites; but those other requisites must still more be striven for without losing sight of this: and when the slightest postponement is made of it to any other end, the sacrifice, often necessary, is never unattended with evil. Bentham has pointed out how complete this sacrifice is in modern European societies: how exclusively, partial and sinister interests are the ruling power there, with only such check as is imposed by public opinion – which being thus, in the existing order of things, perpetually apparent as a source of good, he was led by natural partiality to exaggerate its intrinsic excellence. This sinister interest of rulers Bentham hunted through all its disguises, and especially through those which hide it from the men themselves who are influenced by it. The greatest service rendered by him to the philosophy of universal human nature, is, perhaps, his illustration of what he terms 'interest-begotten prejudice' – the common tendency of man to make a duty and a virtue of following his self-interest. The idea, it is true, was far from being peculiarly Bentham's: the artifices by which we persuade ourselves that we are not yielding to our selfish inclinations when we are, had attracted the notice of all moralists, and had been probed by religious writers to a depth as much below Bentham's, as their knowledge of the profundities and windings of the human heart was superior to his. But it is selfish interest in the form of class-interest, and the class-morality founded thereon, which Bentham has illustrated: the manner in which any set of persons who mix much together, and have a common interest, are apt to make that common interest their standard of virtue, and the social feelings of the members of the class are made to play into the hands of their selfish ones; whence the union so often exemplified in history, between the most heroic personal disinterestedness and the most odious class-selfishness. This was one of Bentham's leading ideas, and almost the only one by which he contributed to the elucidation of history: much of which, except so far as this explained it, must have been entirely inexplicable to him. The idea was given him by Helvetius, whose book, *De l'Esprit*, is one continued and most acute commentary on it; and, together with the other great idea of Helvetius, the influence of circumstances on character, it will make his name live by the side of Rousseau, when most of the other French metaphysicians of the eighteenth century will be extant as such only in literary history.

In the brief view which we have been able to give of Bentham's philosophy, it may surprise the reader that we have said so little about the first principle of it, with which his name is more identified than with anything else; the 'principle of utility', or, as he afterwards named it, 'the greatest-happiness principle'. It is a topic on which much were to be said, if there were room, or if it were in reality necessary for the just estimation of Bentham. On an occasion more suitable for a discussion of the metaphysics of morality, or on which the elucidations necessary to make an opinion on so abstract a subject intelligible could be conveniently given, we should be fully prepared to state what we think on this subject. At present we shall only say, that while, under proper explanations, we entirely agree with Bentham in his principle, we do not hold with him that all right thinking on the details of morals depends on its express assertion. We think utility, or happiness, much too complex and indefinite an end to be sought except through the medium of various secondary ends, concerning which there may be, and often is, agreement among persons who differ in their ultimate standard; and about which there does in fact prevail a much greater unanimity among thinking persons, than might be supposed from their diametrical divergence on the great questions of moral metaphysics. As mankind are much more nearly of one nature, than of one opinion about their own nature, they are more easily brought to agree in their intermediate principles, *vera illa et media axiomata*, as Bacon says, than in their first principles: and the attempt to make the bearings of actions upon the ultimate end more evident than they can be made by referring them to the intermediate ends, and to estimate their value by a direct reference to human happiness, generally terminates in attaching most importance, not to those effects which are really the greatest, but to those which can most easily be pointed to and individually identified. Those who adopt utility as a standard can seldom apply it truly except through the secondary principles; those who reject it, generally do no more than erect those secondary principles into first principles. It is when two or more of the secondary principles conflict, that a direct appeal to some first principle becomes necessary; and then commences the practical importance of the utilitarian controversy; which is, in other respects, a question of arrangement and logical subordination rather than of practice; important principally in a purely scientific point of view, for the sake of the systematic unity and coherency of ethical philosophy. It is probable, however, that to the principle of utility we owe all that Bentham did; that it was necessary to him to find a first principle which he could receive as self-evident, and to which he could attach all his other doctrines as logical consequences: that to him systematic unity was an indispensable condition of his confidence in his own intellect. And there is something further to be remarked. Whether happiness be or be not the end to which morality should be referred – that it be referred to an *end* of some sort, and not left in the dominion of vague feeling or inexplicable internal conviction, that it be made a matter of reason and calculation, and not merely of sentiment, is essential to the very idea of moral philosophy; is, in fact, what renders argument or discussion on moral questions possible. That the morality of actions depends on the consequences which they tend to produce, is the doctrine of rational persons of all schools; that the good or evil of those consequences is measured solely by pleasure or pain, is all of the doctrine of the school of utility, which is peculiar to it.

In so far as Bentham's adoption of the principle of utility induced him to fix his attention upon the consequences of actions as the consideration determining their morality, so far he was indisputably in the right path: though to go far in it without wandering, there was needed a greater knowledge of the formation of character, and of the consequences of actions upon the agent's own frame of mind, than Bentham possessed. His want of power to estimate this class of consequences, together with his want of the degree of modest deference which, from those who have not competent experience of their own, is due to the experience of others on that part of the subject, greatly limit the value of his speculations on questions of practical ethics.

He is chargeable also with another error, which it would be improper to pass over, because nothing has tended more to place him in opposition to the common feelings of mankind, and to give to his philosophy that cold, mechanical and ungenial air which characterizes the popular idea of a Benthamite. This error, or rather one-sidedness, belongs to him not as a utilitarian, but as a moralist by profession, and in common with almost all professed moralists, whether religious or philosophical: it is that of treating the *moral* view of actions and characters, which is unquestionably the first and most important mode of looking at them, as if it were the sole one: whereas it is only one of three, by all of which our sentiments towards the human being may be, ought to be, and without entirely crushing our own nature cannot but be, materially influenced. Every human action has three aspects: its *moral* aspect, or that of its *right* and *wrong*; its *aesthetic* aspect, or that of its *beauty*; its *sympathetic* aspect, or that of its *lovableness*. The first addresses itself to our reason and conscience; the second to our imagination; the third to our human fellow-feeling. According to the first, we approve or disapprove; according to the second, we admire or despise; according to the third, we love, pity or dislike. The morality of an action depends on its foreseeable consequences; its beauty, and its lovableness, or the reverse, depend on the qualities which it is evidence of. Thus, a lie is *wrong*, because its effect is to mislead, and because it tends to destroy the confidence of man in man; it is also *mean*, because it is cowardly – because it proceeds from not daring to face the consequences of telling the truth – or at best is evidence of want of that *power* to compass our ends by straightforward means, which is conceived as properly belonging to every person not deficient in energy or in understanding. The action of Brutus in sentencing his sons was *right*, because it was executing a law essential to the freedom of his country, against persons of whose guilt there was no doubt: it was *admirable*, because it evinced a rare degree of patriotism, courage, and self-control; but there was nothing *lovable* in it; it affords either no presumption in regard to lovable qualities, or a presumption of their deficiency. If one of the sons had engaged in the conspiracy from affection for the other, his action would have been lovable, though neither moral nor admirable. It is not possible for any sophistry to confound these three modes of viewing an action; but it is very possible to adhere to one of them exclusively, and lose sight of the rest. Sentimentality consists in setting the last two of the three above the first; the error of moralists in general, and of Bentham, is to sink the two latter entirely. This is pre-eminently the case with Bentham: he both wrote and felt as if the moral standard ought not only to be paramount (which it ought), but to be alone; as if it ought to be the sole master of all our actions, and even of all our sentiments; as if either to admire or like, or despise or dislike a person for any action which neither does good nor harm, or which does not do a good or a harm proportioned to the sentiment entertained, were an injustice and a prejudice. He carried this so far, that there were certain phrases which, being expressive of what he considered to be this groundless liking or aversion, he could not bear to hear pronounced in his presence. Among these phrases were those of *good* and *bad taste*. He thought it an insolent piece of dogmatism in one person to praise or condemn another in a matter of taste: as if men's likings and dislikings, on things in themselves indifferent, were not full of the most important inferences as to every point of their character; as if a person's tastes did not show him to be wise or a fool, cultivated or ignorant, gentle or rough, sensitive or callous, generous or sordid, benevolent or selfish, conscientious or depraved.

Connected with the same topic are Bentham's peculiar opinions on poetry. Much more has been said than there is any foundation for, about his contempt for the pleasures of imagination, and for the fine arts. Music was throughout life his favourite amusement; painting, sculpture, and the other arts addressed to the eye, he was so far from holding in any contempt, that he occasionally recognizes them as means employable for important social ends; though his ignorance of the deeper springs of human character prevented him (as it prevents most Englishmen) from suspecting how profoundly such things enter into the moral nature of man, and into the education both of the individual and of the race. But towards poetry in the narrower sense, that which employs the language of words, he entertained no favour. Words, he thought, were perverted from their proper office when they were employed in uttering anything but precise logical truth. He says, somewhere in his works, that 'quantity of pleasure being equal, push-pin is as good as poetry': but this is only a paradoxical way of stating what he would equally have said of the things which he most valued and admired. Another aphorism is attributed to him, which is much more characteristic of his view of this subject: 'All poetry is misrepresentation.' Poetry, he thought, consisted essentially in exaggeration for effect: in proclaiming some one view of a thing very emphatically, and suppressing all the limitations and qualifications. This trait of character seems to us a curious example of what Mr Carlyle strikingly calls 'the completeness of limited men'. Here is a philosopher who is happy within his narrow boundary as no man of indefinite range ever was; who flatters himself that he is so completely emancipated from the essential law of poor human intellect, by which it can only see one thing at a time well, that he can even turn round upon the imperfection and lay a solemn interdict upon it. Did Bentham really suppose that it is in poetry only that propositions cannot be exactly true, cannot contain in themselves all the limitations and qualifications with which they require to be taken when applied to practice? We have seen how far his own prose propositions are from realizing this Utopia: and even the attempt to approach it would be incompatible not with poetry merely, but with oratory, and popular writing of every kind. Bentham's charge is true to the fullest extent; all writing which undertakes to make men feel truths as well as see them, does take up one point at a time, does seek to impress that, to drive that home, to make it sink into and colour the whole mind of the reader or hearer. It is justified in doing so, if the portion of truth which it thus enforces be that which is called for by the occasion. All writing addressed to the feelings has a natural tendency to exaggeration; but Bentham should have remembered that in this, as in many things, we must aim at too much, to be assured of doing enough.

From the same principle in Bentham came the intricate and involved style, which makes his later writings books for the student only, not the general reader. It was from his perpetually aiming at impracticable precision. Nearly all his earlier, and many parts of his later writings, are models, as we have already observed, of light, playful and popular style: Benthamiana might be made of passages worthy of Addison or Goldsmith. But in his later years and more advanced studies, he fell into a Latin or German structure of sentence, foreign to the genius of the English language. He could not bear, for the sake of clearness and the reader's ease, to say, as ordinary men are content to do, a little more than the truth in one sentence, and correct it in the next. The whole of the qualifying remarks which he intended to make, he insisted upon imbedding as parentheses in the very middle of the sentence itself. And thus the sense of being so long suspended, and attention being required to the accessory ideas before the principal idea had been properly seized, it became difficult, without some practice, to make out the train of thought. It is fortunate that so many of the most important parts of his writings are free from this defect. We regard it as a *reductio ad absurdum* of his objection to poetry. In trying to write in a manner against which the same objection should not lie, he could stop nowhere short of utter unreadableness, and after all attained no more accuracy than is compatible with opinions as imperfect and one-sided as those of any poet or sentimentalist breathing. Judge then in what state literature and philosophy would be, and what chance they would have of influencing the multitude, if his objection were allowed, and all styles of writing banished which would not stand his test.

We must here close this brief and imperfect view of Bentham and his doctrines; in which many parts of the subject have been entirely untouched, and no part done justice to, but which at least proceeds from an intimate familiarity with his writings, and is nearly the first attempt at an impartial estimate of his character as a philosopher, and of the result of his labours to the world.

After every abatement, and it has been seen whether we have made our abatements sparingly – there remains to Bentham an indisputable place among the great intellectual benefactors of mankind. His writings will long form an indispensable part of the education of the highest order of practical things; and the collected edition of them ought to be in the hands of every one who would either understand his age, or take any beneficial part in the great business of it.

Editor's Note

'Coleridge' was first published in the *London and Westminster Review*, March 1840; the text printed here is taken from *Dissertations and Discussions*.

'Coleridge'
BY J. S. MILL

The name of Coleridge is one of the few English names of our time which are likely to be oftener pronounced, and to become symbolical of more important things, in proportion as the inward workings of the age manifest themselves more and more in outward facts. Bentham excepted, no Englishman of recent date has left his impress so deeply in the opinions and mental tendencies of those among us who attempt to enlighten their practice by philosophical meditation. If it be true, as Lord Bacon affirms, that a knowledge of the speculative opinions of the men between twenty and thirty years of age is the great source of political prophecy, the existence of Coleridge will show itself by no slight or ambiguous traces in the coming history of our country; for no one has contributed more to shape the opinions of those among its younger men, who can be said to have opinions at all.

The influence of Coleridge, like that of Bentham, extends far beyond those who share in the peculiarities of his religious or philosophical creed. He has been the great awakener in this country of the spirit of philosophy, within the bounds of traditional opinions. He has been, almost as truly as Bentham, 'the great questioner of things established', for a questioner needs not necessarily be an enemy. By Bentham, beyond all others, men have been led to ask themselves, in regard to any ancient or received opinion, Is it true? and by Coleridge, What is the meaning of it? The one took his stand outside the received opinion, and surveyed it as an entire stranger to it: the other looked at it from within, and endeavoured to see it with the eyes of a believer in it; to discover by what apparent facts it was at first suggested, and by what appearances it has ever since been rendered continually credible – has seemed, to a succession of persons, to be a faithful interpretation of their experience. Bentham judged a proposition true or false as it accorded or not with the result of his own inquiries; and did not search very curiously into what might be meant by the proposition, when it obviously did not mean what he thought true. With Coleridge, on the contrary, the very fact that any doctrine had been believed by thoughtful men, and received by whole nations or generations of mankind, was part of the problem to be solved, was one of the phenomena to be accounted for. And as Bentham's short and easy method of referring all to the selfish interests of aristocracies, or priests, or lawyers, or some other species of impostors, could not satisfy a man who saw so much farther into the complexities of the human intellect and feelings – he considered the long or extensive prevalence of any opinion as a presumption that it was not altogether a fallacy; that, to its first authors at least, it was the result of a struggle to express in words something which had a reality to them, though perhaps not to many of those who have since received the doctrine by mere tradition. The long duration of a belief, he thought, is at least proof of an adaptation in it to some portion or other of the human mind; and if, on digging down to the root, we do not find, as is generally the case, some truth, we shall find some natural want or requirement of human nature which the doctrine in question is fitted to satisfy: among which wants the instincts of selfishness and of credulity have a place, but by no means an exclusive one. From this difference in the points of view of the two philosophers, and from the too rigid adherence of each of his own, it was to be expected that Bentham should continually miss the truth which is in the traditional opinions, and Coleridge that which is out of them, and at variance with them. But it was also likely that each would find, or show the way to finding, much of what the other missed.

It is hardly possible to speak of Coleridge, and his position among his contemporaries, without reverting to Bentham: they are connected by two of the closest bonds of association – resemblance and contrast. It would be difficult to find two persons of philosophic eminence more exactly the contrary of one another. Compare their modes of treatment of any subject, and you might fancy them inhabitants of different worlds. They seem to have scarcely a principle or a premise in common. Each of them sees scarcely anything but what the other does not see. Bentham would have regarded Coleridge with a peculiar measure of the good-humoured contempt with which he was accustomed to regard all modes of philosophizing different from his own. Coleridge would probably have made Bentham one of the exceptions to the enlarged and liberal appreciation which (to the credit of *his* mode of philosophizing) he extended to most thinkers of any eminence, from whom he differed. But contraries, as logicians say, are but *quae in eodem genere maxime distant*, the things which are farthest from one another in the same kind. These two agreed in being the men who, in their age and country, did most to enforce, by precept and example, the necessity of a philosophy. They agreed in making it their occupation to recall opinions to first principles; taking no proposition for granted without examining into the grounds of it, and ascertaining that it possessed the kind and degree of evidence suitable to its nature. They agreed in recognizing that sound theory is the only foundation for sound practice, and that whoever despises theory, let him give himself what airs of wisdom he may, is self-convicted of being a quack. If a book were to be compiled containing all the best things ever said on the rule-of-thumb school of political craftsmanship, and on the insufficiency for practical purposes of what the mere practical man calls experience, it is difficult to say whether the collection would be more indebted to the writings of Bentham or of Coleridge. They agreed, too, in perceiving that the groundwork of all other philosophy must be laid in the philosophy of the mind. To lay this foundation deeply and strongly, and to raise a superstructure in accordance with it, were the objects to which their lives were devoted. They employed, indeed, for the most part, different materials; but as the materials of both were real observations, the genuine product of experience – the results will in the end be found not hostile, but supplementary, to one another. Of their methods of philosophizing, the same thing may be said: they were different, yet both were legitimate logical processes. In every respect the two men are each other's 'completing counterpart': the strong points of each correspond to the weak points of the other. Whoever could master the premises and combine the methods of both, would possess the entire English philosophy of their age. Coleridge used to say that every one is born either a Platonist or an Aristotelian: it may be similarly affirmed, that every Englishman of the present day is by implication either a Benthamite or a Coleridgian; holds views of human affairs which can only be proved true on the principles either of Bentham or of Coleridge. In one respect, indeed, the parallel fails. Bentham so improved and added to the system of philosophy he adopted, that for his successors he may almost be accounted its founder; while Coleridge, though he has left on the system he inculcated, such traces of himself as cannot fail to be left by any mind of original powers, was anticipated in all the essentials of his doctrine by the great Germans of the latter half of the last century, and was accompanied in it by the remarkable series of their French expositors and followers. Hence, although Coleridge is to Englishmen the type and the main source of that doctrine, he is the creator rather of the shape in which it has appeared among us, than of the doctrine itself.

The time is yet far distant when, in the estimation of Coleridge, and of his influence upon the intellect of our time, anything like unanimity can be looked for. As a poet, Coleridge has taken his place. The healthier taste, and more intelligent canons of poetic criticism, which he was himself mainly instrumental in diffusing, have at length assigned to him his proper rank, as one among the great, and (if we look to the powers shown rather than to the amount of actual achievement) among the greatest, names in our literature. But as a philosopher, the class of thinkers has scarcely yet arisen by whom he is to be judged. The limited philosophical public of this country is as yet too exclusively divided between those to whom Coleridge and the views which he promulgated or defended are everything, and those to whom they are nothing. A true thinker can only be justly estimated when his thoughts have worked their way into minds formed in a different school; have been wrought and moulded into consistency with all other true and relevant thoughts; when the noisy conflict of half-truths, angrily denying one another, has subsided, and ideas which seemed mutually incompatible, have been found only to require mutual limitations. This time has not yet come for Coleridge. The spirit of philosophy in England, like that of religion, is still rootedly sectarian. Conservative thinkers and Liberals, transcendentalists and admirers of Hobbes and Locke, regard each other as out of the pale of philosophical intercourse; look upon each other's speculations as vitiated by an original taint, which makes all study of them, except for purposes of attack, useless if not mischievous. An error much the same as if Kepler had refused to profit by Ptolemy's or Tycho's observations, because those astronomers believed that the sun moved round the earth; or as if Priestley and Lavoisier, because they differed on the doctrine of phlogiston, had rejected each other's chemical experiments. It is even a still greater error than either of these. For, among the truths long recognized by Continental philosophers, but which very few Englishmen have yet arrived at, one is, the importance, in the present imperfect state of mental and social science, of antagonist modes of thought: which, it will one day be felt, are as necessary to one another in speculation, as mutually checking powers are in a political constitution. A clear insight, indeed, into this necessity is the only rational or enduring basis of philosophical tolerance; the only condition under which liberality in matters of opinion can be anything better than a polite synonym for indifference between one opinion and another.

All students of man and society who possess that first requisite for so difficult a study, a due sense of its difficulties, are aware that the besetting danger is not so much of embracing falsehood for truth, as of mistaking part of the truth for the whole. It might be plausibly maintained that in almost every one of the leading controversies, past or present, in social philosophy, both sides were in the right in what they affirmed, though wrong in what they denied; and that if either could have been made to take the other's view in addition to its own, little more would have been needed to make its doctrine correct. Take for instance the question how far mankind have gained by civilization. One observer is forcibly struck by the multiplication of physical comforts; the advancement and diffusion of knowledge; the decay of superstition; the facilities of mutual intercourse; the softening of manners; the decline of war and personal conflict; the progressive limitation of the tyranny of the strong over the weak; the great works accomplished throughout the globe by the co-operation of multitudes: and he becomes that very common character, the worshipper of 'our enlightened age'. Another fixes his attention, not upon the value of these advantages, but upon the high price which is paid for them; the relaxation of individual energy and courage; the loss of proud and self-relying independence; the slavery of so large a portion of mankind to artificial wants; their effeminate shrinking from even the shadow of pain; the dull unexciting monotony of their lives, and the passionless insipidity, and absence of any marked individuality, in their characters; the contrast between the narrow mechanical understanding, produced by a life spent in executing by fixed rules a fixed task, and the varied powers of the man of the woods, whose subsistence and safety depend at each instant upon his capacity of extemporarily adapting means to ends; the demoralizing effect of great inequalities in wealth and social rank; and the sufferings of the great mass of the people of civilized countries, whose wants are scarcely better provided for than those of the savage, while they are bound by a thousand fetters in lieu of the freedom and excitement which are his compensations. One who attends to these things, and to these exclusively, will be apt to infer that savage life is preferable to civilized; that the work of civilization should as far as possible be undone; and from the premises of Rousseau, he will not improbably be led to the practical conclusions of Rousseau's disciple, Robespierre. No two thinkers can be more entirely at variance than the two we have supposed – the worshippers of Civilization and of Independence, of the present and of the remote past. Yet all that is positive in the opinions of either of them is true; and we see how easy it would be to choose one's path, if either half of the truth were the whole of it, and how great may be the difficulty of framing, as it is necessary to do, a set of practical maxims which combine both.

So again, one person sees in a very strong light the need which the great mass of mankind have of being ruled over by a degree of intelligence and virtue superior to their own. He is deeply impressed with the mischief done to the uneducated and uncultivated by weaning them of all habits of reverence, appealing to them as a competent tribunal to decide the most intricate questions, and making them think themselves capable, not only of being a light to themselves, but of giving the law to their superiors in culture. He sees, further, that cultivation, to be carried beyond a certain point, requires leisure; that leisure is the natural attribute of a hereditary aristocracy; that such a body has all the means of acquiring intellectual and moral superiority; and he needs be at no loss to endow them with abundant motives to it. An aristocracy indeed, being human, are, as he cannot but see, not exempt, any more than their inferiors, from the common need of being controlled and enlightened by a still greater wisdom and goodness than their own. For this, however, his reliance is upon reverence for a Higher above them, sedulously inculcated and fostered by the course of their education. We thus see brought together all the elements of a conscientious zealot for an aristocratic government, supporting and supported by an established Christian church. There is truth, and important truth, in this thinker's premises. But there is a thinker of a very different description, in whose premises there is an equal portion of truth. This is he who says, that an average man, even an average member of an aristocracy, if he can postpone the interests of other people to his own calculations or instincts of self-interest, will do so; that all governments in all ages have done so, as far as they were permitted, and generally to a ruinous extent; and that the only possible remedy is a pure democracy, in which the people are their own governors, and can have no selfish interest in oppressing themselves.

Thus it is in regard to every important partial truth; there are always two conflicting modes of thought, one tending to give to that truth too large, the other to give it too small, a place: and the history of opinion is generally an oscillation between these extremes. From the imperfection of the human faculties, it seldom happens that, even in the minds of eminent thinkers, each partial view of their subject passes for its worth, and none for more than its worth. But even if this just balance exist in the mind of the wiser teacher, it will not exist in his disciples, still less in the general mind. He cannot prevent that which is new in his doctrine, and on which, being new, he is forced to insist the most strongly, from making a disproportionate impression. The impetus necessary to overcome the obstacles which resist all novelties of opinion, seldom fails to carry the public mind almost as far on the contrary side of the perpendicular. Thus every excess in either direction determines a corresponding reaction; improvement consisting only in this, that the oscillation, each time, departs rather less widely from the centre, and an ever-increasing tendency is manifested to settle finally in it.

Now the Germano-Coleridgian doctrine is, in our view of the matter, the result of such a reaction. It expresses the revolt of the human mind against the philosophy of the eighteenth century. It is ontological, because that was experimental; conservative, because that was innovative; religious, because so much of that was infidel; concrete and historical, because that was abstract and metaphysical; poetical, because that was matter-of-fact and prosaic. In every respect it flies off in the contrary direction to its predecessor; yet faithful to the general law of improvement last noticed, it is less extreme in its opposition, it denies less of what is true in the doctrine it wars against, than had been the case in any previous philosophic reaction; and in particular, far less than when the philosophy of the eighteenth century triumphed, and so memorably abused its victory, over that which preceded it.

We may begin our consideration of the two systems either at one extreme or the other; with their highest philosophical generalizations, or with their practical conclusions. The former seems preferable, because it is in their highest generalities that the difference between the two systems is most familiarly known.

Every consistent scheme of philosophy requires as its starting point, a theory respecting the sources of human knowledge, and the objects which the human faculties are capable of taking cognizance of. The prevailing theory in the eighteenth century, on this most comprehensive of questions, was that proclaimed by Locke, and commonly attributed to Aristotle – that all knowledge consists of generalizations from experience. Of nature, or anything whatever external to ourselves, we know, according to this theory, nothing, except the facts which present themselves to our senses, and such other facts as may, by analogy, be inferred from these. There is no knowledge *a priori*; no truths cognizable by the mind's inward light, and grounded on intuitive evidence. Sensation, and the mind's consciousness of its own acts, are not only the exclusive sources, but the sole materials of our knowledge. From this doctrine, Coleridge, with the German philosophers since Kant (not to go farther back) and most of the English since Reid, strongly dissents. He claims for the human mind a capacity, within certain limits, of perceiving the nature and properties of 'Things in themselves'. He distinguishes in the human intellect two faculties, which, in the technical language common to him with the Germans, he calls Understanding and Reason. The former faculty judges of phenomena, or the appearances of things, and forms generalizations from these: to the latter it belongs, by direct intuition, to perceive things, and recognize truths, not cognizable by our senses. These perceptions are not indeed innate, nor could ever have been awakened in us without experience; but they are not copies of it: experience is not their prototype, it is only the occasion by which they are irresistibly suggested. The appearances in nature excite in us, by an inherent law, ideas of those invisible things which are the causes of the visible appearances, and on whose law those appearances depend: and we then perceive that these things must have pre-existed to render the appearances possible; just as (to use a frequent illustration of Coleridge's) we see, before we know that we have eyes, but when once this is known to us, we perceive that eyes must have pre-existed to enable us to see. Among the truths which are thus known *a priori*, by occasion of experience, but not themselves the subjects of experience, Coleridge includes the fundamental doctrines of religion and morals, the principles of mathematics, and the ultimate laws even of physical nature; which he contends cannot be proved by experience, though they must necessarily be consistent with it, and would, if we knew them perfectly, enable us to account for all observed facts, and to predict all those which are as yet unobserved.

It is not necessary to remind any one who concerns himself with such subjects, that between the partisans of these two opposite doctrines there reigns a *bellum internecinum*. Neither side is sparing in the imputation of intellectual and moral obliquity to the perceptions, and of pernicious consequences to the creed, of its antagonists. Sensualism is the common term of abuse for the one philosophy, mysticism for the other. The one doctrine is accused of making men beasts, the other lunatics. It is the unaffected belief of numbers on one side of the controversy, that their adversaries are actuated by a desire to break loose from moral and religious obligation; and of numbers on the other that their opponents are either men fit for Bedlam, or who cunningly pander to the interests of hierarchies and aristocracies, by manufacturing superfine new arguments in favour of old prejudices. It is almost needless to say that those who are freest with these mutual accusations, are seldom those who are most at home in the real intricacies of the question, or who are best acquainted with the argumentative strength of the opposite side, or even of their own. But without going to these extreme lengths, even sober men on both sides take no charitable view of the tendencies of each other's opinions.

It is affirmed that the doctrine of Locke and his followers, that all knowledge is experience generalized, leads by strict logical consequence to atheism: that Hume and other sceptics were right when they contended that it is impossible to prove a God on grounds of experience; and Coleridge (like Kant) maintains positively, that the ordinary argument for a Deity, from marks of design in the universe, or, in other words, from the resemblance of the order in nature to the effects of human skill and contrivance, is not tenable. It is further said that the same doctrine annihilates moral obligation; reducing morality either to the blind impulses of animal sensibility, or to a calculation of prudential consequences, both equally fatal to its essence. Even science, it is affirmed, loses the character of science in this view of it, and becomes empiricism; a mere enumeration and arrangement of facts, not explaining nor accounting for them: since a fact is only then accounted for when we are made to see in it the manifestation of laws, which, as soon as they are perceived at all, are perceived to be *necessary*. These are the charges brought by the transcendental philosophers against the school of Locke, Hartley and Bentham. They in their turn allege that the transcendentalists make imagination, and not observation, the criterion of truth; that they lay down principles under which a man may enthrone his wildest dreams in the chair of philosophy, and impose them on mankind as intuitions of the pure reason: which has, in fact, been done in all ages, by all manner of mystical enthusiasts. And even if, with gross inconsistency, the private revelations of any individual Böhme or Swedenborg be disowned, or, in other words, outvoted (the only means of discrimination which, it is contended, the theory admits of), this is still only substituting, as the test of truth, the dreams of the majority for the dreams of each individual. Whoever form a strong enough party, may at any time set up the immediate perceptions of *their* reason, that is to say, any reigning prejudice, as a truth independent of experience; a truth not only requiring no proof, but to be believed in opposition to all that appears proof to the mere understanding; nay, the more to be believed, because it cannot be put into words and into the logical form of a proposition without a contradiction in terms: for no less authority than this is claimed by some transcendentalists for their *a priori* truths. And thus a ready mode is provided, by which whoever is on the strongest side may dogmatize at his ease, and instead of proving his propositions, may rail at all who deny them, as bereft of 'the vision and the faculty divine', or blinded to its plainest revelations by a corrupt heart.

This is a very temperate statement of what is charged by these two classes of thinkers against each other. How much of either representation is correct, cannot conveniently be discussed in this place. In truth, a system of consequences from an opinion, drawn by an adversary, is seldom of much worth. Disputants are rarely sufficiently masters of each other's doctrines, to be good judges what is fairly deducible from them, or how a consequence which seems to flow from one part of the theory may or may not be defeated by another part. To combine the different parts of a doctrine with one another, and with all admitted truths, is not indeed a small trouble, nor one which a person is often inclined to take for other people's opinions. Enough if each does it for his own, which he has a greater interest in, and is more disposed to be just to. Were we to search among men's recorded thoughts for the choicest manifestations of human imbecility and prejudice, our specimens would be mostly taken from their opinions of the opinions of one another. Imputations of horrid consequences ought not to bias the judgement of any person capable of independent thought. Coleridge himself says (in the 25th Aphorism of his *Aids to Reflection*), 'He who begins by loving Christianity better than truth, will proceed by loving his own sect or church better than Christianity, and end in loving himself better than all.'

As to the fundamental difference of opinion respecting the sources of our knowledge (apart from the corollaries which either party may have drawn from its own principle, or imputed to its opponent's), the question lies far too deep in the recesses of psychology for us to discuss it here. The lists having been open ever since the dawn of philosophy, it is not wonderful that the two parties should have been forced to put on their strongest armour, both of attack and of defence. The question would not so long have remained a question, if the more obvious arguments on either side had been unanswerable. Each party has been able to urge in its own favour numerous and striking facts, to reconcile which with the opposite theory has required all the metaphysical resources which that theory could command. It will not be wondered at, then, that we here content ourselves with a bare statement of our opinion. It is, that the truth, on this much-debated question, lies with the school of Locke and of Bentham. The nature and laws of Things in themselves, or of the hidden causes of the phenomena which are the objects of experience, appear to us radically inaccessible to the human faculties. We see no ground for believing that anything can be the object of our knowledge except our experience, and what can be inferred from our experience by the analogies of experience itself; nor that there is any idea, feeling, or power in the human mind, which, in order to account for it, requires that its origin should be referred to any other source. We are therefore at issue with Coleridge on the central idea of his philosophy; and we find no need of, and no use for, the peculiar technical terminology which he and his masters the Germans have introduced into philosophy, for the double purpose of giving logical precision to doctrines which we do not admit, and of marking a relation between those abstract doctrines and many concrete experimental truths, which this language, in our judgement, serves not to elucidate, but to disguise and obscure. Indeed, but for these peculiarities of language, it would be difficult to understand how the reproach of mysticism (by which nothing is meant in common parlance but unintelligibleness) has been fixed upon Coleridge and the Germans in the minds of many, to whom doctrines substantially the same, when taught in a manner more superficial and less fenced round against objections, by Reid and Dugald Stewart, have appeared the plain dictates of 'common sense', successfully asserted against the subtleties of metaphysics.

Yet, though we think the doctrines of Coleridge and the Germans, in the pure science of mind, erroneous, and have no taste for their peculiar terminology, we are far from thinking that even in respect of this, the least valuable part of their intellectual exertions, those philosophers have lived in vain. The doctrines of the school of Locke stood in need of an entire renovation: to borrow a physiological illustration from Coleridge, they required, like certain secretions of the human body, to be re-absorbed into the system and secreted afresh. In what form did that philosophy generally prevail throughout Europe? In that of the shallowest set of doctrines which perhaps were ever passed off upon a cultivated age as a complete psychological system – the ideology of Condillac and his school; a system which affected to resolve all the phenomena of the human mind into sensation, by a process which essentially consisted in merely *calling* all states of mind, however heterogeneous, by that name; a philosophy now acknowledged to consist solely of a set of verbal generalizations, explaining nothing, distinguishing nothing, leading to nothing. That men should begin by sweeping this away, was the first sign that the age of real psychology was about to commence. In England the case, though different, was scarcely better. The philosophy of Locke, as a popular doctrine, had remained nearly as it stood in his own book; which, as its title implies, did not pretend to give an account of any but the intellectual part of our nature; which, even within that limited sphere, was but the commencement of a system, and though its errors and defects as such have been exaggerated beyond all just bounds, it did expose many vulnerable points to the searching criticism of the new school. The least imperfect part of it, the purely logical part, had almost dropped out of sight. With respect to those of Locke's doctrines which are properly metaphysical, however the sceptical part of them may have been followed up by others, and carried beyond the point at which he stopped, the only one of his successors who attempted, and achieved, any considerable improvement and extension of the analytical part, and thereby added anything to the explanation of the human mind on Locke's principles, was Hartley. But Hartley's doctrines, so far as they are true, were so much in advance of the age, and the way had been so little prepared for them by the general tone of thinking which yet prevailed, even under the influence of Locke's writings, that the philosophic world did not deem them worthy of being attended to. Reid and Stewart were allowed to run them down uncontradicted: Brown, though a man of a kindred genius, had evidently never read them; and but for the accident of their being taken up by Priestley, who transmitted them as a kind of heirloom to his Unitarian followers, the name of Hartley might have perished, or survived only as that of a visionary physician, the author of an exploded physiological hypothesis. It perhaps required all the violence of the assaults made by Reid and the German school upon Locke's system, to recall men's minds to Hartley's principles, as alone adequate to the solution, upon that system, of the peculiar difficulties which those assailants pressed upon men's attention as altogether insoluble by it. We may here notice that Coleridge, before he adopted his later philosophical views, was an enthusiastic Hartleian; so that his abandonment of the philosophy of Locke cannot be imputed to unacquaintance with the highest form of that philosophy which had yet appeared. That he should pass through that highest form without stopping at it, is itself a strong presumption that there were more difficulties in the question than Hartley had solved. That anything has since been done to solve them we probably owe to the revolution in opinion, of which Coleridge was one of the organs; and even in abstract metaphysics his writings, and those of his school of thinkers, are one of the richest mines from whence the opposite school can draw the materials for what has yet to be done to perfect their own theory.

If we now pass from the purely abstract to the concrete and practical doctrines of the two schools, we shall see still more clearly the necessity of the reaction, and the great service rendered to philosophy by its authors. This will be best manifested by a survey of the state of practical philosophy in Europe, as Coleridge and his compeers found it, towards the close of the last century.

The state of opinion in the latter half of the eighteenth century was by no means the same on the Continent of Europe and in our own island; and the difference was still greater in appearance than it was in reality. In the more advanced nations of the Continent, the prevailing philosophy had done its work completely: it had spread itself over every department of human knowledge; it had taken possession of the whole Continental mind: and scarcely one educated person was left who retained any allegiance to the opinions or the institutions of ancient times. In England, the native country of compromise, things had stopped far short of this; the philosophical movement had been brought to a halt in an early stage, and a peace had been patched up by concessions on both sides, between the philosophy of the time and its traditional institutions and creeds. Hence the aberrations of the age were generally, on the Continent, at that period, the extravagances of new opinions; in England, the corruptions of old ones.

To insist upon the deficiencies of the Continental philosophy of the last century, or, as it is commonly termed, the French philosophy, is almost superfluous. That philosophy is indeed as unpopular in this country as its bitterest enemy could desire. If its faults were as well understood as they are much railed at, criticism might be considered to have finished its work. But that this is not yet the case, the nature of the imputations currently made upon the French philosophers, sufficiently proves; many of these being as inconsistent with a just philosophic comprehension of their system of opinions, as with charity towards the men themselves. It is not true, for example, that any of them denied moral obligation, or sought to weaken its force. So far were they from meriting this accusation, that they could not even tolerate the writers who, like Helvetius, ascribed a selfish origin to the feelings of morality, resolving them into a sense of interest. Those writers were as much cried down among the *philosophes* themselves, and what was true and good in them (and there is much that is so) met with as little appreciation, then as now. The error of the philosophers was rather that they trusted too much to those feelings; believed them to be more deeply rooted in human nature than they are; to be not so dependent, as in fact they are, upon collateral influences. They thought them the natural and spontaneous growth of the human heart; so firmly fixed in it, that they would subsist unimpaired, nay invigorated, when the whole system of opinions and observances with which they were habitually intertwined was violently torn away.

To tear away was, indeed, all that these philosophers, for the most part, aimed at: they had no conception that anything else was needful. At their millennium, superstition, priestcraft, error and prejudice of every kind, were to be annihilated; some of them gradually added that despotism and hereditary privileges must share the same fate; and, this accomplished, they never for a moment suspected that all the virtues and graces of humanity could fail to flourish, or that when the noxious weeds were once rooted out, the soil would stand in any need of tillage.

In this they committed the very common error, of mistaking the state of things with which they had always been familiar, for the universal and natural condition of mankind. They were accustomed to see the human race agglomerated in large nations, all (except here and there a madman or a malefactor) yielding obedience more or less strict to a set of laws prescribed by a few of their own number, and to a set of moral rules prescribed by each other's opinion; renouncing the exercise of individual will and judgement, except within the limits imposed by these laws and rules; and acquiescing in the sacrifice of their individual wishes when the point was decided against them by lawful authority; or persevering only in hopes of altering the opinion of the ruling powers. Finding matters to be so generally in this condition, the philosophers apparently concluded that they could not possibly be in any other; and were ignorant, by what a host of civilizing and restraining influences a state of things so repugnant to man's self-will and love of independence has been brought about, and how imperatively it demands the continuance of those influences as the condition of its own existence. The very first element of the social union, obedience to a government of some sort, has not been found so easy a thing to establish in the world. Among a timid and spiritless race, like the inhabitants of the vast plains of tropical countries, passive obedience may be of natural growth; though even there we doubt whether it has ever been found among any people with whom fatalism, or in other words, submission to the pressure of circumstances as the decree of God, did not prevail as a religious doctrine. But the difficulty of inducing a brave and warlike race to submit their individual *arbitrium* to any common umpire, has always been felt to be so great, that nothing short of supernatural power has been deemed adequate to overcome it; and such tribes have always assigned to the first institution of civil society a divine origin. So differently did those judge who knew savage man by actual experience, from those who had no acquaintance with him except in the civilized state. In modern Europe itself, after the fall of the Roman empire, to subdue the feudal anarchy and bring the whole people of any European nation into subjection to government (although Christianity in the most concentrated form of its influence was co-operating in the work) required thrice as many centuries as have elapsed since that time.

Now if these philosophers had known human nature under any other type than that of their own age, and of the particular classes of society among whom they lived, it would have occurred to them, that wherever this habitual submission to law and government has been firmly and durably established, and yet the vigour and manliness of character which resisted its establishment have been in any degree preserved, certain requisites have existed, certain conditions have been fulfilled, of which the following may be regarded as the principal.

First: there has existed, for all who were accounted citizens – for all who were not slaves, kept down by brute force – a system of *education*, beginning with infancy and continued through life, of which, whatever else it might include, one main and incessant ingredient was *restraining discipline*. To train the human being in the habit, and thence the power, of subordinating his personal impulses and aims, to what were considered the ends of society; of adhering, against all temptation, to the course of conduct which those ends prescribed; of controlling in himself all the feelings which were liable to militate against those ends, and encouraging all such as tended towards them; this was the purpose, to which every outward motive that the authority directing the system could command, and every inward power or principle which its knowledge of human nature enabled it to evoke, were endeavoured to be rendered instrumental. The entire civil and military police of the ancient commonwealths was such a system of training: in modern nations its place has been attempted to be supplied principally by religious teaching. And whenever and in proportion as the strictness of the restraining discipline was relaxed, the natural tendency of mankind to anarchy reasserted itself; the State became disorganized from within; mutual conflict for selfish ends, neutralized the energies which were required to keep up the contest against natural causes of evil; and the nation, after a longer or briefer interval of progressive decline, became either the slave of a despotism, or the prey of a foreign invader.

The second condition of permanent political society has been found to be, the existence, in some form or other, of the feeling of allegiance, or loyalty. This feeling may vary in its objects, and is not confined to any particular form of government; but whether in a democracy or in a monarchy, its essence is always the same; *viz*, that there be in the constitution of the State *something* which is settled, something permanent, and not to be called in question; something which, by general agreement, has a right to be where it is, and to be secure against disturbance, whatever else may change. This feeling may attach itself, as among the Jews (and indeed in most of the commonwealths of antiquity), to a common God or gods, the protectors and guardians of their State. Or it may attach itself to certain persons, who are deemed to be, whether by divine appointment, by long prescription, or by the general recognition of their superior capacity and worthiness, the rightful guides and guardians of the rest. Or it may attach itself to laws; to ancient liberties, or ordinances. Or finally (and this is the only shape in which the feeling is likely to exist hereafter) it may attach itself to the principles of individual freedom and political and social equality, as realized in institutions which as yet exist nowhere, or exist only in a rudimentary state. But in all political societies which have had a durable existence, there has been some fixed point; something which men agreed in holding sacred; which, wherever freedom of discussion was a recognized principle, it was of course lawful to contest in theory, but which no one could either fear or hope to see shaken in practice; which, in short (except perhaps during some temporary crisis), was in the common estimation placed beyond discussion. And the necessity of this may easily be made evident. A State never is, nor, until mankind are vastly improved, can hope to be, for any long time exempt from internal dissension; for there neither is, nor has ever been, any state of society in which collisions did not occur between the immediate interests and passions of powerful sections of the people. What, then, enables society to weather these storms, and pass through turbulent times without any permanent weakening of the securities for peaceable existence? Precisely this – that however important the interests about which men fell out, the conflict did not affect the fundamental principles of the system of social union which happened to exist; nor threaten large portions of the community with the subversion of that on which they had built their calculations, and with which their hopes and aims had become identified. But when the questioning of these fundamental principles is (not the occasional disease, or salutary medicine, but) the habitual condition of the body politic, and when all the violent animosities are called forth, which spring naturally from such a situation, the State is virtually in a position of civil war; and can never long remain free from it in act and fact.

The third essential condition of stability in political society, is a strong and active principle of cohesion among the members of the same community or state. We need scarcely say that we do not mean nationality in the vulgar sense of the term; a senseless antipathy to foreigners; an indifference to the general welfare of the human race, or an unjust preference of the supposed interests of our own country; a cherishing of bad peculiarities because they are national; or a refusal to adopt what has been found good by other countries. We mean a principle of sympathy, not of hostility; of union, not of separation. We mean a feeling of common interest among those who live under the same government, and are contained within the same natural or historical boundaries. We mean, that one part of the community do not consider themselves as foreigners with regard to another part; that they set a value on their connection, feel that they are one people, that their lot is cast together, that evil to any of their fellow countrymen is evil to themselves; and do not desire selfishly to free themselves from their share of any common inconvenience by severing the connection. How strong this feeling was in those ancient commonwealths which attained any durable greatness, every one knows. How happily Rome, in spite of all her tyranny, succeeded in establishing the feeling of a common country among the provinces of her vast and divided empire, will appear when any one who has given due attention to the subject shall take the trouble to point it out. In modern times the countries which have had that feeling in the strongest degree have been the most powerful countries; England, France, and, in proportion to their territory and resources, Holland and Switzerland; while England in her connection with Ireland, is one of the most signal examples of the consequences of its absence. Every Italian knows why Italy is under a foreign yoke; every German knows what maintains despotism in the Austrian empire; the evils of Spain flow as much from the absence of nationality among the Spaniards themselves, as from the presence of it in their relations with foreigners; while the completest illustration of all is afforded by the republics of South America, where the parts of one and the same state adhere so slightly together, that no sooner does any province think itself aggrieved by the general government, than it proclaims itself a separate nation.

These essential requisites of civil society the French philosophers of the eighteenth century unfortunately overlooked. They found, indeed, all three – at least the first and second, and most of what nourishes and invigorates the third – already undermined by the vices of the institutions, and of the men, that were set up as the guardians and bulwarks of them. If innovators, in their theories, disregarded the elementary principles of the social union, Conservatives, in their practice, had set the first example. The existing order of things had ceased to realize those first principles: from the force of circumstances, and from the short-sighted selfishness of its administrators, it had ceased to possess the essential conditions of permanent society, and was therefore tottering to its fall. But the philosophers did not see this. Bad as the existing system was in the days of its decrepitude, according to them it was still worse when it actually did what it now only pretended to do. Instead of feeling that the effect of a bad social order in sapping the necessary foundations of society itself is one of the worst of its many mischiefs, the philosophers saw only, and saw with joy, that it was sapping its own foundations. In the weakening of all government they saw only the weakening of bad government; and thought they could not better employ themselves than in finishing the task so well begun – in discrediting all that still remained of restraining discipline, because it rested on the ancient and decayed creeds against which they made war; in unsettling everything which was still considered settled, making men doubtful of the few things of which they still felt certain; and in uprooting what little remained in the people's minds of reverence for anything above them, of respect to any of the limits which custom and prescription had set to the indulgence of each man's fancies or inclinations, or of attachment to any of the things which belonged to them as a nation, and which made them feel their unity as such.

Much of all this was, no doubt, unavoidable, and not justly matter of blame. When the vices of all constituted authorities, added to natural causes of decay, have eaten the heart out of old institutions and beliefs, while at the same time the growth of knowledge, and the altered circumstances of the age, would have required institutions and creeds different from these even if they had remained uncorrupt, we are far from saying that any degree of wisdom on the part of speculative thinkers could avert the political catastrophes, and the subsequent moral anarchy and unsettledness, which we have witnessed and are witnessing. Still less do we pretend that those principles and influences which we have spoken of as the conditions of the permanent existence of the social union, once lost, can ever be, or should be attempted to be, revived in connection with the same institutions or the same doctrines as before. When society requires to be rebuilt, there is no use in attempting to rebuild it on the old plan. By the union of the enlarged views and analytic powers of speculative men with the observation and contriving sagacity of men of practice, better institutions and better doctrines must be elaborated;

and until this is done we cannot hope for much improvement in our present condition. The effort to do it in the eighteenth century would have been premature, as the attempts of the Economistes (who, of all persons then living, came nearest to it, and who were the first to form clearly the idea of a Social Science), sufficiently testify. The time was not ripe for doing effectually any other work than that of destruction. But the work of the day should have been so performed as not to impede that of the morrow. No one can calculate what struggles, which the cause of improvement has yet to undergo, might have been spared if the philosophers of the eighteenth century had done anything like justice to the past. Their mistake was, that they did not acknowledge the historical value of much which had ceased to be useful, nor saw that institutions and creeds, now effete, had rendered essential services to civilization, and still filled a place in the human mind, and in the arrangements of society, which could not without great peril, be left vacant. Their mistake was, that they did not recognize in many of the errors which they assailed, corruptions of important truths, and in many of the institutions most cankered with abuse, necessary elements of civilized society, though in a form and vesture no longer suited to the age; and hence they involved, as far as in them lay, many great truths, in a common discredit with the errors which had grown up around them. They threw away the shell without preserving the kernel; and attempting to new-model society without the binding forces which hold society together, met with such success as might have been anticipated.

Now we claim, in behalf of the philosophers of the reactionary school – of the school to which Coleridge belongs – that exactly what we blame the philosophers of the eighteenth century for not doing, they have done.

Every reaction in opinion, of course, brings into view that portion of the truth which was overlooked before. It was natural that a philosophy which anathematized all that had been going on in Europe from Constantine to Luther, or even to Voltaire, should be succeeded by another, at once a severe critic of the new tendencies of society, and an impassioned vindicator of what was good in the past. This is the easy merit of all Tory and Royalist writers. But the peculiarity of the Germano-Coleridgian school is, that they saw beyond the immediate controversy, to the fundamental principles involved in all such controversies. They were the first (except a solitary thinker here and there) who inquired with any comprehensiveness or depth into the inductive laws of the existence and growth of human society. They were the first to bring prominently forward the three requisites which we have enumerated, as essential principles of all permanent forms of social existence, as principles, we say, and not as mere accidental advantages inherent in the particular polity or religion which the writer happened to patronize. They were the first who pursued, philosophically and in the spirit of Baconian investigation, not only this inquiry, but others ulterior and collateral to it. They thus produced, not a piece of party advocacy, but a philosophy of society, in the only form in which it is yet possible, that of a philosophy of history; not a defence of particular ethical or religious doctrines, but a contribution, the largest yet made by any class of thinkers, towards the philosophy of human culture.

The brilliant light which has been thrown upon history during the last half century, has proceeded almost wholly from this school. The disrespect in which history was held by the *philosophes* is notorious; one of the soberest of them, D'Alembert we believe, was the author of the wish that all record whatever of past events could be blotted out. And indeed the ordinary mode of writing history, and the ordinary mode of drawing lessons from it, were almost sufficient to excuse this contempt. But the *philosophes* saw, as usual, what was not true, not what was. It is no wonder that they who looked on the greater part of what had been handed down from the past as sheer hindrances to man's attaining a well-being which would otherwise be of easy attainment, should content themselves with a very superficial study of history. But the case was otherwise with those who regarded the maintenance of society at all, and especially its maintenance in a state of progressive advancement, as a very difficult task, actually achieved, in however imperfect a manner, for a number of centuries, against the strongest obstacles. It was natural that they should feel a deep interest in ascertaining how this had been effected; and should be led to inquire, both what were the requisites of the permanent existence of the body politic, and what were the

conditions which had rendered the preservation of these permanent requisites compatible with perpetual and progressive
improvement. And hence that series of great writers and thinkers,
from Herder to Michelet, by whom history, which was till then
'a tale told by an idiot, full of sound and fury, signifying nothing',
has been made a science of causes and effects; who, by making
the facts and events of the past have a meaning and an intelligible
place in the gradual evolution of humanity, have at once given
history, even to the imagination, an interest like romance, and
afforded the only means of predicting and guiding the future, by
unfolding the agencies which have produced and still maintain
the present.

The same causes have naturally led the same class of thinkers
to do what their predecessors never could have done, for the
philosophy of human culture. For the tendency of their speculations compelled them to see in the character of the national
education existing in any political society, at once the principal
cause of its permanence as a society, and the chief source of its
progressiveness: the former by the extent to which that education
operated as a system of restraining discipline; the latter by the
degree in which it called forth and invigorated the active faculties.
Besides, not to have looked upon the culture of the inward man
as the problem of problems, would have been incompatible with
the belief which many of these philosophers entertained in Christianity, and the recognition by all of them of its historical value,
and the prime part which it has acted in the progress of mankind.
But here, too, let us not fail to observe, they rose to principles,
and did not stick in the particular case. The culture of the human
being had been carried to no ordinary height, and human nature
had exhibited many of its noblest manifestations, not in Christian
countries only, but in the ancient world, in Athens, Sparta,
Rome; nay, even barbarians, as the Germans, or still more
unmitigated savages, the wild Indians, and again the Chinese, the
Egyptians, the Arabs, all had their own education, their own
culture; a culture which, whatever might be its tendency upon
the whole, had been successful in some respect or other. Every
form of polity, every condition of society, whatever else it had
done, had formed its type of national character. What that type

was, and how it had been made what it was, were questions which the metaphysician might overlook, the historical philosopher could not. Accordingly, the views respecting the various elements of human culture and the causes influencing the formation of national character, which pervade the writings of the Germano-Coleridgian school, throw into the shade everything which had been effected before, or which has been attempted simultaneously by any other school. Such views are, more than anything else, the characteristic feature of the Goethian period of German literature; and are richly diffused through the historical and critical writings of the new French school, as well as of Coleridge and his followers.

In this long, though most compressed, dissertation on the Continental philosophy preceding the reaction, and on the nature of the reaction, so far as directed against that philosophy, we have unavoidably been led to speak rather of the movement itself, than of Coleridge's particular share in it; which, from his posteriority in date, was necessarily a subordinate one. And it would be useless, even did our limits permit, to bring together from the scattered writings of a man who produced no systematic work, any of the fragments which he may have contributed to an edifice still incomplete, and even the general character of which, we can have rendered very imperfectly intelligible to those who are not acquainted with the thing itself. Our object is to invite to the study of the original sources, not to supply the place of such a study. What was peculiar to Coleridge will be better manifested, when we now proceed to review the state of popular philosophy immediately preceding him in our own island; which was different, in some material respects, from the contemporaneous Continental philosophy.

In England, the philosophical speculations of the age had not, except in a few highly metaphysical minds (whose example rather served to deter than to invite others), taken so audacious a flight, nor achieved anything like so complete a victory over the counteracting influences, as on the Continent. There is in the English mind, both in speculation and in practice, a highly salutary shrinking from all extremes. But as this shrinking is rather an instinct of caution than a result of insight, it is too ready to satisfy

201

itself with any medium, merely because it is a medium, and to acquiesce in a union of the disadvantages of both extremes instead of their advantages. The circumstances of the age, too, were unfavourable to decided opinions. The repose which followed the great struggles of the Reformation and the Commonwealth; the final victory over Popery and Puritanism, Jacobitism and Republicanism, and the lulling of the controversies which kept speculation and spiritual consciousness alive; the lethargy which came upon all governors and teachers, after their position in society became fixed; and the growing absorption of all classes in material interests – caused a character of mind to diffuse itself, with less of deep inward workings, and less capable of interpreting those it had, than had existed for centuries. The age seemed smitten with an incapacity of producing deep or strong feeling, such as at least could ally itself with meditative habits. There were few poets, and none of a high order; and philosophy fell mostly into the hands of men of a dry prosaic nature, who had not enough of the materials of human feeling in them to be able to imagine any of its more complex and mysterious manifestations; all of which they either left out of their theories, or introduced them with such explanations as no one who had experienced the feelings could receive as adequate. An age like this, an age without earnestness, was the natural era of compromises and half-convictions.

To make out a case for the feudal and ecclesiastical institutions of modern Europe was by no means impossible: they had a meaning, had existed for honest ends, and an honest theory of them might be made. But the administration of those institutions had long ceased to accord with any honest theory. It was impossible to justify them in principle, except on grounds which condemned them in practice; and grounds of which there was at any rate little or no recognition in the philosophy of the eighteenth century. The natural tendency, therefore, of that philosophy, everywhere but in England, was to seek the extinction of those institutions. In England it would doubtless have done the same, had it been strong enough: but as this was beyond its strength, an adjustment was come to between the rival powers. What neither party cared about, the *ends* of existing institutions, the work that was to be done by teachers and governors, was flung overboard. The wages of that work the teachers and governors did care about, and those wages were secured to them. The existing institutions in Church and State were to be preserved inviolate, in outward semblance at least, but were required to be, practically, as much a nullity as possible. The Church continued to 'rear her mitred front in courts and palaces', but not as in the days of Hildebrand or Becket, as the champion of arts against arms, of the serf against the seigneur, peace against war, or spiritual principles and powers against the domination of animal force. Nor even (as in the days of Latimer and John Knox) as a body divinely commissioned to train the nation in a knowledge of God and obedience to his laws, whatever became of temporal principalities and powers, and whether this end might most effectually be compassed by their assistance or by trampling them under foot. No; but the people of England liked old things, and nobody knew how the place might be filled which the doing away with so conspicuous an institution would leave vacant, and *quieta ne movere* was the favourite doctrine of those times; therefore, on condition of not making too much noise about religion, or taking it too much in earnest, the church was supported, even by philosophers – as a 'bulwark against fanaticism', a sedative to the religious spirit, to prevent it from disturbing the harmony of society or the tranquillity of states. The clergy of the establishment thought they had a good bargain on these terms, and kept its conditions very faithfully.

The State, again, was no longer considered, according to the old ideal, as a concentration of the force of all the individuals of the nation in the hands of certain of its members, in order to the accomplishment of whatever could be best accomplished by systematic co-operation. It was found that the State was a bad judge of the wants of society; that it in reality cared very little for them; and when it attempted anything beyond that police against crime, and arbitration of disputes, which are indispensable to social existence, the private sinister interest of some class or individual was usually the prompter of its proceedings. The natural inference would have been that the constitution of the State was somehow not suited to the existing wants of society; having indeed descended, with scarcely any modifications that could be avoided, from a time when the most prominent exigencies of society were quite different. This conclusion, however, was shrunk from; and it required the peculiarities of very recent times, and the speculations of the Bentham school, to produce even any considerable tendency that way. The existing Constitution, and all the arrangements of existing society, continued to be applauded as the best possible. The celebrated theory of the three powers was got up, which made the excellence of our Constitution consist in doing less harm than would be done by any other form of government. Government altogether was regarded as a necessary evil, and was required to hide itself, to make itself as little felt as possible. The cry of the people was not 'help us', 'guide us', 'do for us the things we cannot do, and instruct us, that we may do well those which we can' – and truly such requirements from such rulers would have been a bitter jest: the cry was 'let us alone'. Power to decide questions of *meum* and *tuum*, to protect society from open violence, and from some of the most dangerous modes of fraud, could not be withheld; these functions the Government was left in possession of, and to these it became the expectation of the public that it should confine itself.

Such was the prevailing tone of English belief in temporals; what was it in spirituals? Here too a similar system of compromise had been at work. Those who pushed their philosophical speculations to the denial of the received religious belief, whether they went to the extent of infidelity or only of heterodoxy, met with little encouragement; neither religion itself, nor the received forms of it, were at all shaken by the few attacks which were made upon them from without. The philosophy, however, of the time, made itself felt as effectually in another fashion; it pushed its way *into* religion. The *a priori* arguments for a God were first dismissed. This was indeed inevitable. The internal evidences of Christianity shared nearly the same fate; if not absolutely thrown aside, they fell into the background, and were little thought of. The doctrine of Locke, that we have no *innate* moral sense, perverted into the doctrine that we have no moral sense at all, made it appear that we had not any capacity of judging from the doctrine itself, whether it was worthy to have come from a righteous Being. In forgetfulness of the most solemn warnings of the Author of Christianity, as well as of the Apostle who was the main diffuser of it through the world, belief in his religion was left to stand upon miracles – a species of evidence which, according to the universal belief of the early Christians themselves, was by no means peculiar to true religion: and it is melancholy to see on what frail reeds able defenders of Christianity preferred to rest, rather than upon that better evidence which alone gave to their so-called evidences any value as a collateral confirmation. In the interpretation of Christianity, the palpablest *bibliolatry* prevailed: if (with Coleridge) we may so term that superstitious worship of particular texts, which persecuted Galileo, and, in our own day, anathematized the discoveries of geology. Men whose faith in Christianity rested on the literal infallibility of the sacred volume, shrank in terror from the idea that it could have been included in the scheme of Providence that the human opinions and mental habits of the particular writers should be allowed to mix with and colour their mode of conceiving and of narrating the divine transactions. Yet this slavery to the letter has not only raised every difficulty which envelops the most unimportant passage in the Bible, into an objection to revelation, but has paralysed many a well-meant effort to bring Christianity home, as a consistent scheme, to human experience and capacities of apprehension; as if there was much of it which it was more prudent to leave *in nubibus*, lest, in the attempt to make the mind seize hold of it as a reality, some text might be found to stand in the way. It might have been expected that this idolatry of the words of Scripture would at least have saved its doctrines from being tampered with by human notions: but the contrary proved to be the effect; for the vague and sophistical mode of interpreting texts, which was necessary in order to reconcile what was manifestly irreconcilable, engendered a habit of playing fast and loose with Scripture, and finding in, or leaving out of it, whatever one pleased. Hence, while Christianity was, in theory and in intention, received and submitted to, with even 'prostration of the understanding' before it, much alacrity was in fact displayed in *accommodating* it to the received philosophy, and even to the popular notions of the time. To take only one example, but so signal a one as to be *instar omnium*. If there is any one requirement of Christianity less doubtful than another, it is that of being spiritually minded; of loving and practising good from a pure love, simply because it is good. But one of the crotchets of the philosophy of the age was, that all virtue is self-interest; and accordingly, in the textbook adopted by the Church (in one of its universities) for instruction in moral philosophy, the reason for doing good is declared to be, that God is stronger than we are, and is able to damn us if we do not. This is no exaggeration of the sentiments of Paley, and hardly even of the crudity of his language.

Thus, on the whole, England had neither the benefits, such as they were, of the new ideas nor of the old. We were just sufficiently under the influences of each, to render the other powerless. We had a Government, which we respected too much to attempt to change it, but not enough to trust it with any power, or look to it for any services that were not compelled. We had a Church, which had ceased to fulfil the honest purposes of a church, but which we made a great point of keeping up as the pretence or *simulacrum* of one. We had a highly spiritual religion (which we were instructed to obey from selfish motives), and the most mechanical and worldly notions on every other subject; and we were so much afraid of being wanting in reverence to each particular syllable of the book which contained our religion, that we let its most important meanings slip through our fingers, and entertained the most grovelling conceptions of its spirit and general purposes. This was not a state of things which could recommend itself to any earnest mind. It was sure in no great length of time to call forth two sorts of men – the one demanding the extinction of the institutions and creeds which had hitherto existed; the other that they be made a reality: the one pressing the new doctrines to their utmost consequences; the other reasserting the best meaning and purposes of the old. The first type attained its greatest height in Bentham; the last in Coleridge.

We hold that these two sorts of men, who seem to be, and believe themselves to be, enemies, are in reality allies. The powers they wield are opposite poles of one great force of progression. What was really hateful and contemptible was the state which preceded them, and which each, in its way, has been striving now for many years to improve. Each ought to hail with rejoicing the advent of the other. But most of all ought an enlightened Radical or Liberal to rejoice over such a Conservative as Coleridge. For such a Radical must know, that the Constitution and Church of England, and the religious opinions and political maxims professed by their supporters, are not mere frauds, nor sheer nonsense – have not been got up originally, and all along maintained, for the sole purpose of picking people's pockets; without aiming at, or being found conducive to, any honest end during the whole process. Nothing, of which this is a sufficient account, would have lasted a tithe of five, eight, or ten centuries, in the most improving period and (during much of that period) the most improving nation in the world. These things, we may depend upon it, were not always without much good in them, however little of it may now be left: and Reformers ought to hail the man as a brother Reformer who points out what this good is; what it is which we have a right to expect from things established – which they are bound to do for us, as the justification of their being established: so that they may be recalled to it and compelled to do it, or the impossibility of their any longer doing it may be conclusively manifested. What is any case for reform good for, until it has passed this test? What mode is there of determining whether a thing is fit to exist, without first considering what purposes it exists for, and whether it be still capable of fulfilling them?

We have not room here to consider Coleridge's Conservative philosophy in all its aspects, or in relation to all the quarters from which objections might be raised against it. We shall consider it with relation to Reformers, and especially to Benthamites. We would assist them to determine whether they would have to do with Conservative philosophers or with Conservative dunces; and whether, since there are Tories, it be better that they should learn their Toryism from Lord Eldon, or even Sir Robert Peel, or from Coleridge.

Take, for instance, Coleridge's view of the grounds of a Church Establishment. His mode of treating any institution is to investigate what he terms the Idea of it, or what in common parlance would be called the principle involved in it. The idea or principle of a national church, and of the Church of England in that character, is, according to him, the reservation of a portion of the land, or of a right to a portion of its produce, as a fund – for what purpose? For the worship of God? For the performance of religious ceremonies? No; for the advancement of knowledge, and the civilization and cultivation of the community. This fund he does not term Church property, but 'the nationalty', or national property. He considers it as destined for:

the support and maintenance of a permanent class or order, with the following duties. A certain smaller number were to remain at the fountainheads of the humanities, in cultivating and enlarging the knowledge already possessed, and in watching over the interests of physical and moral science; being likewise the instructors of such as constituted, or were to constitute, the remaining more numerous classes of the order. The members of this latter and far more numerous body were to be distributed throughout the country, so as not to leave even the smallest integral part or division without a resident guide, guardian and instructor; the objects and final intention of the whole order being these – to preserve the stores and to guard the treasures of past civilization, and thus to bind the present with the past; to perfect and add to the same, and thus to connect the present with the future; but especially to diffuse through the whole community, and to every native entitled to its laws and rights, that quantity and quality of knowledge which was indispensable both for the understanding of those rights, and for the performance of the duties correspondent; finally, to secure for the nation, if not a superiority over the neighbouring states, yet an equality at least, in that character of general civilization, which equally with, or rather more than, fleets, armies, and revenue, forms the ground of its defensive and offensive power.

This organized body, set apart and endowed for the cultivation and diffusion of knowledge, is not, in Coleridge's view, necessarily a religious corporation.

Religion may be an indispensable ally, but is not the essential constitutive end, of that national institute, which is unfortunately, at least improperly, styled the Church; a name which, in its best sense, is exclusively appropriate to the Church of Christ . . . The *clerisy* of the nation, or national church in its primary acceptation and original intention, comprehended the learned of all denominations, the sages and professors of the law and jurisprudence, of medicine and physiology, of music, of military and civil architecture, with the mathematical as the common organ of the preceding; in short, all the so-called liberal arts and sciences, the possession and application of which constitute the civilization of a country, as well as the theological. The last was, indeed, placed at the head of all; and of good right did it claim the precedence. But why? Because under the name of theology or divinity were contained the interpretation of languages, the conservation and tradition of past events, the momentous epochs and revolutions of the race and nation, the continuation of the records, logic, ethics, and the determination of ethical science, in application to the rights and duties of men in all their various relations, social and civil; and lastly, the ground-knowledge, the *prima scientia*, as it was named – philosophy, or the doctrine and discipline of ideas.

Theology formed only a part of the objects, the theologians formed only a portion of the clerks or clergy, of the national Church. The theological order had precedency indeed, and deservedly; but not because its members were priests, whose office was to conciliate the invisible powers, and to superintend the interests that survive the grave; nor as being exclusively, or even principally, sacerdotal or templar, which, when it did occur, is to be considered as an accident of the age, a misgrowth of ignorance and oppression, a falsification of the constitutive principle, not a constituent part of the same. No; the theologians took the lead, because the science of theology was the root and the trunk of the knowledge of civilized man: because it gave unity and the circulating sap of life to all other sciences, by virtue of which alone they could be contemplated as forming collectively the living tree of knowledge. It had the precedency because, under the name theology, were comprised all the main aids, instruments, and materials of national education, the *nisus formativus* of the body politic, the shaping and informing spirit, which, educing or eliciting the latent man in all the natives of the soil, trains them up to be citizens of the country, free subjects of the realm. And, lastly, because to divinity belong those fundamental truths which are the common groundwork of our civil and our religious duties, not less indispensable to a right view of our temporal concerns than to a rational faith respecting our immortal well-being. Not without celestial observations can even terrestrial charts be accurately constructed. [*Church and State*, Ch. V.]

The nationalty, or national property, according to Coleridge, 'cannot rightfully, and without foul wrong to the nation never has been, alienated from its original purposes', from the promotion of 'a continuing and progressive civilization', to the benefit of individuals, or any public purpose of merely economical or material interest. But the State may withdraw the fund from its actual holders, for the better execution of its purposes. There is no sanctity attached to the means, but only to the ends. The fund is not dedicated to any particular scheme of religion, nor even to religion at all; religion has only to do with it in the character of an instrument of civilization, and in common with all the other instruments.

I do not assert that the proceeds from the nationalty cannot be rightfully vested, except in what we now mean by clergymen and the established clergy. I have everywhere implied the contrary . . . In relation to the national church, Christianity, or the Church of Christ, is a blessed accident, a providential boon, a grace of God . . . As the olive tree is said in its growth to fertilize the surrounding soil, to invigorate the roots of the vines in its immediate neighbourhood, and to improve the strength and flavour of the wines; such is the relation of the Christian and the national Church. But as the olive is not the same plant with the vine, or with the elm or poplar (that is, the State) with which the vine is wedded; and as the vine, with its prop, may exist, though in less perfection, without the olive, or previously to its implantation; even so is Christianity, and *a fortiori* any particular scheme of theology derived, and supposed by its partisans to be deduced, from Christianity, no essential part of the being of the national Church, however conducive or even indispensable it may be to its well-being. [Chap. VI.]

What would Sir Robert Inglis, or Sir Robert Peel, or Mr Spooner say to such a doctrine as this? Will they thank Coleridge for this advocacy of Toryism? What would become of the three years' debates on the Appropriation Clause, which so disgraced this country before the face of Europe? Will the ends of practical Toryism be much served by a theory under which the Royal Society might claim a part of the Church property with as good right as the bench of bishops, if, by endowing that body like the French Institute, science could be better promoted? A theory by which the State, in the conscientious exercise of its judgement, having decided that the Church of England does not fulfil the object for which the nationalty was intended, might transfer its endowments to any other ecclesiastical body, or to any other body not ecclesiastical, which it deemed more competent to fulfil those objects; might establish any other sect, or all sects, or no sect at all, if it should deem that in the divided condition of religious opinion in this country, the State can no longer with advantage attempt the complete religious instruction of its people, but must for the present content itself with providing secular instruction, and such religious teaching, if any, as all can take part in; leaving each sect to apply to its own communion that which they all agree in considering as the keystone of the arch? We believe this to be the true state of affairs in Great Britain at the present time. We are far from thinking it other than a serious evil. We entirely acknowledge, that in any person fit to be a teacher, the view he takes of religion will be intimately connected with the view he will take of all the greatest things which he has to teach. Unless the same teachers who give instruction on those other subjects, are at liberty to enter freely on religion, the scheme of education will be, to a certain degree, fragmentary and incoherent. But the State at present has only the option of such an imperfect scheme, or of entrusting the whole business to perhaps the most unfit body for the exclusive charge of it that could be found among persons of any intellectual attainments, namely, the established clergy as at present trained and composed. Such a body would have no chance of being selected as the exclusive administrators of the nationalty, on any foundation but that of divine right; the ground avowedly taken by the only other school of Conservative philosophy which is attempting to raise its head in this country – that of the new Oxford theologians.

Coleridge's merit in this matter consists, as it seems to us, in two things. First, that by setting in a clear light what a national church establishment ought to be, and what, by the very fact of its existence, it must be held to pretend to be, he has pronounced the severest satire upon what in fact it is. There is some difference, truly, between Coleridge's church, in which the schoolmaster forms the first step in the hierarchy, 'who, in due time, and under condition of a faithful performance of his arduous duties, should succeed to the pastorate', and the Church of England such as we now see. But to say the Church, and mean only the clergy, 'constituted', according to Coleridge's conviction, 'the first and fundamental apostasy'. He, and the thoughts which have proceeded from him, have done more than would have been effected in thrice the time by Dissenters and Radicals, to make the Church ashamed of the evil of her ways, and to determine that movement of improvement from within, which has begun where it ought to begin, at the Universities and among the younger clergy, and which, if this sect-ridden country is ever to be really taught, must proceed *pari passu* with the assault carried on from without.

Secondly, we honour Coleridge for having rescued from the discredit in which the corruptions of the English Church had involved everything connected with it, and for having vindicated against Bentham and Adam Smith and the whole eighteenth century, the principle of an endowed class, for the cultivation of learning, and for diffusing its results among the community. That such a class is likely to be behind, instead of before, the progress of knowledge, is an induction erroneously drawn from the peculiar circumstances of the last two centuries, and in contradiction to all the rest of modern history. If we have seen much of the abuses of endowments, we have not seen what this country might be made by a proper administration of them, as we trust we shall not see what it would be without them. On this subject we are entirely at one with Coleridge, and with the other great defender of endowed establishments, Dr Chalmers; and we consider the definitive establishment of this fundamental principle, to be one of the permanent benefits which political science owes to the Conservative philosophers.

Coleridge's theory of the Constitution is not less worthy of notice than his theory of the Church. The Delolme and Blackstone doctrine, the balance of the three powers, he declares he never could elicit one ray of common sense from, no more than from the balance of trade. There is, however, according to him, an Idea of the Constitution, of which he says:

Because our whole history, from Alfred onwards, demonstrates the continued influence of such an idea, or ultimate aim, in the minds of our forefathers, in their characters and functions as public men, alike in what they resisted and what they claimed; in the institutions and forms of polity which they established, and with regard to those against which they more or less successfully contended; and because the result has been a progressive, though not always a direct or equable, advance in the gradual realization of the idea; and because it is actually, though (even because it is an idea) not adequately, represented in a correspondent scheme of means really existing; we speak, and have a right to speak, of the idea itself as actually existing, that is, as a principle existing in the only way in which a principle can exist – in the minds and consciences of the persons whose duties it prescribes, and whose rights it determines.

This fundamental idea

is at the same time the final criterion by which all particular frames of government must be tried: for here only can we find the great constructive principles of our representative system: those principles in the light of which it can alone be ascertained what are excrescences, symptoms of distemperature, and marks of degeneration, and what are native growths, or changes naturally attendant on the progressive development of the original germ, symptoms of immaturity, perhaps, but not of disease; or, at worst, modifications of the growth by the defective or faulty, but remediless or only gradually remediable, qualities of the soil and surrounding elements

Of these principles he gives the following account:

It is the chief of many blessings derived from the insular character and circumstances of our country, that our social institutions have formed themselves out of our proper needs and interests: that long and fierce as the birth-struggle and growing pains have been, the antagonist powers have been of our own system, and have been allowed to work out their final balance with less disturbance from external forces than was possible in the Continental States . . . Now, in every country of civilized men, or acknowledging the rights of property, and by means of determined boundaries and common laws united into one people or nation, the two antagonist powers or opposite interests of the State, under which all other State interests are comprised, are those of *permanence* and of *progression*.

The interest of permanence, or the Conservative interest, he considers to be naturally connected with the land, and with landed property. This doctrine, false in our opinion as a universal principle, is true of England, and of all countries where landed property is accumulated in large masses.

'On the other hand,' he says, 'the progression of a State, in the arts and comforts of life, in the diffusion of the information and

213

knowledge useful or necessary for all; in short, all advances in civilization, and the rights and privileges of citizens, are especially connected with, and derived from, the four classes – the mercantile, the manufacturing, the distributive, and the professional.' (We must omit the interesting historical illustrations of this maxim.) 'These four last-mentioned classes I will designate by the name of the Personal Interest, as the exponent of all moveable and personal possessions, including skill and acquired knowledge, the moral and intellectual stock in trade of the professional man and the artist, no less than the raw materials, and the means of elaborating, transporting, and distributing them.'

The interest of permanence, then, is provided for by a representation of the landed proprietors; that of progression, by a representation of personal property and of intellectal acquirement: and while one branch of the legislature, the peerage, is essentially given over to the former, he considers it a part both of the general theory and of the actual English constitution, that the representatives of the latter should form 'the clear and effectual majority of the Lower House'; or if not, that at least, by the added influence of public opinion, they should exercise an effective preponderance there. That 'the very weight intended for the effectual counterpoise of the great landholders' has 'in the course of events, been shifted into the opposite scale'; that the members for the towns 'now constitute a large proportion of the political power and influence of the very class of men whose personal cupidity and whose partial views of the landed interest at large they were meant to keep in check'; – these things he acknowledges: and only suggests a doubt, whether roads, canals, machinery, the press, and other influences favourable to the popular side, do not constitute an equivalent force to supply the deficiency.

How much better a Parliamentary Reformer, then, is Coleridge, than Lord John Russell, or any Whig who stickles for maintaining this unconstitutional omnipotence of the landed interest. If these became the principles of Tories, we should not wait long for further reform, even in our organic institutions. It is true Coleridge disapproved of the Reform Bill, or rather of the principle, or the no-principle, on which it was supported. He saw in it (as we may surmise) the dangers of a change amounting almost to a revolution, without any real tendency to remove those defects in the machine, which alone could justify a change so extensive. And that this is nearly a true view of the matter, all parties seem to be now agreed. The Reform Bill was not calculated greatly to improve the general composition of the legislature. The good it has done, which is considerable, consists chiefly in this, that being so great a change, it has weakened the superstitious feeling against great changes. Any good, which is contrary to the selfish interest of the dominant class, is still only to be effected by a long and arduous struggle: but improvements which threaten no powerful body in their social importance or in their pecuniary emoluments, are no longer resisted, as they once were, because of their greatness – because of the very benefit which they promised. Witness the speedy passing of the Poor Law Amendment and the Penny Postage Acts.

Meanwhile, though Coleridge's theory is but a mere commencement, not amounting to the first lines of a political philosophy, has the age produced any other theory of government which can stand a comparison with it as to its first principles? Let us take, for example, the Benthamic theory. The principle of this may be said to be, that since the general interest is the object of government, a complete control over the government ought to be given to those whose interest is identical with the general interest. The authors and propounders of this theory were men of extraordinary intellectual powers, and the greater part of what they meant by it is true and important. But when considered as the foundation of a science, it would be difficult to find among theories proceeding from philosophers one less like a philosophical theory, or, in the works of analytical minds, anything more entirely unanalytical. What can a philosopher make of such complex notions as 'interest' and 'general interest', without breaking them down into the elements of which they are composed? If by men's interest be meant what would appear such to a calculating bystander, judging what would be good for a man during his whole life, and making no account, or but little, of the gratification of his present passions, his pride, his envy, his vanity, his cupidity, his love of pleasure, his love of ease – it may be questioned whether, in this sense, the interest of an aristocracy, and still more that of a monarch, would not be as accordant with the general interest as that of either the middle or the poorer classes; and if men's interest, in this understanding of it, usually governed their conduct, absolute monarchy would probably be the best form of government. But since men usually do what they like, often being perfectly aware that it is not for their ultimate interest, still more often that it is not for the interest of their posterity, and when they do believe that the object they are seeking is permanently good for them, almost always overrating its value, it is necessary to consider, not who are they whose permanent interest, but who are they whose immediate interests and habitual feelings, are likely to be most in accordance with the end we seek to obtain. And as that end (the general good) is a very complex state of things, comprising as its component elements many requisites which are neither of one and the same nature, nor attainable by one and the same means – political philosophy must begin by a classification of these elements, in order to distinguish those of them which go naturally together (so that the provision made for one will suffice for the rest), from those which are ordinarily in a state of antagonism, or at least of separation, and require to be provided for apart. This preliminary classification being supposed, things would, in a perfect government, be so ordered, that corresponding to each of the great interests of society, there would be some branch or some integral part of the governing body, so constituted that it should not be merely deemed by philosophers, but should actually and constantly deem itself, to have its strongest interests involved in the maintenance of that one of the ends of society which it is intended to be the guardian of. This, we say, is the thing to be aimed at, the type of perfection in a political constitution. Not that there is a possibility of making more than a limited approach to it in practice. A government must be composed out of the elements already existing in society, and the distribution of power in the constitution cannot vary much or long from the distribution of it in society itself. But wherever the circumstances of society allow any choice, wherever wisdom and contrivance are at all available, this, we conceive, is the principle of guidance; and whatever anywhere exists is imperfect and a failure, just so far as it recedes from this type.

Such a philosophy of government, we need hardly say, is in its infancy: the first step to it, the classification of the exigencies of society, has not been made. Bentham, in his *Principles of Civil Law*, has given a specimen, very useful for many other purposes, but not available, nor intended to be so, for founding a theory of representation upon it. For that particular purpose we have seen nothing comparable as far as it goes, notwithstanding its manifest insufficiency, to Coleridge's division of the interests of society into the two antagonistic interests of Permanence and Progression. The Continental philosophers have, by a different path, arrived at the same division; and this is about as far, probably, as the science of political institutions has yet reached.

In the details of Coleridge's political opinions there is much good, and much that is questionable, or worse. In political economy especially he writes like an arrant driveller, and it would have been well for his reputation had he never meddled with the subject. But this department of knowledge can now take care of itself. On other points we meet with far-reaching remarks, and a tone of general feeling sufficient to make a Tory's hair stand on end. Thus, in the work from which we have most quoted, he calls the State policy of the last half-century 'a Cyclops with one eye, and that in the back of the head' – its measures 'either a series of anachronisms, or a truckling to events instead of the science that should command them'. He styles the great Common-wealthsmen 'the stars of that narrow interspace of blue sky between the black clouds of the First and Second Charles's reigns'. The *Literary Remains* are full of disparaging remarks on many of the heroes of Toryism and Church-of-Englandism. He sees, for instance, no difference between Whitgift and Bancroft, and Bonner and Gardiner, except that the last were the most consistent – that the former sinned against better knowledge; and one of the most poignant of his writings is a character of Pitt, the very reverse of panegyrical. As a specimen of his practical views, we have mentioned his recommendation that the parochial clergy should begin by being schoolmasters. He urges 'a different division and subdivision of the kingdom' instead of 'the present barbarism, which forms an obstacle to the improvement of the country of much greater magnitude that men are generally aware'. But we must confine ourselves to instances in which he has helped to bring forward great principles, either implied in the old English opinions and institutions, or at least opposed to the new tendencies.

For example, he is at issue with the *let alone* doctrine, or the theory that governments can do no better than to do nothing; a doctrine generated by the manifest selfishness and incompetence of modern European governments, but of which, as a general theory, we may now be permitted to say, that one half of it is true, and the other half false. All who are on a level with their age now readily admit that government ought not to *interdict* men from publishing their opinions, pursuing their employments, or buying and selling their goods, in whatever place or manner they deem the most advantageous. Beyond suppressing force and fraud, governments can seldom, without doing more harm than good, attempt to chain up the free agency of individuals. But does it follow from this that government cannot exercise a free agency of its own? – that it cannot beneficially employ its powers, its means of information, and its pecuniary resources (so far surpassing those of any other association, or of any individual), in promoting the public welfare by a thousand means which individuals would never think of, would have no sufficient motives to attempt, or no sufficient power to accomplish? To confine ourselves to one, and that a limited view of the subject: a State ought to be considered as a great benefit society, or mutual insurance company, for helping (under the necessary regulations for preventing abuse) that large proportion of its members who cannot help themselves.

Let us suppose, [says Coleridge,] the negative ends of a State already attained, namely, its own safety by means of its own strength, and the protection of person and property for all its members; there will then remain its positive ends: 1. To make the means of subsistence more easy to each individual: 2. To secure to each of its members the hope of bettering his own condition or that of his children: 3. The development of those faculties which are essential to his humanity, that is to his rational and moral being.

In regard to the two former ends, he of course does not mean that they can be accomplished merely by making laws to that effect; or that, according to the wild doctrines now afloat, it is the fault of the government if every one has not enough to eat and drink. But he means that government can do something directly, and very much indirectly, to promote even the physical comfort of the people; and that if, besides making a proper use of its own powers, it would exert itself to teach the people what is in theirs, indigence would soon disappear from the face of the earth.

Perhaps, however, the greatest service which Coleridge has rendered to politics in his capacity of a Conservative philosopher, though its fruits are mostly yet to come, is in reviving the idea of a *trust* inherent in landed property. The land, the gift of nature, the source of subsistence to all, and the foundation of everything that influences our physical well-being, cannot be considered a subject of property, in the same absolute sense in which men are deemed proprietors of that in which no one has any interest but themselves – that which they have actually called into existence by their own bodily exertion. As Coleridge points out, such a notion is altogether of modern growth.

The very idea of individual or private property in our present acceptation of the term, and according to the current notion of the right to it, was originally confined to moveable things; and the more moveable, the more susceptible of the nature of property.

By the early institutions of Europe, property in land was a public function, created for certain public purposes, and held under condition of their fulfilment; and as such, we predict, under the modifications suited to modern society, it will again come to be considered. In this age, when everything is called in question, and when the foundation of private property itself needs to be argumentatively maintained against plausible and persuasive sophisms, one may easily see the danger of mixing up what is not really tenable with what is – and the impossibility of maintaining an absolute right in an individual to an unrestricted control, a *jus utendi et abutendi*, over an unlimited quantity of the mere raw material of the globe, to which every other person could originally make out as good a natural title as himself. It will certainly not be much longer tolerated that agriculture should be carried on (as Coleridge expresses it) on the same principles as those of trade; 'that a gentleman should regard his estate as a merchant his cargo, or a shopkeeper his stock', that he should be allowed to deal with it as if it only existed to yield rent to him, not food to the numbers whose hands till it; and should have a right, and a right possessing all the sacredness of property, to turn them out by hundreds and make them perish on the high road, as has been done before now by Irish landlords. We believe it will soon be thought, that a mode of property in land which has brought things to this pass, has existed long enough.

We shall not be suspected (we hope) of recommending a general resumption of landed possessions, or the depriving any one, without compensation, of anything which the law gives him. But we say that when the State allows any one to exercise ownership over more land than suffices to raise by his own labour his subsistence and that of his family, it confers on him power over other human beings – power affecting them in their most vital interests; and that no notion of private property can bar the right which the State inherently possesses, to require that the power which it has so given shall not be abused. We say, also, that, by giving this direct power over so large a portion of the community, indirect power is necessarily conferred over all the remaining portion; and this, too, it is the duty of the State to place under proper control. Further, the tenure of land, the various rights connected with it, and the system on which its cultivation is carried on, are points of the utmost importance both to the economical and to the moral well-being of the whole community. And the State fails in one of its highest obligations, unless it takes these points under its particular superintendence; unless, to the full extent of its power, it takes means of providing that the manner in which land is held, the mode and degree of its division, and every other peculiarity which influences the mode of its cultivation, shall be the most favourable possible for making the best use of the land: for drawing the greatest benefit from its productive resources, for securing the happiest existence to those employed on it, and for setting the greatest number of hands free to employ their labour for the benefit of the community in other ways. We believe that these opinions will become, in no very long period, universal throughout Europe. And we gratefully bear testimony to the fact, that the first among us who has given the sanction of philosophy to so great a reform in the popular and current notions, is a Conservative philosopher.

Of Coleridge as a moral and religious philosopher (the character which he presents most prominently in his principal works), there is neither room, nor would it be expedient for us to speak more than generally. On both subjects, few men have ever combined so much earnestness with so catholic and unsectarian a spirit. 'We have imprisoned,' says he, 'our own conceptions by the lines which we have drawn in order to exclude the conceptions of others. *J'ai trouvé que la plupart des sectes ont raison dans une bonne partie de ce qu'elles avancent, mais non pas tant en ce qu'elles nient.*' That almost all sects, both in philosophy and religion, are right in the positive part of their tenets, though commonly wrong in the negative, is a doctrine which he professes as strongly as the eclectic school in France. Almost all errors he holds to be 'truths misunderstood', 'half-truths taken as the whole', though not the less, but the more dangerous on that account. Both the theory and practice of enlightened tolerance in matters of opinion, might be exhibited in extracts from his writings more copiously than in those of almost any other writer we know; though there are a few (and but a few) exceptions to his own practice of it. In the theory of ethics, he contends against the doctrine of general consequences, and holds that, *for man*, 'to obey the simple unconditional commandment of eschewing every act that implies a self-contradiction' – so to act as to 'be able, without involving any contradiction, to will that the maxim of thy conduct should be the law of all intelligent beings – is the one universal and sufficient principle and guide of morality'. Yet even a utilitarian can have little complaint to make of a philosopher who lays it down that 'the *outward* object of virtue' is 'the greatest producible sum of happiness of all men', and that 'happiness in its proper sense is but the continuity and sum total of the pleasure which is allotted or happens to a man'.

But his greatest object was to bring into harmony religion

and philosophy. He laboured incessantly to establish that 'the Christian faith – in which,' says he, 'I include every article of belief and doctrine professed by the first reformers in common' is not only divine truth, but also 'the perfection of Human Intelligence'. All that Christianity has revealed, philosophy, according to him, can prove, though there is much which it could never have discovered; human reason, once strengthened by Christianity, can evolve all the Christian doctrines from its own sources. Moreover, 'if infidelity is not to overspread England as well as France', the Scripture, and every passage of Scripture, must be submitted to this test; inasmuch as 'the compatibility of a document with the conclusions of self-evident reason, and with the laws of conscience, is a condition *a priori* of any evidence adequate to the proof of its having been revealed by God'; and this, he says, is no philosophic novelty, but a principle 'clearly laid down both by Moses and St Paul'. He thus goes quite as far as the Unitarians in making man's reason and moral feelings a test of revelation; but differs *toto caelo* from them in their rejection of its mysteries, which he regards as the highest philosophic truths, and says that 'the Christian to whom, after a long profession of Christianity, the mysteries remain as much mysteries as before, is in the same state as a schoolboy with regard to his arithmetic, to whom the *facit* at the end of the examples in his cyphering-book is the whole ground for his assuming that such and such figures amount to so and so'.

These opinions are not likely to be popular in the religious world, and Coleridge knew it: 'I quite calculate,' said he once, 'on my being one day or other holden in worse repute by many Christians than the Unitarians and even Infidels.' 'It must be undergone by every one who loves the truth for its own sake beyond all other things.' For our part, we are not bound to defend him; and we must admit that, in his attempt to arrive at theology by way of philosophy, we see much straining, and most frequently, as it appears to us, total failure. The question, however, is not whether Coleridge's attempts are successful, but whether it is desirable or not that such attempts should be made. Whatever some religious people may think, philosophy will and must go on, ever seeking to understand whatever can be made understandable; and, whatever some philosophers may think, there is little prospect at present that philosophy will take the place of religion, or that any philosophy will be speedily received in this country, unless supposed not only to be consistent with, but even to yield collateral support to, Christianity. What is the use, then, of treating with contempt the idea of a religious philosophy? Religious philosophies are among the things to be looked for, and our main hope ought to be that they may be such as fulfil the conditions of a philosophy – the very foremost of which is, unrestricted freedom of thought. There is no philosophy possible where fear of consequences is a stronger principle than love of truth; where speculation is paralysed, either by the belief that conclusions honestly arrived at will be punished by a just and good Being with eternal damnation, or by seeing in every text of Scripture a foregone conclusion, with which the results of inquiry must, at any expense of sophistry and self-deception, be made to quadrate.

From both these withering influences, that have so often made the acutest intellects exhibit specimens of obliquity and imbecility in their theological speculations which have excited the pity of subsequent generations, Coleridge's mind was perfectly free. Faith – the faith which is placed among religious duties – was, in his view, a state of the will and of the affections, not of the understanding. Heresy, in 'the literal sense and scriptural import of the word', is, according to him, 'wilful error, or belief originating in some perversion of the will'; he says, therefore, that there may be orthodox heretics, since indifference to truth may as well be shown on the right side of the question as on the wrong; and denounces, in strong language, the contrary doctrine of the 'pseudo-Athanasius', who 'interprets Catholic faith by belief', an act of the understanding alone. The 'true Lutheran doctrine', he says, is, that 'neither will truth, as a mere conviction of the understanding, save, nor error condemn. To love truth sincerely is spiritually to have truth; and an error becomes a personal error, not by its aberration from logic or history, but so far as the causes of such error are in the heart, or may be traced back to some antecedent unchristian wish or habit.' 'The unmistakable passions of a factionary and a schismatic, the ostentatious display, the ambitious and dishonest arts of a sect-founder, must be superinduced on the false doctrine before the heresy makes the man a heretic.'

Against the other terror, so fatal to the unshackled exercise of reason on the greatest questions, the view which Coleridge took of the authority of the Scriptures was a preservative. He drew the strongest distinction between the inspiration which he owned in the various writers, and an express dictation by the Almighty of every word they wrote. 'The notion of the absolute truth and divinity of every syllable of the text of the books of the Old and New Testament as we have it', he again and again asserts to be unsupported by the Scripture itself; to be one of those superstitions in which 'there is a heart of unbelief', to be, if possible, still more extravagant' than the Papal infallibility; and declares that the very same arguments are used for both doctrines. God, he believes, informed the minds of the writers with the truths he meant to reveal, and left the rest to their human faculties. He pleaded most earnestly, says his nephew and editor, for this liberty of criticism with respect to the Scriptures, as:

the only middle path of safety and peace between a godless disregard of the unique and transcendent character of the Bible, taken generally, and that scheme of interpretation, scarcely less adverse to the pure spirit of Christian wisdom, which wildly arrays our faith in opposition to our reason, and inculcates the sacrifice of the latter to the former; for he threw up his hands in dismay at the language of some of our modern divinity on this point, as if a faith not founded on insight were aught else than a specious name for wilful positiveness; as if the Father of Lights could require, or would accept, from the only one of his creatures whom he had endowed with reason, the sacrifice of fools! . . . Of the aweless doctrine that God might, if he had so pleased, have given to man a religion which to human intelligence should not be rational, and exacted his faith in it, Coleridge's whole middle and later life was one deep and solemn denial.

He bewails 'bibliolatry' as the pervading error of modern Protestant divinity, and the great stumbling-block of Christianity, and exclaims, 'O might I live but to utter all my meditations on this most concerning point . . . in what sense the Bible may be called the word of God, and how and under what conditions the unity of the Spirit is translucent through the letter, which, read as the letter merely, is the word of this and that pious, but fallible and imperfect, man.' It is known that he did live to write down these meditations; and speculations so important will one day, it is devoutly to be hoped, be given to the world.

Theological discussion is beyond our province, and it is not for us, in this place, to judge these sentiments of Coleridge; but it is clear enough that they are not the sentiments of a bigot, or of one who is to be dreaded by Liberals, less he should illiberalize the minds of the rising generation of Tories and High-Churchmen. We think the danger is rather lest they should find him vastly too liberal. And yet, now when the most orthodox divines, both in the Church and out of it, find it necessary to explain away the obvious sense of the whole first chapter of Genesis, or failing to do that, consent to disbelieve it provisionally, on the speculation that there may hereafter be discovered a sense in which it can be believed, one would think the time gone by for expecting to learn from the Bible what it never could have been intended to communicate, and to find in all its statements a literal truth neither necessary nor conducive to what the volume itself declares to be the ends of revelation. Such at least was Coleridge's opinion: and whatever influence such an opinion may have over Conservatives, it cannot do other than make them less bigots, and better philosophers.

But we must close this long essay: long in itself, though short in its relation to its subject, and to the multitude of topics involved in it. We do not pretend to have given any sufficient account of Coleridge; but we hope we may have proved to some, not previously aware of it, that there is something both in him, and in the school to which he belongs, not unworthy of their better knowledge. We may have done something to show that a Tory philosopher cannot be wholly a Tory, but must often be a better Liberal than Liberals themselves; while he is the natural means of rescuing from oblivion truths which Tories have forgotten, and which the prevailing schools of Liberalism never knew.

And even if a Conservative philosophy were an absurdity, it is well calculated to drive out a hundred absurdities worse than itself. Let no one think that it is nothing, to accustom people to give a reason for their opinion, be the opinion ever so untenable, the reason ever so insufficient. A person accustomed to submit his fundamental tenets to the test of reason, will be more open to the dictates of reason on every other point. Not from him shall we have to apprehend the owl-like dread of light, the drudge-like aversion to change, which were the characteristics of the old unreasoning race of bigots. A man accustomed to contemplate the fair side of Toryism (the side that every attempt at a philosophy of it must bring to view), and to defend the existing system by the display of its capabilities as an engine of public good – such a man, when he comes to administer the system, will be more anxious than another person to realize those capabilities, to bring the fact a little nearer to the specious theory. 'Lord, enlighten thou our enemies', should be the prayer of every true reformer; sharpen their wits, give acuteness to their perceptions, and con-secutiveness and clearness to their reasoning powers: we are in danger from their folly, not from their wisdom; their weakness is what fills us with apprehension, not their strength.

For ourselves, we are not so blinded by our particular opinions as to be ignorant that in this and in every other country of Europe, the great mass of the owners of large property, and of all the classes intimately connected with the owners of large property, are, and must be expected to be, in the main, Conservative. To suppose that so mighty a body can be without immense influence in the commonwealth, or to lay plans for effecting great changes, either spiritual or temporal, in which they are left out of the question, would be the height of absurdity. Let those who desire such changes, ask themselves if they are content that these classes should be, and remain, to a man, banded against them; and what progress they expect to make, or by what means, unless a process of preparation shall be going on in the minds of these very classes; not by the impracticable method of converting them from Con-servatives into Liberals, but by their being led to adopt one liberal opinion after another, as a part of Conservatism itself. The first step to this, is to inspire them with the desire to systematize and rationalize their own actual creed: and the feeblest attempt to do this has an intrinsic value; far more, then, one which has so much in it, both of moral goodness and true insight, as the philosophy of Coleridge.

Editor's Note

'Whewell on Moral Philosophy' was first published in the *Westminster Review*, October 1852. The text printed here is taken from *Dissertations and Discussions*.

'Whewell on Moral Philosophy'

BY J. S. MILL

If the worth of Dr Whewell's writings could be measured by the importance and amplitude of their subjects, no writer of the age could vie with him in merit or usefulness. He has aspired to be not only the historian, but the philosopher and legislator, of almost all the great departments of human knowledge; reducing each to its first principles, and showing how it might be scientifically evolved from these as a connected whole. After endeavouring, in his *History and Philosophy of the Inductive Sciences*, to place physics, and incidentally metaphysics, on a philosophic foundation, he has made an almost equally ambitious attempt on the subjects of morals and government, of which the two works before us are the results. He is thus entitled to the praise of having done his best to wipe off from the two endowed universities, in one of which he holds a high place, the reproach to which they have so long been justly liable, of neglecting the higher regions of philosophy. By his writings and influence, he has been an agent in that revival of speculation on the most difficult and highest subjects, which has been noticeable for some years past within as well as without the pale of Oxford and Cambridge. And inasmuch as mental activity of any kind is better than torpidity, and bad solutions of the great questions of philosophy are preferable to a lazy ignoring of their existence, whoever has taken so active a part as Dr Whewell in this intellectual movement may lay claim to considerable merit.

Unfortunately it is not in the nature of bodies constituted like the English universities, even when stirred up into something like mental activity, to send forth thought of any but one description. There have been universities (those of France and Germany have at some periods been practically conducted on this principle) which brought together into a body the most vigorous thinkers and the ablest teachers, whatever the conclusions to which their thinking might have led them. But in the English universities no thought can find place, except that which can reconcile itself with orthodoxy. They are ecclesiastical institutions; and it is the essence of all churches to vow adherence to a set of opinions made up and prescribed, it matters little whether three or thirteen centuries ago. Men will some day open their eyes, and perceive how fatal a thing it is that the instruction of those who are intended to be the guides and governors of mankind should be confided to a collection of persons thus pledged. If the opinions they are pledged to were every one as true as any fact in physical science, and had been adopted, not as they almost always are, on trust and authority, but as the result of the most diligent and impartial examination of which the mind of the recipient was capable; even then, the engagement under penalties always to adhere to the opinions once assented to, would debilitate and lame the mind, and unfit it for progress, still more for assisting the progress of others. The person who has to think more of what an opinion leads to, than of what is the evidence of it, cannot be a philosopher, or a teacher of philosophers. Of what value is the opinion on any subject, of a man of whom everyone knows that by his profession he must hold that opinion? And how can intellectual vigour be fostered by the teaching of those who, even as a matter of duty, would rather that their pupils were weak and orthodox, than strong with freedom of thought? Whoever thinks that persons thus tied are fitting depositaries of the trust of educating a people, must think that the proper object of intellectual education is not to strengthen and cultivate the intellect, but to make sure of its adopting certain conclusions: that, in short, in the exercise of the thinking faculty, there is something, either religion, or conservatism, or peace, or whatever it be, more important than truth. Not to dilate further on this topic, it is nearly inevitable, that when persons bound by the vows and placed in the circumstances of an established clergy, enter into the paths of higher speculation, and endeavour to make a philosophy, either purpose or instinct will direct them to the kind of philosophy best fitted to prop up the doctrines to which they are pledged. And when these doctrines are so prodigiously in arrear of the general progress of thought, as the doctrines of the Church of England now are, the philosophy resulting will have a tendency not to promote, but to arrest progress.

Without the slightest wish to speak in disparagement of Dr Whewell's labours, and with no ground for questioning his sincerity of purpose, we think the preceding remark thoroughly applicable to his philosophical speculations. We do not say the intention, but certainly the tendency, of his efforts, is to shape the whole of philosophy, physical as well as moral, into a form adapted to serve as a support and a justification to any opinions which happen to be established. A writer who has gone beyond all his predecessors in the manufacture of necessary truths, that is, of propositions which, according to him, may be known to be true independently of proof; who ascribes this self-evidence to the larger generalities of all sciences (however little obvious at first) as soon as they have become familiar – was still more certain to regard all moral propositions familiar to him from his early years as self-evident truths. His *Elements of Morality* could be nothing better than a classification and systematizing of the opinions which he found prevailing among those who had been educated according to the approved methods of his own country; or, let us rather say, an apparatus for converting those prevailing opinions, on matters of morality, into reasons for themselves.

This, accordingly, is what we find in Dr Whewell's volumes: while we have sought in vain for the numerous minor merits, which give a real scientific value to his previous works. If the *Philosophy of the Inductive Sciences* was, as we think, an erroneous philosophy, it contained much that was not unfit to find place in a better, and was often calculated to suggest deeper thoughts than it possessed of its own. But in the *Elements of Morality* he leaves the subject so exactly as he found it – the book is so mere a catalogue of received opinions, containing nothing to correct any of them, and little which can work with any potency even to confirm them – that it can scarcely be counted as anything more than one of the thousand waves on the dead sea of commonplace, affording nothing to invite or to reward a separate examination. We should not, therefore, have felt called upon to concern ourselves specially about it, if Dr Whewell had not, in his more recent publication, *Lectures on the History of Moral Philosophy in England*, undertaken to characterize and criticize, from his own point of view, all other English writers on moral philosophy; and particularly those who derive their ethical conclusions, not from internal intuition, but from an external standard. So long as he contented himself with giving what we think bad reasons for common opinions, there was not much inducement to interfere with them; but assaults on the only methods of philosophizing from which any improvement in ethical opinions can be looked for, ought to be repelled. And in doing this it is necessary to extend our comments to some of Dr Whewell's substantive opinions also. When he argues in condemnation of any external standard, and especially of utility, or tendency to happiness, as the principle or test of morality, it is material to examine how he gets on without it; how he fares in the attempt to construct a coherent theory of morals on any other basis. We shall make use of his larger work in so far only as it is evidence on this point.

Even with the *Lectures*, considered as giving an account of English speculations on moral philosophy previous to the age of Bentham and Paley, it is not our purpose to meddle: Hobbes, therefore, and Locke, must be left in the hands of Dr Whewell, without any attempt either to correct his estimate of their opinions, or to offer any judgement of our own. This historical sketch suggests, however, one remark of an historical character, not new to any one who is conversant with the writings of English thinkers on ethical subjects. During the greater part of the eighteenth century, the received opinions in religion and ethics were chiefly attacked, as by Shaftesbury, and even by Hume, on the ground of instinctive feelings of virtue, and the theory of a moral taste or sense. As a consequence of this, the defenders of established opinions, both lay and clerical, commonly professed utilitarianism. To the many writers on the side of orthodoxy, of the utilitarian school mentioned by Dr Whewell, might be added several, of at least equal note, whom he has omitted; as John Brown, the author of *Essays on the Characteristics*; Soame Jenyns, and his more celebrated reviewer, Dr Johnson; all of whom, as explicitly as Bentham, laid down the doctrine that utility is the foundation of morals. This series of writers attained its culmination in Paley, whose treatise, proclaiming without evasion or circumlocution, not only expediency as the end, but (a very different doctrine) simple self-interest as the motive, of virtue, and deducing from these premises all the orthodox conclusions, became the textbook of moral philosophy in one of the two universities of the Church of England. But a change ensued, and the utilitarian doctrine, which had been the favourite theory of the defenders of orthodoxy, began to be used by its assailants. In the hands of the French philosophers, and in those of Godwin and of Bentham – who, though earlier than Godwin in date, was later in acquiring popular influence – a moral philosophy founded on utility led to many conclusions very unacceptable to the orthodox. For a whole generation, so effectual a fight was kept up against those conclusions, by bayonets in the field, and prosecutions in the courts of justice, that there seemed no necessity for taking much concern about the premises: but when those carnal weapons fell into disuse, and the spirit which had wielded them was laid – when the battle of established opinions in Church and State had again to be fought by argument, a demand arose for metaphysics and moral philosophy, of the kind most remote from that which appeared so full of danger to received opinions. Utility was now abjured as a deadly heresy, and the doctrine of *a priori* or self-evident morality, an end in itself, independent of all consequences, became the orthodox theory. Having once entered into this course, and gone in search of a philosophical system to be extracted from the mind itself, without any external evidence, the defenders of orthodoxy were insensibly led to seek their system where it exists in the most elaborate shape – in the German metaphysicians. It was not without reluctance that they found themselves engaged in this path; for German metaphysics in Germany lay under as grave a suspicion of religious scepticism, as the rival philosophy in England or France. But it was found on trial, that philosophy of this cast admitted of easy adaptation, and would bend to the very Thirty-nine Articles; as it is the essence of a philosophy which seeks its evidence in internal conviction, that it bears its testimony with equal ease for any conclusions in favour of which there is a predisposition, and is sceptical with the sceptical, and mystical with the mystical.

Accordingly, the tone of religious metaphysics, and of the ethical speculations connected with religion, is now altogether Germanized; and Dr Whewell, by his writings, has done no little to impress upon the metaphysics of orthodoxy this change of character.

It has always been indistinctly felt that the doctrine of *a priori* principles is one and the same doctrine, whether applied to the ὄν or the δέον – to the knowledge of truth or to that of duty; that it belongs to the same general tendency of thought, to extract from the mind itself, without any outward standard, principles and rules of morality, and to deem it possible to discover, by mere introspection into our minds, the laws of external nature. Both forms of this mode of thought attained a brilliant development in Descartes, the real founder of the modern anti-inductive school of philosophy. The Cartesian tradition was never lost, being kept alive by direct descent through Spinoza, Leibnitz and Kant, to Schelling and Hegel; but the speculations of Bacon and Locke, and the progress of the experimental sciences, gave a long period of predominance to the philosophy of experience; and though many followed out that philosophy into its natural alliances, and acknowledged not only observation and experiment as rulers of the speculative world, but utility of the practical, others thought that it was scientifically possible to separate the two opinions, and professed themselves Baconians in the physical department, remaining Cartesians in the moral. It will probably be thought by posterity to be the principal merit of the German metaphysicians of the last and present age, that they have proved the impossibility of resting on this middle ground of compromise; and have convinced all thinkers of any force, that if they adhere to the doctrine of *a priori* principles of morals, they must follow Descartes and Hegel in ascribing the same character to the principles of physics.

On the present occasion, it is only with the moral branch of the subject that we have to deal; and we shall begin by showing in what manner Dr Whewell states the question between us.

Schemes of morality, that is, modes of deducing the rules of human action, are of two kinds: those which assert it to be the law of human action to aim at some external object, (external, that is, to the mind which aims,) as, for example, those which in ancient or modern times have asserted pleasure, or utility, or the greatest happiness of the greatest number, to be the true end of human action; and those which would regulate human action by an internal principle or relation, as conscience or a moral faculty, or duty, or rectitude, or the superiority of reason to desire. These two kinds of schemes may be described respectively as *dependent* and *independent* morality. Now, it is here held that independent morality is the true scheme. We maintain, with Plato, that reason has a natural and rightful authority over desire and affection; with Butler, that there is a difference of kind in our principles of action; with the general voice of mankind, that we must do what is right, at whatever cost of pain and loss. We deny the doctrine of the ancient Epicureans, that pleasure is the supreme good; of Hobbes, that moral rules are only the work of men's mutual fear; of Paley, that what is expedient is right, and that there is no difference among pleasures except their intensity and duration; and of Bentham, that the rules of human action are to be obtained by casting up the pleasures which actions produce. But though we thus take our stand upon the ground of independent morality, as held by previous writers, we hope that we are (by their aid mainly) able to present it in a more systematic and connected form than has yet been done. ['Introductory Lecture'.]

There is in this mode of stating the question, great unfairness to the doctrine of 'dependent morality', as Dr Whewell terms it, though the word independent is fully as applicable to it as to the intuition doctrine. He appropriates to his own side of the question all the expressions, such as conscience, duty, rectitude, with which the reverential feelings of mankind towards moral ideas are associated, and cries out, *I* am for these noble things, *you* are for pleasure, or utility. We cannot accept this as a description of the matter in issue. Dr Whewell is assuming to himself what belongs quite as rightfully to his antagonists. We are as much for conscience, duty, rectitude, as Dr Whewell. The terms, and all the feelings connected with them, are as much a part of the ethics of utility as of that of intuition. The point in dispute is, what acts are the proper objects of those feelings; whether we ought to take the feelings as we find them, as accident or design has made them, or whether the tendency of actions to promote happiness affords a test to which the feelings of morality should conform. In the same spirit, Dr Whewell announces it as *his* opinion, as the side *he* takes in this great controversy, 'that we must do what is right, at whatever cost of pain and loss'. As if this was not everybody's opinion: as if it was not the very meaning of the word right. The matter in debate is, what *is* right, not whether what is right ought to be done. Dr Whewell represents his opponents as denying an identical proposition, in order that he may claim a monopoly of high principle for his own opinions. The same unfairness pervades the whole phraseology. It is not only Dr Whewell who 'maintains, with Plato, that reason has a rightful authority over desire and affection'. Everybody maintains it; only, what *is* reason? And by what rule is it to guide and govern the desires and affections? The description of Bentham, as obtaining his rule of conduct by 'casting up the pleasures which actions produce', ought to be 'casting up the pleasures and pains which actions produce': a very different thing.

As might be expected from the historical character of the *Lectures*, the discussion of opinions mostly assumes the form of criticism on writers. Dr Whewell's objections to utility, or the 'greatest happiness', as the standard of morals are chiefly contained in his animadversions on Paley and on Bentham. It would be quite open to a defender of the principle of utility, to refuse encumbering himself with a defence of either of those authors. The principle is not bound up with what they have said in its behalf, nor with the degree of felicity which they may have shown in applying it. As for Paley, we resign him without compunction to the tender mercies of Dr Whewell. It concerns Dr Whewell more than ourselves to uphold the reputation of a writer, who, whatever principle of morals he professed, seems to have had no object but to insert it as a foundation underneath the existing set of opinions, ethical and political; who, when he had laid down utility as the fundamental axiom, and the recognition of general rules as the condition of its application, took his leave of scientific analysis, and betook himself to picking up utilitarian reasons by the wayside, in proof of all accredited doctrines, and in defence of most tolerated practices. Bentham was a moralist of another stamp. With him, the first use to be made of his ultimate principle, was to erect on it, as a foundation, secondary or middle principles, capable of serving as premises for a body of ethical doctrine not derived from existing opinions, but fitted to be their test. Without such middle principles, a universal principle, either in science or in morals, serves for little but a thesaurus of commonplaces for the discussion of questions, instead of a means of deciding them. If Bentham has been regarded by subsequent adherents of morality grounded on the 'greatest happiness', as in a peculiar sense the founder of that system of ethics, it is not because, as Dr Whewell imagines, he either thought himself, or was thought by others, to be the 'discoverer of the principle', but because he was the first who, keeping clear of the direct and indirect influences of all doctrines inconsistent with it, deduced a set of subordinate generalities from utility alone, and by these consistently tested all particular questions. This great service, previously to which a scientific doctrine of ethics on the foundation of utility was impossible, has been performed by Bentham (though with a view to the exigencies of legislation more than to those of morals) in a manner, as far as it goes, eminently. We must at the same time qualify our approbation by adding, not that his practical conclusions in morals were often wrong, for we think that as far as they went they were mostly right; but that there were large deficiencies and hiatuses in his scheme of human nature and life, and a consequent want of breadth and comprehension in his secondary principles, which led him often to deduce just conclusions from premises so narrow as to provoke many minds to a rejection of what was nevertheless truth. It is by his *method* chiefly that Bentham, as we think, justly earned a position in moral science analogous to that of Bacon in physical. It is because he was the first to enter into the right mode of working ethical problems, though he worked many of them, as Bacon did physical, on insufficient data. Dr Whewell's shafts, however, seldom touch Bentham where he is really vulnerable; they are mostly aimed at his strong points.

Before commencing his attack on Bentham's opinions, Dr Whewell gives a sketch of his life. In this there is an apparent desire to be just to Bentham, as far as the writer's opinions allow. But there is in some of the strictures a looseness of expression, scarcely excusable in an extemporaneous lecture, and still less in a printed book. 'He showed very early that peculiar one-sidedness in his mode of asserting and urging his opinions, which made him think all moderation with regard to his opponents superfluous and absurd.' What is here called 'one-sidedness in his mode of asserting and urging his opinions', must mean one-sidedness in the opinions themselves. It could not be Bentham's 'mode of asserting his opinions', that 'made him think' whatever he did think. This is as if any one should say, 'his speaking only English made him unable to understand French', or 'his peculiar habit of fighting made him think it superfluous and absurd to keep the peace'. Again, 'Bentham appears to have been one of those persons to whom everything which passes through their own thoughts assumes quite a different character and value from that which the same thing had when it passed through the thoughts of other persons.' If a thought in a person's own mind did not assume a different character from what the same thought had in other minds, people might as well think by deputy.

A more serious injustice to Bentham is that of citing, as is constantly done in this volume, the book called *Deontology*, as the authentic exposition of Bentham's philosophy of morals. Dr Whewell would, no doubt, justify this by saying that the book in question is the only treatise expressly and exclusively on morals, which we have from Bentham. It is true that we have no other; but the *Deontology* was not, and does not profess to be written by Bentham. Still less ought that book to be represented as the embodiment of the opinions and mental characteristics of all who share Bentham's general conception of ethics. After charging the compiler of the *Deontology* with profound ignorance, and saying that it is almost 'superfluous to notice misstatements so gross and partiality so blind', Dr Whewell adds that 'such misrepresentations and such unfairness are the usual style of controversy of him [Bentham] and his disciples; and it is fit that we, in entering upon the consideration of their writings, should be aware of this.' Who are the persons here included under the name of Bentham's 'disciples', we are not enabled to judge; nor are we aware that Bentham ever had any disciples, in Dr Whewell's sense of the term. As far as our means of observation have gone, which in this matter are considerably greater than Dr Whewell's, those who, from the amount of their intellectual obligations to Bentham, would be the most likely to be classed by Dr Whewell as Benthamites, were and are persons in an unusual degree addicted to judging and thinking for themselves; persons remarkable for learning willingly from all masters, but swearing blind fealty to none. It is also a fact, with which Dr Whewell cannot be altogether unacquainted, that among them there have been men of the widest and most accurate acquirements in history and philosophy, against whom the accusation of ignorance of the opinions which they controverted would be as unfounded as the imputation of blind partiality. We protest against including them and Bentham in an imaginary sect, of which the *Deontology* is to be considered the gospel. Bentham's merits or demerits must stand on what is contained in the books written by himself.

Among these, the one in which the doctrine of utility is expressly discussed, and contrasted with the various ethical doctrines opposed to it, is the *Introduction to the Principles of Morals and Legislation*, published in 1789. On this Dr Whewell comments as follows:

The first chapter of this work is 'On the Principle of Utility': the second 'On Principles adverse to that of Utility'. These adverse principles are stated to be two: The Principle of Asceticism, and the Principle of Sympathy. [Bentham calls it the Principle of Sympathy and Antipathy, which is already a considerable difference.] The principle of asceticism is that principle which approves of actions in proportion as they tend to *diminish* human happiness, and, conversely, disapproves of them as they tend to augment it. The principle of sympathy is that which approves or disapproves of certain actions 'merely because a man finds himself disposed to approve or disapprove of them, holding up that approbation or disapprobation as a sufficient reason for itself, and disclaiming the necessity of looking out for any extrinsic grounds'. And these two principles are, it seems, according to Bentham's view, the only principles which are, or which can be, opposed to the principle of utility!

Now it is plain that these are not only not fair representations of any principles ever held by moralists, or by any persons speaking gravely and deliberately, but that they are too extravagant and fantastical to be accepted even as caricatures of any such principles. For who ever approved of actions because they tend to make mankind miserable? Or who ever said anything which could, even in an intelligible way of exaggeration, be so represented? . . . But who then are the ascetic school who are thus ridiculed? We could not, I think, guess from the general description thus given; but from a note, it appears that he had the Stoical philosophers and the religious ascetics in his mind. With regard to the Stoics, it would of course be waste of time and thought to defend them from such coarse buffoonery as this, which does not touch their defects, whatever these may be. . .

Not solely for the due estimation of Bentham, but for the right understanding of the utilitarian controversy, it is important to know what the truth is, respecting the points here in issue between Bentham and Dr Whewell.

Undoubtedly no one has set up, in opposition to the 'greatest happiness' principle, a 'greatest unhappiness' principle, as the standard of virtue. But it was Bentham's business not merely to discuss the avowed principles of his opponents, but to draw out those which, without being professed as principles, were implied in detail, or were essential to support the judgements passed in particular cases. His own doctrine being that the increase of pleasure and the prevention of pain were the proper ends of all moral rules, he had for his opponents all who contended that pleasure could ever be an evil or pain a good in itself, apart from its consequences. Now this, whatever Dr Whewell may say, the religious ascetics really did. They held that self-mortification, or even self-torture, practised for its own sake, and not for the sake of any useful end, was meritorious. It matters not that they may have expected to be rewarded for these merits by consideration in this world, or by the favour of an invisible tyrant in a world to come. So far as this life was concerned, their doctrine required it to be supposed that pain was a thing to be sought, and pleasure to be avoided. Bentham generalized this into a maxim, which he called the principle of asceticism. The Stoics did not go so far as the ascetics; they stopped half-way. They did not say that pain is a good, and pleasure an evil. But they said, and boasted of saying, that pain is no evil, and pleasure no good: and this is all, and more than all, that Bentham imputes to them, as may be seen by any one who reads that chapter of his book. This, however, was enough to place them, equally with the ascetics, in direct opposition to Bentham, since they denied his supreme end to be an end at all. And hence he classed them and the ascetics together, as professing the direct negation of the utilitarian standard.

In the other division of his opponents he placed those who, though they did not deny pleasure to be a good and pain an evil, refused to consider the pain or the pleasure which an action or a class of actions tends to produce, as the criterion of its morality. As the former category of opponents were described by Bentham as followers of the 'principle of asceticism', so he described these as followers of 'the principle of sympathy and antipathy'; not because they had themselves generalized their principle of judgement, or would have acknowledged it when placed undisguised before them; but because, at the bottom of what they imposed on themselves and others as reasons, he could find nothing else; because they all, in one phrase or another, placed the test of right and wrong in a feeling of approbation or disapprobation, thus making the feeling its own reason and its own justification. This portion of Bentham's doctrine can only be fairly exhibited in his own words.

It is manifest that this [the principle of sympathy and antipathy] is rather a principle in name than in reality; it is not a positive principle of itself, so much as a term employed to signify the negation of all principle. What one expects to find in a principle is something that points out some external consideration as a means of warranting and guiding the internal sentiments of approbation and disapprobation: this expectation is but ill fulfilled by a proposition which does neither more nor less than hold up each of these sentiments as a ground and standard for itself.

In looking over the catalogue of human actions (says a partisan of this principle) in order to determine which of them are to be marked with the seal of disapprobation, you need but to take counsel of your own feelings; whatever you find in yourself a propensity to condemn, is wrong for that very reason. For the same reason it is also meet for punishment: in what proportion it is adverse to utility, or whether it be adverse to utility at all, is a matter that makes no difference. In that same proportion also is it meet for punishment: if you hate much, punish much; if you hate little, punish little: punish as you hate. If you hate not at all, punish not at all: the fine feelings of the soul are not to be overborne and tyrannized by the harsh and rugged dictates of political utility.

The various systems that have been formed concerning the standard of right and wrong, may all be reduced to the principle of sympathy and antipathy. One account may serve for all of them. They consist, all of them, in so many contrivances for avoiding the obligation of appealing to any external standard, and for prevailing upon the reader to accept of the author's sentiment or opinion as a reason for itself. The phrase is different, but the principle the same.

It is curious enough to observe the variety of inventions men have hit upon, and the variety of phrases they have brought forward, in order to conceal from the world, and if possible from themselves, this very general, and therefore very pardonable self-sufficiency.

One man says, he has a thing made on purpose to tell him what is right and what is wrong, and that it is called a *moral sense*; and then he goes to work at his ease, and says, such a thing is right, and such a thing is wrong – why? 'because my moral sense tells me it is.'

Another man comes and alters the phrase; leaving out *moral*, and putting in *common* in the room of it. He then tells you, that his common sense teaches him what is right and wrong, as much as the other's moral sense did: meaning, by common sense, a sense of some kind or other, which, he says, is possessed by all mankind; the sense of those, whose sense is not the same as the author's being struck out of the account as not worth taking. This contrivance does better than the other; for a moral sense being a new thing, a man may feel about him a good while without being able to find it out; but common sense is as old as the creation; and there is no man but would be ashamed to be thought not to have as much of it as his neighbours. It has another great advantage; by appearing to share power, it lessens envy: for when a man gets up upon this ground, in order to anathematize those who differ from him, it is not by a *sic volo sic jubeo*, but by a *velitis jubeatis*.

Another man comes, and says, that as to a moral sense indeed, he cannot find that he has any such thing; that, however, he has an *understanding*, which will do quite as well. This understanding, he says, is the standard of right and wrong: it tells him so and so. All good and wise men understand as he does: if other men's understandings differ in any point from his, so much the worse for them; it is a sure sign they are either defective or corrupt.

Another man says, that there is an eternal and immutable rule of right; that that rule of right dictates so and so; and then he begins giving you his sentiments upon anything that comes uppermost; and these sentiments (you are to take for granted) are so many branches of the eternal rule of right.

Another man, or perhaps the same man (it's no matter), says, that there are certain practices conformable, and others repugnant, to the fitness of things; and then he tells you, at his leisure, what practices are conformable and what repugnant; just as he happens to like a practice or dislike it.

A great multitude of people are continually talking of the law of nature; and then they go on giving you their sentiments about what is right and what is wrong; and these sentiments, you are to understand, are so many chapters and sections of the law of nature.

We have one philosopher who says, there is no harm in anything in the world but in telling a lie; and that if, for example, you were to murder your own father, this would only be a particular way of saying, he was not your father. Or course, when this philosopher sees anything that he does not like, he says, it is a particular way of telling a lie. It is saying, that the act ought to be done, or may be done, when, *in truth*, it ought not to be done. [Chap. II.]

To this Dr Whewell thinks it a sufficient answer to call it extravagant ridicule, and to ask, 'Who ever asserted that he approved or disapproved of actions merely because he found himself disposed to do so, and that this was reason sufficient in itself for his moral judgements?' Dr Whewell will find that this by no means disposes of Bentham's doctrine. Bentham did not mean that people 'ever asserted' that they approved or condemned actions only because they felt disposed to do so. He meant that they do it without asserting it; that they find certain feelings of approbation and disapprobation in themselves, take for granted that these feelings are the right ones, and when called on to say anything in justification of their approbation or disapprobation, produce phrases which mean nothing but the fact of the approbation or disapprobation itself. If the hearer or reader feels in the same way, the phrases pass muster; and a great part of all the ethical reasoning in books and in the world is of this sort. All this is not only true, but cannot consistently be denied by those who, like Dr Whewell, consider the moral feelings as their own justification. Dr Whewell will doubtless say that the feelings they appeal to are not their own individually, but a part of universal human nature. Nobody denies that they say so: a feeling of liking or aversion to an action, confined to an individual, would have no chance of being accepted as a reason. The appeal is always to something which is assumed to belong to all mankind. But it is not of much consequence whether the feeling which is set up as its own standard is the feeling of an individual human being, or of a multitude. A feeling is not proved to be right, and exempted from the necessity of justifying itself, because the writer or speaker is not only conscious of it in himself, but expects to find it in other people; because instead of saying 'I', he says 'you and I'. If it is alleged that the intuitive school require, as an authority for the feeling, that it should *in fact* be universal, we deny it. They assume the utmost latitude of arbitrarily determining whose votes deserve to be counted. They either ignore the existence of dissentients, or leave them out of the account, on the pretext that they have the feeling which they deny having, or if not, that they ought to have it. This falsification of the universal suffrage which is ostensibly appealed to, is not confined, as is often asserted, to cases in which the only dissentients are barbarous tribes. The same measure is dealt out to whole ages and nations, the most conspicuous for the cultivation and development of their mental faculties; and to individuals among the best and wisest of their respective countries. The explanation of the matter is, the inability of persons in general to conceive that feelings of right and wrong, which have been deeply implanted in their minds by the teaching they have from infancy received from all around them, can be sincerely thought by any one else to be mistaken or misplaced. This is the mental infirmity which Bentham's philosophy tends especially to correct, and Dr Whewell's to perpetuate. Things which were really believed by all mankind, and for which all were convinced that they had the unequivocal evidence of their senses, have been proved to be false: as that the sun rises and sets. Can immunity from similar error be claimed for the moral feelings? when all experience shows that those feelings are eminently artificial, and the product of culture; that even when reasonable, they are no more spontaneous than the growth of corn and wine (which are quite as natural), and that the most senseless and pernicious feelings can as easily be raised to the utmost intensity by inculcation, as hemlock and thistles would be reared to luxuriant growth by sowing them instead of wheat. Bentham, therefore, did not judge too severely a kind of ethics whereby any implanted sentiment which is tolerably general may be erected into a moral law, binding, under penalties, on all mankind. The contest between the morality which appeals to an external standard, and that which grounds itself on internal convicion, is the contest of progressive morality against stationary – of reason and argument against the deification of mere opinion and habit. The doctrine that the existing order of things is the natural order, and that, being natural, all innovation upon it is criminal, is as vicious in morals, as it is now at last admitted to be in physics, and in society and government.

Let us now consider Dr Whewell's objections to utility as the foundation of ethics.

Let it be taken for granted, as a proposition which is true, if the terms which it involves be duly understood, that actions are right and virtuous in proportion as they promote the happiness of mankind; the actions being considered upon the whole, and with regard to all their consequences. Still, I say, we cannot make this truth the basis of morality, for two reasons: first, we cannot calculate all the consequences of any action, and thus cannot estimate the degree in which it promotes human happiness; second, happiness is derived from moral elements, and therefore we cannot properly derive morality from happiness. The calculable happiness resulting from actions cannot determine their virtue: first, because the resulting happiness is not calculable; and secondly, because the virtue is one of the things which determine the resulting happiness.

The first of these arguments is an irrelevant truism. 'We cannot calculate *all* the consequences of any action.' If Dr Whewell can point out any department of human affairs in which we can do *all* that would be desirable, he will have found something new. But because we cannot foresee everything, is there no such thing as foresight? Does Dr Whewell mean to say that no estimate can be formed of consequences, which can be any guide for our conduct, unless we can calculate *all* consequences? That because we cannot predict every effect which may follow from a person's death, we cannot know that the liberty of murder would be destructive to human happiness? Dr Whewell, in his zeal against the morality of consequences, commits the error of proving too much. Whether morality is or is not a question of consequences, he cannot deny that prudence is; and if there is such a thing as prudence, it is because the consequences of actions *can* be calculated. Prudence, indeed, depends on a calculation of the consequences of individual actions, while for the establishment of moral rules it is only necessary to calculate the consequences of classes of actions – a much easier matter. It is certainly a very effectual way of proving that morality does not depend on expediency, to maintain that there is no such thing as expediency – that we have no means of knowing whether anything is expedient or not. Unless Dr Whewell goes this length, to what purpose is what he says about the uncertainty of consequences? Uncertain or certain, we are able to guide ourselves by them, otherwise human life could not exist. And there is hardly any one concerned in the business of life, who has not daily to decide questions of expediency far more knotty than those which Dr Whewell so coolly pronounces to be insoluble.

But let us examine more closely what Dr Whewell finds to say for the proposition, that 'if we ask whether a given action will increase or diminish the total amount of human happiness, it is impossible to answer with any degree of certainty'.

Take ordinary cases. I am tempted to utter a flattering falsehood: to gratify some sensual desire contrary to ordinary moral rules. How shall I determine, on the greatest happiness principle, whether the act is virtuous, or the contrary? In the first place, the direct effect of each act is to give pleasure, to another by flattery, to myself by sensual gratification; and pleasure is the material of happiness, in the scheme we are now considering. But by the flattering lie I promote falsehood, which is destructive of confidence, and so, of human comfort. Granted that I do this in some degree – although I may easily say that I shall never allow myself to speak falsely, except when it will give pleasure; and thus I may maintain that I shall not shake confidence in any case in which it is of any value. But granted that I do, in some degree, shake the general fabric of mutual human confidence by my flattering lie, still the question remains, *how much* I do this: whether in such a degree as to overbalance the pleasure, which is the primary and direct consequence of the act. How small must be the effect of my solitary act upon the whole scheme of human action and habit! How clear and decided is the direct affect of increasing the happiness of my hearer! And in the same way we may reason concerning the sensual gratification. Who will know it? Who will be influenced by it of those who do know it? What appreciable amount of pain will it produce in its consequences, to balance the palpable pleasure, which according to our teachers, is the only real good? It appears to me that it is impossible to answer these questions in any way which will prove on these principles, mendacious flattery, and illegitimate sensuality, to be vicious and immoral. They may possibly produce, take in all their effects, a balance of evil; but if they do, it is by some process which we cannot trace with any clearness, and the result is one which we cannot calculate with any certainty, or even probability; and therefore, on this account, because the resulting evil of such falsehood and sensuality is not calculable or appreciable, we cannot, by calculation of resulting evil, show falsehood and sensuality to be vices. And the like is true of other vices; and, on this ground, the construction of a scheme of morality on Mr Bentham's plan is plainly impossible.

Dr Whewell supposes his self-deceiving utilitarian to be very little master of his own principles. If the effect of a 'solitary act upon the whole scheme of human action and habit' is small, the addition which the accompanying pleasure makes to the general mass of human happiness is small likewise. So small, in the great majority of cases, are both, that we have no scales to weigh them against each other, taken singly. We must look at them multiplied, and in large masses. The portion of the tendencies of an action which belong to it not individually, but as a violation of a general rule, are as certain and as calculable as any other consequences; only they must be examined not in the individual case, but in classes of cases. Take, for example, the case of murder. There are many persons to kill whom would be to remove men who are a cause of no good to any human being, of cruel physical and moral suffering to several, and whose whole influence tends to increase the mass of unhappiness and vice. Were such a man to be assassinated, the balance of traceable consequences would be greatly in favour of the act. The counter-consideration, on the principle of utility, is, that unless persons were punished for killing, and taught not to kill; that if it were thought allowable for any one to put to death at pleasure any human being whom he believes that the world would be well rid of, nobody's life would be safe. To this Dr Whewell answers:

How does it appear that the evil, that is, the pain, arising from violating a general rule once, is too great to be overbalanced by the pleasurable consequences of that single violation? The actor says, I acknowledge the general rule – I do not deny its value; but I do not intend that this one act should be drawn into consequence.

But it does not depend on him whether or not it shall be drawn into consequence. If one person may break through the rule on his own judgement, the same liberty cannot be refused to others; and since no one could rely on the rule's being observed, the rule would cease to exist. If a hundred infringements would produce all the mischief implied in the abrogation of the rule, a hundredth part of that mischief must be debited to each one of the infringements, though we may not be able to trace it home individually. And this hundredth part will generally far outweigh any good expected to arise from the individual act. We say generally, not universally; for the admission of exceptions to rules is a necessity equally felt in all systems of morality. To take an obvious instance, the rule against homicide, the rule against deceiving, the rule against taking advantage of superior physical strength, and various other important moral rules, are suspended against enemies in the field, and partially against malefactors in private life: in each case suspended as far as is required by the peculiar nature of the case. That the moralities arising from the special circumstances of the action may be so important as to overrule those arising from the class of acts to which it belongs, perhaps to take it out of the category of virtues into that of crimes, or *vice versa*, is a liability common to all ethical systems.

And here it may be observed that Dr Whewell, in his illustration drawn from flattering lies, gives to the side he advocates a colour of rigid adherence to principle, which the fact does not bear out. Is none of the intercourse of society carried on by those who hold the common opinions, by means of what is here meant by 'flattering lies'? Does no one of Dr Whewell's way of thinking say, or allow it to be thought, that he is glad to see a visitor whom he wishes away? Does he never ask acquaintances or relatives to stay when he would prefer them to go, or invite them when he hopes that they will refuse? Does he never show any interest in persons and things he cares nothing for, or send people away believing in his friendly feeling, to whom his real feeling is indifference, or even dislike? Whether these things are right, we are not now going to discuss. For our part, we think that flattery should be only permitted to those who can flatter without lying, as all persons of sympathizing feelings and quick perceptions can. At all events, the existence of exceptions to moral rules is no stumbling-block peculiar to the principle of utility. The essential is, that the exception should be itself a general rule; so that, being of definite extent, and not leaving the expediencies to the partial judgement of the agent in the individual case, it may not shake the stability of the wider rule in the cases to which the reason of the exception does not extend. This is an ample foundation for 'the construction of a scheme of morality'. With respect to the means of inducing people to conform in their actions to the scheme so formed, the utilitarian system depends, like all other schemes of morality, on the external motives supplied by law and opinion, and the internal feelings produced by education or reason. It is thus no worse off in this respect than any other scheme – we might rather say, much better; inasmuch as people are likely to be more willing to confirm to rules when a reason is given for them.

Dr Whewell's second argument against the happiness principle is, that the morality of actions cannot depend on the happiness they produce, because the happiness depends on the morality.

Why should a man be truthful and just? Because acts of veracity and justice, even if they do not produce immediate gratification to him and his friends in other ways (and it may easily be that they do not), at least produce pleasure in this way, that they procure him his own approval and that of all good men. To us this language is intelligible and significant; but the Benthamite must analyse it further. What does it mean according to him? A man's own approval of his act, means that he thinks it virtuous. And therefore the matter stands thus. He (being a Benthamite) thinks it virtuous, because it gives him pleasure; and it gives him pleasure because he thinks it virtuous. This is a vicious circle, quite as palpable as any of those in which Mr Bentham is so fond of representing his adversaries as revolving. And in like manner with regard to the approval of others. The action is virtuous, says the Benthamite, because it produces pleasure; namely, the pleasure arising from the approval of neighbours; they approve it and think it virtuous, he also says, because it gives pleasure. The virtue depends upon the pleasure, the pleasure depends upon the virtue. Here again is a circle from which there is no legitimate egress. We may grant that, taking into account all the elements of happiness – the pleasures of self-approval – of peace of mind and harmony within us, and of the approval of others – of the known sympathy of all good men – we may grant that, including these elements virtue always does produce an overbalance of happiness; but then we cannot make this moral truth the basis of morality, because we cannot extricate the happiness and the virtue the one from the other, so as to make the first, the happiness, the foundation of the second, the virtue.

In Dr Whewell's first argument against utility, he was obliged to assert that it is impossible for human beings to know that some actions are useful and others hurtful. In the present, he forgets against what principle he is combating, and draws out an elaborate argument against something else. What he now appears to be contending against, is the doctrine (whether really held by any one or not), that the test of morality is the greatest happiness of the agent himself. It argues total ignorance of Bentham, to represent him as saying that an action is virtuous because it produces 'the approbation of neighbours', and as making so 'fluctuating' a thing as 'public opinion', and such a 'loose and wide abstraction as education', the 'basis of morality'. When Bentham talks of public opinion in connection with morality, he is not talking of the 'basis of morality' at all. He was the last person to found the morality of actions upon anybody's opinion of them. He founded it upon facts: namely, upon the observed tendencies of the actions. Nor did he ever dream of defining morality to be the self-interest of the agent. His 'greatest happiness principle' was the greatest happiness of mankind, and of all sensitive beings. When he talks of education, and of 'the popular or moral sanction', meaning the opinion of our fellow creatures, it is not as constituents or tests of virtue, but as *motives* to it; as means of making the self-interest of the individual *accord* with the greatest happiness principle.*

*It is curious that while Dr Whewell here confounds the Happiness theory of Morals with the theory of Motives sometimes called the Selfish System, and attacks the latter as Bentham's, under the name of the former, Dr Whewell himself, in his larger work, adopts the Selfish theory. Happiness, he says (meaning, as he explains, our own happiness), is 'our being's end and aim'; we cannot desire anything else unless by identifying it with our happiness. (*Elements of Morality*,

Dr Whewell's remark, therefore, that the approval of our fellow creatures, presupposing moral ideas, cannot be the foundation of morality, has no application against Bentham, nor against the principle of utility. It may, however, be pertinently remarked, that the moral ideas which this approval presupposes, are no other than those of utility and hurtfulness. There is no great stretch of hypothesis in supposing that in proportion as mankind are aware of the tendencies of actions to produce happiness or misery, they will like and commend the first, abhor and reprobate the second. How these feelings of natural complacency and natural dread and aversion directed towards actions, come to assume the peculiar character of what we term *moral* feelings, is not a question of ethics but of metaphysics, and very fit to be discussed in its proper place. Bentham did not concern himself with it. He left it to other thinkers. It sufficed him that the perceived influence of actions on human happiness is cause enough, both in reason and in fact, for strong feelings of favour to some actions and of hatred towards others. From the sympathetic reaction of these feelings in the imagination and self-consciousness of the agent, naturally arise the more complex feelings of self-approbation and self-reproach, or, to avoid all disputed questions, we will merely say of satisfaction and dissatisfaction with ourselves. All this must be admitted, whatever else may be denied. Whether the greatest happiness is the principle of morals or not, people do

Vol. I.). To this we should have nothing to object, if by identification was meant that what we desire unselfishly must first, by a mental process, become an actual part of what we seek as our own happiness; that the good of others becomes our pleasure because we have learnt to find pleasure in it: this is, we think, the true philosophical account of the matter. But we do not understand this to be Dr Whewell's meaning: for in an argument to prove that there is no virtue without religion, he says that religion alone can assure us of the identity of happiness with duty. Now, if the happiness connected with duty were the happiness we find *in* our duty, self-consciousness would give us a full account of this, without religion. The happiness, therefore, which Dr Whewell means, must consist, not in the thing itself, but in a reward appended to it: and when he says that there can be no morality unless we believe that happiness is identical with duty, and that we cannot believe this apart from 'the belief in God's government of the world', he must mean that no one would act virtuously unless he believed that God would reward him for it. In Dr Whewell's view of morality, therefore, disinterestedness has no place.

desire their own happiness, and do consequently like the conduct in other people which they think promotes it, and dislike that which visibly endangers it. This is absolutely all that Bentham postulates. Grant this, and you have his popular sanction, and its reaction on the agent's own mind, two influences tending, in proportion to mankind's enlightenment, to keep the conduct of each in the line which promotes the general happiness. Bentham thinks that there is no other true morality than this, and that the so-called moral sentiments, whatever their origin or composition, should be trained to act in this direction only. And Dr Whewell's attempt to find anything illogical or incoherent in this theory, only proves that he does not yet understand it.

Dr Whewell puts the last hand to his supposed refutation of Bentham's principle, by what he thinks a crushing *reductio ad absurdum*. The reader might make a hundred guesses before discovering what this is. We have not yet got over our astonishment, not at Bentham, but at Dr Whewell. See, he says, to what consequences your greatest-happiness principle leads! Bentham says that it is as much a moral duty to regard the pleasures and pains of other animals as those of human beings. We cannot resist quoting the admirable passage which Dr Whewell cites from Bentham, with the most *naïf* persuasion that everybody will regard it as reaching the last pitch of paradoxical absurdity.

Under the Gentoo and Mahometan religion the interests of the rest of the animal kingdom seem to have met with some attention. Why have they not, universally, with as much as those of human creatures, allowance made for the difference in point of sensibility? Because the laws that are, have been the work of mutual fear; a sentiment which the less rational animals have not had the same means as man has of turning to account. Why ought they not? No reason can be given. The day may come when the rest of the animal creation may acquire those rights which never could have been withholden from them but by the hand of tyranny. It may come one day to be recognized that the number of the legs, the villosity of the skin, or the termination of the *os sacrum*, are reasons insufficient for abandoning a sensitive being to the caprice of a tormentor. What else is it that should trace the insuperable line? Is it the faculty of reason, or perhaps the faculty of discourse? But a full-grown horse or dog is beyond comparison a more rational, as well as a more conversable animal, than an infant of a day, a week, or even a month old. But suppose the case were otherwise, what would it avail? The question is not, can they reason? nor, can they speak? but, can they suffer?

This noble anticipation, in 1780, of the better morality of which a first dawn has been seen in the laws enacted nearly fifty years afterwards against cruelty to animals, is in Dr Whewell's eyes the finishing proof that the morality of happiness is absurd!

The pleasures of animals are elements of a very different order from the pleasures of man. We are bound to endeavour to augment the pleasures of man, not only because they are pleasures, but because they are human pleasures. We are bound to men by the universal tie of humanity, of human brotherhood. We have no such tie to animals.

This then is Dr Whewell's noble and disinterested ideal of virtue. Duties, according to him, are only duties to ourselves and our like.

We are to be *humane* to them, because we are *human*, not because we and they alike feel *animal* pleasures . . . The morality which depends upon the increase of pleasure alone, would make it our duty to increase the pleasure of pigs or of geese rather than that of men, if we were sure that the pleasures we could give them were greater than the pleasures of men . . . It is not only not an obvious, but to most persons not a tolerable doctrine, that we may sacrifice the happiness of men provided we can in that way produce an overplus of pleasure to cats, dogs and hogs.

It is 'to most persons' in the Slave States of America not a tolerable doctrine that we may sacrifice any portion of the happiness of white men for the sake of a greater amount of happiness to black men. It would have been intolerable five centuries ago 'to most persons' among the feudal nobility, to hear it asserted that the greatest pleasure or pain of a hundred serfs ought not to give way to the smallest of a nobleman. According to the standard of Dr Whewell, the slavemasters and the nobles were right. They too felt themselves 'bound' by a 'tie of brotherhood' to the white men and to the nobility, and felt no such tie to the negroes and serfs. And if a feeling on moral subjects is right because it is natural, their feeling was justifiable. Nothing is more natural to human beings, nor, up to a certain point in cultivation, more universal, than to estimate the pleasures and pains of others as deserving of regard exactly in proportion to their likeness to ourselves. These superstitions of selfishness had the characteristics by which Dr Whewell recognizes his moral rules; and his opinion on the rights of animals shows that in this case at least he is consistent. We are perfectly willing to stake the whole question on this one issue. Granted that any practice causes more pain to animals than it gives pleasure to man; is that practice moral or immoral? And if, exactly in proportion as human beings raise their heads out of the slough of selfishness, they do not with one voice answer 'immoral', let the morality of the principle of utility be for ever condemned.

There cannot be a fitter transition than this subject affords, from the Benthamic standard of ethics to that of Dr Whewell. It is not enough to object to the morality of utility. It is necessary also to show that there is another and a better morality. This is what Dr Whewell proposes to himself in his Introductory Lecture, and in the whole of his previous work, *Elements of Morality*. We shall now, therefore, proceed to examine Dr Whewell's achievements as the constructor of a scientific foundation for the theory of morals.

'The moral rule of human action,' Dr Whewell says, is that 'we must do what is right.' (*Lectures*.) Here, at all events, is a safe proposition; since to deny it would be a contradiction in terms. But what is meant by 'right'? According to Dr Whewell, 'what we must do'. This, he says, is the very definition of right.

The definition of *rightful*, or of the adjective *right*, is, I conceive, contained in the maxim which I have already quoted as proceeding from the general voice of mankind: namely this, that we must do what is right at whatever cost. That an action is right is a reason for doing it, which is paramount to all other reasons, and overweighs them all when they are on the contrary side. It is painful; but it is right: therefore we must do it. It is a loss; but it is right: therefore we must do it. It is unkind; but it is right: therefore we must do it. These are self-evident [he might have said identical] propositions. That a thing is right, is a *supreme* reason for doing it. *Right* implies this supreme, unconquerable reason; and does this especially and exclusively. No other word does imply such an irresistible cogency in its effect, except in so far as it involves the same notion. What we *ought* to do, what we *should* do, that we *must* do, though it bring pain and loss. But why Because it is *right*. The expressions all run together in their meaning. And this *supreme* rule, that we must do what is right, is also the *moral* rule of human action.

Right means that which we *must* do, and the rule of action is, that we must do what is right; that we must do that which we must do. This we will call vicious circle the first. But let us not press hardly on Dr Whewell at this stage; perhaps he only means that the foundation of morals is the conviction that there is *something* which we must do at all risks; and he admits that we have still to find what this something is. 'What *is* right; what it is that we ought to do, we must have some means of determining, in order to complete our moral scheme.'

Attempting then to pick out Dr Whewell's leading propositions, and exhibit them in connection, we find, first, that 'the supreme rule of human action, Rightness', ought to control the desires and affections, or otherwise that these are 'to be regulated so that they may be right'. This does not help towards showing what *is* right.

But secondly, we come to a 'condition which is obviously requisite'. In order that the desires and affections which relate to 'other men' may be right, 'they must conform to this primary and universal condition, that they do not violate the *rights* of others. The condition may not be sufficient, but it is necessary.'

This promises something. In tracing to its elements the idea of Right, the adjective, we are led to the prior, and it is to be presumed more elementary idea, of Rights, the substantive. But now, what are rights? And how came they to be rights?

Before answering these questions, Dr Whewell gives a classification of rights 'commonly recognized among men'. He says, they are of five sorts, 'those of person, property, family, state and contract'. But how do we discover that they are rights? And what is meant by calling them rights? Much to our surprise, Dr Whewell refers us, on both these points, to the law. And he asks, 'in what manner do we rise from mere legal rights to moral rightness?' and replies, 'we do so in virtue of this principle: that the supreme rule of man's actions must be a rule which has authority over the whole of man; over his intentions as well as his actions; over his affections, his desires, his habits, his thoughts, his wishes.' We must not only not violate the rights of others, but we must not desire to violate them. 'And thus we rise from legal obligation to moral duty; from legality to virtue; from blamelessness in the forum of man to innocence in the court of conscience.'

And this Dr Whewell actually gives as his scheme of morality. His rule of right is, to infringe no rights conferred by the law, and to cherish no dispositions which could make us desire such infringements! According to this, the early Christians, the religious reformers, the founders of all free governments, Clarkson, Wilberforce, and all enemies of the rights of slaveowners, must be classed among the wicked. If this is Dr Whewell's morality, it is the very Hobbism which he reprobates, and this in its worst sense. But though Dr Whewell says that this is his morality, he presently unsays it.

Our morality is not derived from the special commands of existing laws, but from the fact that laws exist, and from our classification of their subjects. Personal safety, property, contracts, family and civil relations, are everywhere the subjects of law, and are everywhere protected by law; therefore we judge that these things must be the subjects of morality, and must be reverently regarded by morality. But we are not thus bound to approve of all the special appointments with regard to those subjects, which may exist at a given time in the laws of a given country. On the contrary, we may condemn the laws as being contrary to morality. We cannot frame a morality without recognizing property, and property exists through law; but yet the law of property, in a particular country, may be at variance with that moral purpose for which, in our eyes, laws exist. Law is the foundation and necessary condition of justice; but yet laws may be unjust, and when unjust ought to be changed.

The practical enormities consequent on Dr Whewell's theory are thus got rid of; but when these are gone, there is nothing of the theory left. He undertook to explain how we may know what is right. It appeared at first that he was about to give a criterion, when he said that it is not right to violate legal rights. According to this, when we want to know what is right, we have to consult the law, and see what rights it recognizes. But now it seems that these rights may be contrary to right; and all we can be sure of is, that it is right there should be rights of some sort. And we learn that, after all, it is for a 'moral purpose' that in Dr Whewell's opinion 'laws exist'. So that while the meaning of *ought* is that we ought to respect rights, it is a previous condition that these rights must be such as *ought* to be respected. Morality must conform to law, but law must first conform to morality. This is vicious circle the second. Dr Whewell has broken out of the first; he has made, this time, a larger sweep; the curve he describes is wider, but it still returns into itself.

An adherent of 'dependent morality' would say that, instead of deriving right from rights, we must have a rule of right before it can be decided what ought to be rights; and that, both in law and in morals, the rights which ought to exist are those which for the general happiness it is expedient should exist. And Dr Whewell anticipates that some one may even do him what he thinks the injustice of supposing this to be his opinion. He introduces an objector as saying, 'that by making our morality begin from rights, we really do found it upon expediency, notwithstanding our condemnation of systems so founded. For, it may be said, rights such as property exist only because they are expedient.' Dr Whewell hastens to repel this imputation; and here is his theory. 'We reply as before, that rights are founded on the whole nature of man, in such a way that he cannot have a human existence without them. He is a moral being, and must have rights, *because morality cannot exist where rights are not.*' Was ever an unfortunate metaphysician driven into such a corner? We wanted to know what morality is, and Dr Whewell said that it is conforming to rights. We ask how he knows that there are rights, and he answers, because otherwise there could be no morality. This is vicious circle the third, and the most wonderful of the three. The Indians placed their elephant on the back of a tortoise, but they did not at the same time place the tortoise on the back of the elephant.

Dr Whewell has failed in what it was impossible to succeed in. Every attempt to dress up an appeal to intuition in the forms of reasoning, must break down in the same manner. The system must, from the conditions of the case, revolve in a circle. If morality is not to gravitate to any end, but to hang self-balanced in space, it is useless attempting to suspend one point of it upon another point. The fact of moral rules supposes a certain assemblage of ideas. It is to no purpose detaching these ideas one from another, and saying that one of them must exist because another does. Press the moralist a step farther, and he can only say that the other must exist because of the first. The house must have a centre because it has wings, and wings because it has a centre. But the question was about the whole house, and how it comes to exist. It would be much simpler to say plainly, that it exists because it exists. This is what Dr Whewell is in the end obliged to come to; and he would have saved himself a great deal of bad logic, if he had begun with it.*

So much as to the existence of moral rules: now as to what they are.

We do not rest our rules of action upon the tendency of actions to produce the happiness of others, or of mankind in general; because we cannot solve a problem so difficult as to determine which of two courses of action will produce the greatest amount of human happiness: and we see a simpler and far more satisfactory mode of deducing such rules; namely, by considering that there must be such rules; that they must be rules for man; for man living among men; and for the whole of man's being. Since we are thus led directly to moral rules, by the consideration of the internal condition of man's being, we cannot think it is wise to turn away from this method, and to try to determine such rules by reference to an obscure and unmanageable external condition, the amount of happiness produced.

If these were not Dr Whewell's own words, we should expect to be charged, as he charges Bentham, with caricature. This is

*In Dr Whewell's larger work, we find him resorting, after all, to an 'external object' as the ultimate ground for acknowledging any moral rules whatever. He there says, that 'the reason for doing what is absolutely right, is that it is the will of God, through whom the condition and destination of mankind are what they are.' (Elements of Morality, Vol. I.) In the Lectures, however, he admits that this renders nugatory the ascribing any moral attributes to God. 'If we make holiness, justice, and purity, the mere result of God's commands, we can no longer find any force in the declaration that God is holy, just, and pure; since the assertion then becomes merely an empty identical proposition.' We hope that this indicates a change of opinion since the publication of the earlier work.

given as a scientific statement of the proper mode of discovering what are the rules of morality! We are to 'deduce such rules' from four considerations. First, 'that there must be such rules'; a necessary preliminary, certainly. If we are to build a wall, it is because it has been previously decided that there must be a wall. But we must know what the wall is for; what end it is intended to serve; or we shall not know what sort of wall is required. What end are moral rules intended to serve? No end, according to Dr Whewell. They do not exist for the sake of an end. To have them is part of man's nature, like (it is Dr Whewell's own illustration) the circulation of the blood. It is now then to be inquired *what* rules are part of our nature. This is to be discovered from three things: that they must be 'rules for man; for man living among men; and for the whole of man's being'. This is only saying over again, in a greater number of words, what we want, not how we are to find it. First, they must be 'rules for man'; but we are warned not to suppose that this means for man's benefit; it only means that they are for man to obey. This leaves us exactly where we were before. Next, they are for 'man living among men', that is, for the conduct of man to men: but *how* is man to conduct himself to men? Thirdly, they are 'for the whole of man's being'; that is, according to Dr Whewell's explanation, they are for the regulation of our desires as well as of our actions; but what we wanted to know was, *how* we are to regulate our desires and our actions? Of the four propositions given as premises from which all moral rules are to be deduced, not one points to any difference between one kind of moral rules and another. Whether the rule is to love or to hate our neighbour, it will equally answer all Dr Whewell's conditions. These are the premises which are more 'simple and satisfactory' than such 'obscure and unmanageable' propositions, so utterly impossible to be assured of, as that some actions are favourable, and others injurious, to human happiness! Try a parallel case. Let it be required to find the principles of the art of navigation. Bentham says, we must look to an 'external end'; getting from place to place on the water. No, says Dr Whewell, there is a 'simpler and more satisfactory' mode, *viz*. to consider that there must be such an art; that it must be for a ship; for a ship at sea; and for all the parts of a ship. Would Dr Whewell prevail on any one to suppose that these considerations made it unnecessary to consider, with Bentham, what a ship is intended to do?

This account is all we get from Dr Whewell, in the *Lectures*, of the mode of discovering and recognizing the rules of morality. But perhaps he succeeds better in doing the thing, than in explaining how it ought to be done. At all events, having written two volumes of *Elements of Morality*, he must have performed this feat, either well or ill; he must have found a way of 'deducing moral rules'. We will now, therefore, dismiss Dr Whewell's generalities, and try to estimate his method, not by what he says about it, but by what we see him doing when he carries it into practice.

We turn, then, to his *Elements of Morality*, and to the third chapter of that work, which is entitled, 'Moral Rules exist necessarily'. And here we at once find something well calculated to surprise us. That moral rules must exist, was, it may be remembered, the first of Dr Whewell's four fundamental axioms; and has been presented hitherto as a law of human nature, requiring no proof. It must puzzle some of his pupils to find him here proving it; and still more, to find him proving it from utility.

In enumerating and describing, as we have done, certain desires as among the most powerful springs of human action, we have stated that man's life is scarcely tolerable if these desires are not in some degree gratified; that man cannot be at all satisfied without some security in such gratification; that without property, which gratifies one of these desires, man's free agency cannot exist; that without marriage, which gratifies another, there can be no peace, comfort, tranquillity, or order. And the same may be said of all those springs of actions which we enumerated as mental desires. Without some provision for the tranquil gratification of these desires, society is disturbed, unbalanced, painful. The gratification of such desires must be a part of the order of the society. There must be rules which direct the course and limits of such gratification. Such rules are necessary for the peace of society. [*Elements of Morality*, Vol. I.]

This is a very different mode of treating the subject from that which we observed in the *Lectures*. We are now among reasons: good or bad they may be, but still reasons. Moral rules are here spoken of as means to an end. We now hear of the peace and comfort of society; of making man's life tolerable; of the satisfaction and gratification of human beings; of preventing a disturbed and painful state of society. This is utility – this is pleasure and pain. When real reasons are wanted, the repudiated happiness principle is always the resource. It is true, this is soon followed by a recurrence to the old topics, of the necessity of rules 'for the action of man as man', and the impossibility to 'conceive man as man without conceiving him as subject to rules'. But any meaning it is possible to find in these phrases (which is not much) is all reflected from the utilitarian reasons given just before. Rules are necessary, because mankind would have no security for any of the things which they value, for anything which gives them pleasure or shields them from pain, unless they could rely on one another for doing, and in particular for abstaining from, certain acts. And it is true, that man could not be conceived 'as man', that is, with the average human intelligence, if he were unable to perceive so obvious a utility.

Almost all the *generalia* or moral philosophy prefixed to the *Elements* are in like manner derived from utility. For example: that the desires, until subjected to general rules, bring mankind into conflict and opposition; but that, when general rules are established, the feelings which gather round these 'are sources not of opposition, but of agreement'; that they 'tend to make men unanimous; and that such rules with regard to the affections and desires as tend to control the repulsive and confirm the attractive forces which operate in human society; such as tend to unite men, to establish concord, unanimity, sympathy, agree with that which is the character of moral rules'. (Vol. I.) This is Benthamism – even approaching to Fourierism.

And again, in attempting a classification and definition of virtues, and a parallel one of duties corresponding to them. The definitions of both the one and the other are deduced from utility. After classing virtues under the several heads of benevolence, justice, truth, purity and order, benevolence is defined as 'desire of the good of all men'; and in a wider sense, as the 'absence of all the affections which tend to separate men, and the aggregate of the affections which unite them'. (Vol. I.) Justice, as 'the desire that each person should have his own'. Truth is defined 'an agreement of the verbal expression with the thought', and is declared to be a duty because 'lying and deceit tend to separate and disunite men, and to make all actions implying mutual dependence, that is, all social action and social life, impossible'. Purity is defined 'the control of the appetites by the moral sentiments and the reason'. Order, as a conformity of our internal dispositions to the laws and to moral rules (why not rather to good laws, and good moral rules?). All these definitions, though very open to criticism in detail, are in principle utilitarian.* Though Dr Whewell will not recognize the promotion of happiness as the ultimate principle, he deduces his secondary principles from it, and supports his propositions by utilitarian reasons as far as they will go. He is chiefly distinguished from utilitarian moralists of the more superficial kind, by this, that he ekes out his appeal to utility with appeals to 'our idea of man as man'; and when reasons fail, or are not sufficiently convincing, then 'all men think', or 'we cannot help feeling', serves as a last resort, and closes the discussion.

Of this hybrid character is the ethics of Dr Whewell's *Elements of Morality*. And in this he resembles all other writers of the intuitive school of morals. They are none of them frankly and consistently intuitive. To use a happy expression of Bentham in a different case, they draw from a double fountain – utility and internal conviction; the tendencies of actions, and the feelings with which mankind regard them. This is not a matter of choice with these writers, but of necessity. It arises from the nature of the morality of internal conviction. Utility, as a standard, is capable of being carried out singly and consistently; a moralist can

*The enumeration of duties does not always follow accurately the definition of the corresponding virtues. For example, the definition of purity is one which suits temperance, 'the control of the appetites by the moral sentiments and the reason': but the scheme of duties set forth under this head is rather as if the definition had been 'the conformity of the appetites to the moral opinions and customs of the country'. It is remarkable that a writer who uses the word purity so much out of its common meaning as to make it synonymous with temperance, should charge Bentham (*Lectures*), because he employs the word in another of its acknowledged senses, with arbitrarily altering its signification. Bentham understands by the purity of a pleasure, its freedom from admixture of pain: as we speak of pure gold, pure water, pure truth, of things purely beneficial or purely mischievous: meaning, in each case, freedom from alloy with any other ingredient.

deduce from it his whole system of ethics, without calling to his assistance any foreign principle. It is not so with one who relies on moral intuition; for where will he find his moral intuitions? How many ethical propositions can be enumerated, of which the most reckless assertor will venture to affirm that they have the adhesion of all mankind? Dr Whewell declares unhesitatingly that the moral judgement of mankind, when it is unanimous, must be right. 'What are universally held as virtues, must be dispositions in conformity with this law: what are universally reckoned vices, must be wrong.' This is saying much, when we consider the worth, in other matters nearly allied to these, of what is complimentarily called the general opinion of mankind; when we remember what grovelling superstitions, what witchcraft, magic, astrology, what oracles, ghosts, what gods and demons scattered through all nature, were once universally believed in, and still are so by the majority of the human race. But where are these unanimously recognized vices and virtues to be found? Practices the most revolting to the moral feelings of some ages and nations do not incur the smallest censure from others; and it is doubtful whether there is a single virtue which is held to be a virtue by all nations, in the same sense, and with the same reservations. There are, indeed, some moralities of an utility so unmistakable, so obviously indispensable to the common purposes of life, that as general rules mankind could no more differ about them than about the multiplication table; but even here, there is the widest difference of sentiment about the exceptions. The universal voice of mankind, so often appealed to, is universal only in its discordance. What passes for it is merely the voice of the majority, or, failing that, of any large number having a strong feeling on the subject; especially if it be a feeling of which they cannot give any account, and which, as it is not consciously grounded on any reasons, is supposed to be better than reasons, and of higher authority. With Dr Whewell, a strong feeling, shared by most of those whom he thinks worth counting, is always an *ultima ratio* from which there is no appeal. He forgets that as much might have been pleaded, and in many cases might still be pleaded, in defence of the absurdest superstitions.

It seems to be tacitly supposed that however liable mankind

are to be wrong in their opinions, they are generally right in their feelings, and especially in their antipathies. On the contrary, there is nothing which it is more imperative that they should be required to justify by reasons. The antipathies of mankind are mostly derived from three sources. One of these is an impression, true or false, of utility. They dislike what is painful or dangerous, or what is apparently so. These antipathies, being grounded on the happiness principle, must be required to justify themselves by it. The second class of antipathies are against what they are taught, or imagine, to be displeasing to some visible or invisible power, capable of doing them harm, and whose wrath, once kindled, may be wreaked on those who tolerated, as well as on those who committed, the offence. The third kind of antipathies, often as strong as either of the others, are directed towards mere differences of opinion, or of taste. Any of the three, when nourished by education, and deriving confidence from mutual encouragement, assumes to common minds the character of a moral feeling. But to pretend that any such antipathy, were it ever so general, gives the smallest guarantee of its own justice and reasonableness, or has any claim to be binding on those who do not partake in the sentiment, is as irrational as to adduce the belief in ghosts or witches as a proof of their real existence. I am not bound to abstain from an action because another person dislikes it, however he may dignify his dislike with the name of disapprobation.

We cannot take leave of Dr Whewell's strictures on Bentham, without adverting to some observations made by him on Bentham's character as a jurist rather than as a moralist. In this capacity Dr Whewell does more justice to Bentham, than in the department of moral philosophy. But he finds fault with him for two things: first, for not sufficiently recognizing what Dr Whewell calls the historical element of legislation; and imagining 'that to a certain extent his schemes of law might be made independent of local conditions'. Dr Whewell admits it to be part of Bentham's doctrine, that different countries must to a certain extent have different laws; and is aware that he wrote an *Essay on the Influence of Time and Place in Matters of Legislation*; but thinks him wrong in maintaining that there should be a general plan, of which the details only should be modified by local circumstances; and contends, that different countries require different ground-plans of legislation.

There is in every national code of law a necessary and fundamental historical element; not a few supplementary provisions which may be added or adapted to the local circumstances after the great body of the code has been constructed: not a few touches of local colouring to be put in after the picture is almost painted: but an element which belongs to law from its origin, and penetrates to its roots: a part of the intimate structure; a cast in the original design. The national views of personal status; property, and the modes of acquisition; bargains, and the modes of concluding them; family, and its consequences; government, and its origin; these affect even the most universal aspects and divisions of penal offences; these affect still more every step of the expository process which the civil law applies to rights in defining penal offences. (*Lectures*)

What Dr Whewell designates by the obscure and misleading expression, 'an historical element', and accuses Bentham of paying too little regard to, is the existing opinions and feelings of the people. These may, without doubt, in some sense be called historical, as being partly the product of their previous history; but whatever attention is due to those opinions and feelings in legislation, is due to them not as matter of history, but as social forces in present being. Now Bentham, in common with all other rational persons, admitted that a legislator is obliged to have regard to the opinions and feelings of the people to be legislated for; but with this difference, that he did not look upon those opinions and feelings as affecting, in any great degree, what was desirable to be done, but only what could be done. Take one of Dr Whewell's instances, 'the national views of personal status'. The 'national views' may regard slavery as a legitimate condition of human beings, and Mr Livingston, in legislating for Louisiana, may have been obliged to recognize slavery as a fact, and to make provision for it, and for its consequences, in his code of laws; but he was bound to regard the equality of human beings as the foundation of his legislation, and the concession to the 'historical element' as a matter of temporary expediency; and while yielding to the necessity, to endeavour, by all the means in his power, to educate the nation into better things. And so of the other subjects mentioned by Dr Whewell – property, contracts, family and government. The fact that, in any of these matters, a people prefer some particular mode of legislation, on historical grounds – that is, because they have been long used to it – is no proof of any original adaptation in it to their nature of circumstances, and goes a very little way in recommendation of it as for their benefit now. But it may be a very important element in determining what the legislator can do, and still more, the manner in which he should do it: and in both these respects Bentham allowed it full weight. What he is at issue with Dr Whewell upon, is in deeming it right for the legislator to keep before his mind an ideal of what he would do if the people for whom he made laws were entirely devoid of prejudice or accidental prepossession: while Dr Whewell, by placing their prejudices and accidental prepossessions 'at the basis of the system', enjoins legislation not in simple recognition of existing popular feelings, but in obedience to them.

The other objection made by Dr Whewell to Bentham as a writer on legislation (for we omit the criticism on his classification of offences, as too much a matter of detail for the present discussion), is that he does not fully recognize 'the moral object of law'. Dr Whewell says, in phraseology which we considerably abridge, that law ought not only to preserve and gratify man, but to improve and teach him: not only to take care of him as an animal, but to raise him to a moral life. Punishment, therefore, he says, 'is to be, not merely a means of preventing suffering, but is also to be a moral lesson'. But Bentham, as Dr Whewell is presently forced to admit, says the same: and in fact carries this doctrine so far, as to maintain that legal punishment ought sometimes to be attached to acts for the mere purpose of stigmatizing them, and turning the popular sentiment against them. No one, more than Bentham, recognizes that most important, but most neglected, function of the legislator, the office of an instructor, both moral and intellectual. But he receives no credit for this from Dr Whewell, except that of being false to his principles; for Dr Whewell seems to reckon it an impertinence in anybody to recognize morality as a good, who thinks, as Bentham does, that it is a means to an end. If any one who believes that the moral sentiments should be guided by the happiness of mankind, proposes that moral sentiments, so guided, should be cultivated and fostered, Dr Whewell treats this as a deserting of utilitarian principles, and borrowing or stealing from his.

As an example of 'Bentham's attempt to exclude morality, as such, in his legislation', Dr Whewell refers to 'what he says respecting the laws of marriage, and especially in favour of a liberty of divorce by common consent'. As this is the only opportunity Dr Whewell gives his readers, of comparing his mode of discussing a specific moral question with Bentham's, we shall devote a few words to it.

Having quoted from Bentham the observation that a government which interdicts divorce 'takes upon itself to decide that it understands the interests of individuals better than they do themselves', Dr Whewell answers, that this is an objection to all laws: that in many other cases, 'government, both in its legislation and administration, does assume that it understands the interests of individuals, *and the public interest as affected by them*, better than they do themselves'. The words which we have put in italics, adroitly change the question. Government is entitled to assume that it will take better care than individuals of the public interest, but not better care of their own interest. It is one thing for the legislator to dictate to individuals what they shall do for their own advantage, and another thing to protect the interest of other persons who may be injuriously affected by their acts. Dr Whewell's own instances suffice: 'What is the meaning of restraints imposed for the sake of public health, cleanliness and comfort? Why are not individuals left to do what they like with reference to such matters? Plainly because carelessness, ignorance, indolence, would prevent their doing what is most for their own interest.' Say rather, would lead them to do what is contrary to the interest of other people. The proper object of sanitary laws is not to compel people to take care of their own health, but to prevent them from endangering that of others. To prescribe by law, what they should do for their own health alone, would by most people be justly regarded as something very like tyranny.

Dr Whewell continues:

But is Mr Bentham ready to apply consistently the principle which he

266

thus implies, that in such matters individuals are the best judges of their own interests? Will he allow divorce to take place whenever the two parties agree in desiring it? . . . Such a facility of divorce as this, leaves hardly any difference possible between marriage and concubinage. If a pair may separate when they please, why does the legislator take the trouble to recognize their living together?

Apply this to other cases. If a man can pay his tailor when he and his tailor choose, why does the law take the trouble to recognize them as debtor and creditor? Why recognize, as partners in business, as landlords and tenants, as servants and employers, people who are not tied to each other for life?

Dr Whewell finds what he thinks an inconsistency in Bentham's view of the subject. He thus describes Bentham's opinions.

Marriage for life is, he says, the most natural marriage: if there were no laws except the ordinary law of contracts, this would be the most ordinary arrangement. So far, good. But Mr Bentham, having carried his argument so far, does not go on with it. What conclusion are we to suppose him to intend? This arrangement would be very *general* without law, therefore the legislator should pass a law to make it *universal*? . . . No. The very next sentence is employed in showing the absurdity of making the engagement one from which the parties cannot liberate themselves by mutual consent. And there is no attempt to reduce these arguments, or their results, to a consistency.

Dr Whewell's ideas of inconsistency seem to be peculiar. Bentham, he says, is of opinion, that in the majority of cases it is best for the happiness of married persons that they should remain together. Is it so? (says Dr Whewell) – then why not force them to remain together, even when it would be best for their happiness to separate?

Try again parallel cases. In choosing a profession, a sensible person will fix on one in which he will find it agreeable to remain; therefore, it should not be lawful to change a profession once chosen. A landlord, when he has a good tenant, best consults his own interest by not changing him; therefore, all tenancy should be for life. Electors who have found a good representative will probably do wisely in re-electing him; therefore, members of Parliament should be irremovable.

Dr Whewell intended to show into what errors Bentham was led, by treating the question of marriage apart from 'moral grounds'. Yet part of his complaint is that Bentham does consider moral grounds, which, according to Dr Whewell, he has no right to do. If one married person maltreats the other to procure consent to a divorce:

> Bentham's decision is, that liberty should be allowed to the party maltreated and not to the other . . . Now to this decision I have nothing to object: but I must remark, that the view which makes it tolerable is, its being a decision on moral grounds, such as Mr Bentham would not willingly acknowledge. The man may not take advantage of his own wrong: *that* is a maxim which quite satisfies *us*. But Mr Bentham, who only regards wrong as harm, would, I think, find it difficult to satisfy the man that he was fairly used.

Mr Bentham would have found it difficult to conceive that any one attempting to criticize his philosophy could know so little of its elements. Dr Whewell wonders what the reason can be, on Bentham's principles, for not allowing a man to benefit by his own wrong. Did it never occur to him, that it is to take away from the man his inducement to commit the wrong?

Finally, Dr Whewell says, 'No good rule can be established on this subject without regarding the marriage union in a moral point of view; without assuming it as one great object of the law to elevate and purify men's idea of marriage; to lead them to look upon it as an entire union of interests and feelings, enjoyments and hopes, between the two parties.' We cannot agree in the doctrine that it should be an object of the law to 'lead men to look upon' marriage as being what it is not. Neither Bentham nor any one who thinks with him would deny that this entire union is the completest ideal of marriage; but it is bad philosophy to speak of a relation as if it always *was* the best thing that it possibly can be, and then infer that when it is notoriously not such, as in an immense majority of cases, and even when it is the extreme contrary, as in a considerable minority, it should nevertheless be treated exactly as if the fact corresponded with the theory. The liberty of divorce is contended for, because marriages are not what Dr Whewell says they should be looked upon as being;

because a choice made by an inexperienced person, and not allowed to be corrected, cannot, except by a happy accident, realize the conditions essential to this complete union.

We give these observations not as a discussion of the question, but of Dr Whewell's treatment of it; as part of the comparison which he invites his readers to institute between his method and that of Bentham. Were it our object to confirm the general character we have given of Dr Whewell's philosophy, by a survey in detail of the morality laid down by him, the two volumes of *Elements* afford abundant materials. We could show that Dr Whewell not only makes no improvement on the old moral doctrines, but attempts to set up afresh several of them which have been loosened or thrown down by the stream of human progress.

Thus we find him everywhere inculcating, as one of the most sacred duties, reverence for superiors, even when personally undeserving, and obedience to existing laws, even when bad. 'The laws of the state are to be observed even when they enact slavery.' 'The morality of the individual,' he says, 'depends on his not violating the law of his nation.' It is not even the spirit of the law, but the letter, to which obedience is due. The law, indeed, is accepted by Dr Whewell as the fountain of rights; of those rights which it is the primary moral duty not to infringe. And mere custom is of almost equal authority with express enactment. Even in a matter so personal as marriage, the usage and practice of the country is to be a paramount law. 'In some countries, the marriage of the child is a matter usually managed by the parents; in such cases, it is the child's duty to bring the affections, as far as possible, into harmony with the custom.' 'Reverence and affection' towards 'the constitution of each country', he holds as 'one of the duties of a citizen'.

Again, Dr Whewell affirms, with a directness not usually ventured on in these days by persons of his standing and importance, that to disbelieve either a providential government of the world, or revelation, is morally criminal; for that 'men are blameable in disbelieving truths after they have been promulgated, though they are ignorant without blame before the promulgation'. This is the very essence of religious intolerance, aggravated by the fact, that among the persons thus morally stigmatized are notoriously included many of the best men who ever lived. He goes still further, and lays down the principle of intolerance in its broad generality, saying, that 'the man who holds false opinions' is morally condemnable 'when he has had the means of knowing the truth'; that it is 'his duty to think rationally' (*i.e.* to think the same as Dr Whewell): that it is to no purpose his saying that he has 'done all he could to arrive at truth, since a man has never done *all he can* to arrive at truth'. If a man has never done all he can, neither has his judge done all he can; and the heretic may have more grounds for believing his opinion true, than the judge has for affirming it to be false. But the judge is on the side of received opinions, which, according to Dr Whewell's standard, makes all right.

It is not, however, our object to criticize Dr Whewell as a teacher of the details of morality. Our design goes no farther than to illustrate his controversy with Bentham respecting its first principle. It may, perhaps, be thought that Dr Whewell's arguments against the philosophy of utility are too feeble to require so long a refutation. But feeble arguments easily pass for convincing, when they are on the same side as the prevailing sentiment; and readers in general are so little acquainted with that or any other system of moral philosophy, that they take the word of anybody, especially an author in repute, who professes to inform them what it is; and suppose that a doctrine must be indeed absurd, to which mere truisms are offered as sufficient reply. It was, therefore, not unimportant to show, by a minute examination, that Dr Whewell has misunderstood and misrepresented the philosophy of utility, and that his attempts to refute it, and to construct a moral philosophy without it, have been equally failures.

Editor's Note

Utilitarianism appeared as three articles in *Fraser's Magazine* from October to December 1861. The text printed here is that of the 1871 edition, the last to appear in Mill's lifetime.

Utilitarianism

BY J. S. MILL

Chapter I
General Remarks

There are few circumstances among those which make up the present condition of human knowledge, more unlike what might have been expected, or more significant of the backward state in which speculation on the most important subjects still lingers, than the little progress which has been made in the decision of the controversy respecting the criterion of right and wrong. From the dawn of philosophy, the question concerning the *summum bonum*, or, what is the same thing, concerning the foundation of morality, has been accounted the main problem in speculative thought, has occupied the most gifted intellects, and divided them into sects and schools, carrying on a vigorous warfare against one another. And after more than two thousand years the same discussions continue, philosophers are still ranged under the same contending banners, and neither thinkers nor mankind at large seem nearer to being unanimous on the subject, than when the youth Socrates listened to the old Protagoras, and asserted (if Plato's dialogue be grounded on a real conversation) the theory of utilitarianism against the popular morality of the so-called sophist.

It is true that similar confusion and uncertainty, and in some cases similar discordance, exist respecting the first principles of all the sciences, not excepting that which is deemed the most certain of them, mathematics; without much impairing, generally indeed without impairing at all, the trustworthiness of the conclusions of those sciences. An apparent anomaly, the explanation of which is, that the detailed doctrines of a science are not usually deduced from, nor depend for their evidence upon, what are called its first principles. Were it not so, there would be no science more precarious, or whose conclusions were more insufficiently made out, than algebra; which derives none of its certainty from what are commonly taught to learners as its elements, since these, as laid down by some of its most eminent teachers, are as full of fictions as English law, and of mysteries as theology. The truths which are ultimately accepted as the first principles of a science, are really the last results of metaphysical analysis, practised on the elementary notions with which the science is conversant; and their relation to the science is not that of foundations to an edifice, but of roots to a tree, which may perform their office equally well though they be never dug down to and exposed to light. But though in science the particular truths precede the general theory, the contrary might be expected to be the case with a practical art, such as morals or legislation. All action is for the sake of some end, and rules of action, it seems natural to suppose, must take their whole character and colour from the end to which they are subservient. When we engage in a pursuit, a clear and precise conception of what we are pursuing would seem to be the first thing we need, instead of the last we are to look forward to. A test of right and wrong must be the means, one would think, of ascertaining what is right or wrong, and not a consequence of having already ascertained it.

The difficulty is not avoided by having recourse to the popular theory of a natural faculty, a sense or instinct, informing us of right and wrong. For – besides that the existence of such a moral instinct is itself one of the matters in dispute – those believers in it who have any pretensions to philosophy, have been obliged to abandon the idea that it discerns what is right or wrong in the particular case in hand, as our other senses discern the sight or sound actually present. Our moral faculty, according to all those of its interpreters who are entitled to the name of thinkers, supplies us only with the general principles of moral judgements; it is a branch of our reason, not of our sensitive faculty; and must be looked to for the abstract doctrines of morality, not for perception of it in the concrete. The intuitive, no less than what may be termed the inductive, school of ethics, insists on the necessity of general laws. They both agree that the morality of an individual action is not a question of direct perception, but of the application of a law to an individual case. They recognize also, to a great extent, the same moral laws; but differ as to their evidence, and the source from which they derive their authority. According to the one opinion, the principles of morals are evident *a priori*, requiring nothing to command assent, except that the meaning of the terms be understood. According to the other doctrine, right and wrong, as well as truth and falsehood, are questions of observation and experience. But both hold equally that morality must be deduced from principles; and the intuitive school affirm as strongly as the inductive, that there is a science of morals. Yet they seldom attempt to make out a list of the *a priori* principles which are to serve as the premises of the science; still more rarely do they make any effort to reduce those various principles to one first principle, or common ground of obligation. They either assume the ordinary precepts of morals as of *a priori* authority, or they lay down as the common groundwork of those maxims, some generality much less obviously authoritative than the maxims themselves, and which has never succeeded in gaining popular acceptance. Yet to support their pretensions there ought either to be some one fundamental principle or law, at the root of all morality, or if there be several, there should be a determinate order of precedence among them; and the one principle, or the rule for deciding between the various principles when they conflict, ought to be self-evident.

To inquire how far the bad effects of this deficiency have been mitigated in practice, or to what extent the moral beliefs of mankind have been vitiated or made uncertain by the absence of any distinct recognition of an ultimate standard, would imply a complete survey and criticism of past and present ethical doctrine. It would, however, be easy to show that whatever steadiness or consistency these moral beliefs have attained, has been mainly due to the tacit influence of a standard not recognized. Although the non-existence of an acknowledged first principle has made ethics not so much a guide as a consecration of men's actual sentiments, still, as men's sentiments, both of favour and of aversion, are greatly influenced by what they suppose to be the effects of things upon their happiness, the principle of utility, or as

Bentham latterly called it, the greatest-happiness principle, has had a large share in forming the moral doctrines even of those who most scornfully reject its authority. Nor is there any school of thought which refuses to admit that the influence of actions on happiness is a most material and even predominant consideration in many of the details of morals, however unwilling to acknowledge it as the fundamental principle of morality, and the source of moral obligation. I might go much further, and say that to all those *a priori* moralists who deem it necessary to argue at all, utilitarian arguments are indispensable. It is not my present purpose to criticize these thinkers; but I cannot help referring, for illustration, to a systematic treatise by one of the most illustrious of them, the *Metaphysics of Ethics*, by Kant. This remarkable man, whose system of thought will long remain one of the landmarks in the history of philosophical speculation, does, in the treatise in question, lay down a universal first principle as the origin and ground of moral obligation; it is this: 'So act, that the rule on which thou actest would admit of being adopted as a law by all rational beings.' But when he begins to deduce from this precept any of the actual duties of morality, he fails, almost grotesquely, to show that there would be any contradiction, any logical (not to say physical) impossibility, in the adoption by all rational beings of the most outrageously immoral rules of conduct. All he shows is that the *consequences* of their universal adoption would be such as no one would choose to incur.

On the present occasion, I shall, without further discussion of the other theories, attempt to contribute something towards the understanding and appreciation of the Utilitarian or Happiness theory, and towards such proof as it is susceptible of. It is evident that this cannot be proof in the ordinary and popular meaning of the term. Questions of ultimate ends are not amenable to direct proof. Whatever can be proved to be good, must be so by being shown to be a means to something admitted to be good without proof. The medical art is proved to be good, by its conducing to health; but how is it possible to prove that health is good? The art of music is good, for the reason, among others, that it produces pleasure; but what proof is it possible to give that pleasure is good? If, then, it is asserted that there is a comprehensive formula, including all things which are in themselves good, and that what ever else is good, is not so as an end, but as a mean, the formula may be accepted or rejected, but is not a subject of what is commonly understood by proof. We are not, however, to infer that its acceptance or rejection must depend on blind impulse, or arbitrary choice. There is a larger meaning of the word proof, in which this question is as amenable to it as any other of the disputed questions of philosophy. The subject is within the cognizance of the rational faculty; and neither does that faculty deal with it solely in the way of intuition. Considerations may be presented capable of determining the intellect either to give or withhold its assent to the doctrine; and this is equivalent to proof.

We shall examine presently of what nature are these considerations; in what manner they apply to the case, and what rational grounds, therefore, can be given for accepting or rejecting the utilitarian formula. But it is a preliminary condition of rational acceptance or rejection, that the formula should be correctly understood. I believe that the very imperfect notion ordinarily formed of its meaning, is the chief obstacle which impedes its reception; and that could it be cleared, even from only the grosser misconceptions, the question would be greatly simplified, and a large proportion of its difficulties removed. Before, therefore, I attempt to enter into the philosophical grounds which can be given for assenting to the utilitarian standard, I shall offer some illustrations of the doctrine itself; with the view of showing more clearly what it is, distinguishing it from what it is not, and disposing of such of the practical objections to it as either originate in, or are closely connected with, mistaken interpretations of its meaning. Having thus prepared the ground, I shall afterwards endeavour to throw such light as I can upon the question, considered as one of philosophical theory.

Chapter II
What Utilitarianism Is

A passing remark is all that needs be given to the ignorant blunder of supposing that those who stand up for utility as the test of right and wrong, use the term in that restricted and merely colloquial sense in which utility is opposed to pleasure. An apology is due to the philosophical opponents of utilitarianism, for even the momentary appearance of confounding them with anyone capable of so absurd a misconception; which is the more extraordinary, inasmuch as the contrary accusation, of referring everything to pleasure, and that too in its grossest form, is another of the common charges against utilitarianism: and, as has been pointedly remarked by an able writer, the same sort of persons, and often the very same persons, denounce the theory 'as impracticably dry when the word utility precedes the word pleasure, and as too practicably voluptuous when the word pleasure precedes the word utility'. Those who know anything about the matter are aware that every writer, from Epicurus to Bentham, who maintained the theory of utility, meant by it, not something to be contradistinguished from pleasure, but pleasure itself, together with exemption from pain; and instead of opposing the useful to the agreeable or the ornamental, have always declared that the useful means these, among other things. Yet the common herd, including the herd of writers, not only in newspapers and periodicals, but in books of weight and pretension, are perpetually falling into this shallow mistake. Having caught up the word utilitarian, while knowing nothing whatever about it but its sound, they habitually express by it the rejection, or the neglect, of pleasure in some of its forms; of beauty, of ornament, or of amusement. Nor is the term thus ignorantly misapplied solely in disparagement, but occasionally in compliment; as though it implied superiority to frivolity and the mere pleasures of the moment. And this perverted use is the only one in which the word is popularly known, and the one from which the new generation are acquiring their sole notion of its meaning. Those who introduced the word, but who had for many years discontinued it as a distinctive appellation, may well feel themselves called upon to resume it, if by doing so they can hope to contribute anything towards rescuing it from this utter degredation.*

*The author of this essay has reason for believing himself to be the first person who brought the word utilitarian into use. He did not invent it, but adopted it from a passing expression in Mr Galt's *Annals of the Parish*. After using it as a designation for several years, he and others abandoned it from a growing dislike

The creed which accepts as the foundation of morals, Utility, or the Greatest Happiness Principle, holds that actions are right in proportion as they tend to promote happiness, wrong as they tend to produce the reverse of happiness. By happiness is intended pleasure, and the absence of pain; by unhappiness, pain, and the privation of pleasure. To give a clear view of the moral standard set up by the theory, much more requires to be said; in particular, what things it includes in the ideas of pain and pleasure; and to what extent this is left an open question. But these supplementary explanations do not affect the theory of life on which this theory of morality is grounded – namely, that pleasure, and freedom from pain, are the only things desirable as ends; and that all desirable things (which are as numerous in the utilitarian as in any other scheme) are desirable either for the pleasure inherent in themselves, or as means to the promotion of pleasure and the prevention of pain.

Now, such a theory of life excites in many minds, and among them in some of the most estimable in feeling and purpose, inveterate dislike. To suppose that life has (as they express it) no higher end than pleasure – no better and nobler object of desire and pursuit – they designate as utterly mean and grovelling; as a doctrine worthy only of swine, to whom the followers of Epicurus were, at a very early period, contemptuously likened; and modern holders of the doctrine are occasionally made the subject of equally polite comparisons by its German, French and English assailants.

When thus attacked, the Epicureans have always answered, that it is not they, but their accusers, who represent human nature in a degrading light; since the accusation supposes human beings to be capable of no pleasures except those of which swine are capable. If this supposition were true, the charge could not be gainsaid, but would then be no longer an imputation; for if the sources of pleasure were precisely the same to human beings and

to anything resembling a badge or watchword of sectarian distinction. But as a name for one single opinion, not a set of opinions – to denote the recognition of utility as a standard, not any particular way of applying it – the term supplies a want in the language, and offers, in many cases, a convenient mode of avoiding tiresome circumlocution.

to swine, the rule of life which is good enough for the one would be good enough for the other. The comparison of the Epicurean life to that of beasts is felt as degrading, precisely because a beast's pleasures do not satisfy a human being's conceptions of happiness. Human beings have faculties more elevated than the animal appetites, and when once made conscious of them, do not regard anything as happiness which does not include their gratification. I do not, indeed, consider the Epicureans to have been by any means faultless in drawing out their scheme of consequences from the utilitarian principle. To do this in any sufficient manner, many Stoic as well as Christian elements require to be included. But there is no known Epicurean theory of life which does not assign to the pleasures of the intellect, of the feelings and imagination, and of the moral sentiments, a much higher value as pleasures than to those of mere sensation. It must be admitted, however, that utilitarian writers in general have placed the superiority of mental over bodily pleasures chiefly in the greater permanency, safety, uncostliness, etc., of the former – that is, in their circumstantial advantages rather than in their intrinsic nature. And on all these points utilitarians have fully proved their case; but they might have taken the other, and, as it may be called, higher ground, with entire consistency. It is quite compatible with the principle of utility to recognize the fact, that some *kinds* of pleasure are more desirable and more valuable than others. It would be absurd that while, in estimating all other things, quality is considered as well as quantity, the estimation of pleasures should be supposed to depend on quantity alone.

If I am asked, what I mean by difference of quality in pleasures, or what makes one pleasure more valuable than another, merely as a pleasure, except its being greater in amount, there is but one possible answer. Of two pleasures, if there be one to which all or almost all who have experience of both give a decided preference, irrespective of any feeling of moral obligation to prefer it, that is the more desirable pleasure. If one of the two is, by those who are competently acquainted with both, placed so far above the other that they prefer it, even though knowing it to be attended with a greater amount of discontent, and would not resign it for any quantity of the other pleasure which their nature is capable of, we are justified in ascribing to the preferred enjoyment a superiority in quality, so far outweighing quantity as to render it, in comparison, of small account.

Now it is an unquestionable fact that those who are equally acquainted with, and equally capable of appreciating and enjoying, both, do give a most marked preference to the manner of existence which employs their higher faculties. Few human creatures would consent to be changed into any of the lower animals, for a promise of the fullest allowance of a beast's pleasures; no intelligent human being would consent to be a fool, no instructed person would be an ignoramus, no person of feeling and conscience would be selfish and base, even though they should be persuaded that the fool, the dunce, or the rascal is better satisfied with his lot than they are with theirs. They would not resign what they possess more than he, for the most complete satisfaction of all the desires which they have in common with him. If they ever fancy they would, it is only in cases of unhappiness so extreme, that to escape from it they would exchange their lot for almost any other, however undesirable in their own eyes. A being of higher faculties requires more to make him happy, is capable probably of more acute suffering, and is certainly accessible to it at more points, than one of an inferior type; but in spite of these liabilities, he can never really wish to sink into what he feels to be a lower grade of existence. We may give what explanation we please of this unwillingness; we may attribute it to pride, a name which is given indiscriminately to some of the most and to some of the least estimable feelings of which mankind are capable; we may refer it to the love of liberty and personal independence, an appeal to which was with the Stoics one of the most effective means for the inculcation of it; to the love of power, or to the love of excitement, both of which do really enter into and contribute to it: but its most appropriate appellation is a sense of dignity, which all human beings possess in one form or other, and in some, though by no means in exact, proportion to their higher faculties, and which is so essential a part of the happiness of those in whom it is strong, that nothing which conflicts with it could be, otherwise than momentarily, an object of desire to them. Whoever supposes that this preference takes place at a sacrifice of happiness – that the superior being, in anything like equal circumstances, is not happier than the inferior – confounds the two very different ideas, of happiness, and content. It is indisputable that the being whose capacities of enjoyment are low, has the greatest chance of having them fully satisfied; and a highly endowed being will always feel that any happiness which he can look for, as the world is constituted, is imperfect. But he can learn to bear its imperfections, if they are at all bearable; and they will not make him envy the being who is indeed unconscious of the imperfections, but only because he feels not at all the good which those imperfections qualify. It is better to be a human being dissatisfied than a pig satisfied; better to be Socrates dissatisfied than a fool satisfied. And if the fool, or the pig, is of a different opinion, it is because they only know their own side of the question. The other party to the comparison knows both sides.

It may be objected, that many who are capable of the higher pleasures, occasionally, under the influence of temptation, postpone them to the lower. But this is quite compatible with a full appreciation of the intrinsic superiority of the higher. Men often, from infirmity of character, make their election for the nearer good, though they know it to be the less valuable; and this no less when the choice is between two bodily pleasures, than when it is between bodily and mental. They pursue sensual indulgences to the injury of health, though perfectly aware that health is the greater good. It may be further objected, that many who begin with youthful enthusiasm for everything noble, as they advance in years sink into indolence and selfishness. But I do not believe that those who undergo this very common change, voluntarily choose the lower description of pleasures in preference to the higher. I believe that before they devote themselves exclusively to the one, they have already become incapable of the other. Capacity for the nobler feelings is in most natures a very tender plant, easily killed, not only by hostile influences, but by mere want of sustenance; and in the majority of young persons it speedily dies away if the occupations to which their position in life has devoted them, and the society into which it has thrown them, are not favourable to keeping that higher capacity in exercise. Men lose their high aspirations as they lose their intellectual tastes, because they have not time or opportunity for indulging them; and they addict themselves to inferior pleasures, not because they deliberately prefer them, but because they are either the only ones to which they have access, or the only ones which they are any longer capable of enjoying. It may be questioned whether any one who has remained equally susceptible to both classes of pleasures, ever knowingly and calmly preferred the lower; though many, in all ages, have broken down in an ineffectual attempt to combine both.

From this verdict of the only competent judges, I apprehend there can be no appeal. On a question which is the best worth having of two pleasures, or which of two modes of existence is the most grateful to the feelings, apart from its moral attributes and from its consequences, the judgement of those who are qualified by knowledge of both, or, if they differ, that of the majority among them, must be admitted as final. And there needs be the less hesitation to accept this judgement respecting the quality of pleasures, since there is no other tribunal to be referred to even on the question of quantity. What means are there of determining which is the acutest of two pains, or the intensest of two pleasurable sensations, except the general suffrage of those who are familiar with both? Neither pains nor pleasures are homogeneous, and pain is always heterogeneous with pleasure. What is there to decide whether a particular pleasure is worth purchasing at the cost of a particular pain, except the feelings and judgement of the experienced? When, therefore, those feelings and judgement declare the pleasures derived from the higher faculties to be preferable *in kind*, apart from the question of intensity, to those of which the animal nature, disjoined from the higher faculties, is susceptible, they are entitled on this subject to the same regard.

I have dwelt on this point, as being a necessary part of a perfectly just conception of Utility or Happiness, considered as the directive rule of human conduct. But it is by no means an indispensable condition to the acceptance of the utilitarian standard; for that standard is not the agent's own greatest happiness, but the greatest amount of happiness altogether; and if it may possibly be doubted whether a noble character is always the happier for its nobleness, there can be no doubt that it makes other people happier, and that the world in general is immensely a gainer by it. Utilitarianism, therefore, could only attain its end by the general cultivation of nobleness of character, even if each individual were only benefited by the nobleness of others, and his own, so far as happiness is concerned, were a sheer deduction from the benefit. But the bare enunciation of such an absurdity as this last, renders refutation superfluous.

According to the Greatest Happiness Principle, as above explained, the ultimate end, with reference to and for the sake of which all other things are desirable (whether we are considering our own good or that of other people), is an existence exempt as far as possible from pain, and as rich as possible in enjoyments, both in point of quantity and quality; the test of quality, and the rule for measuring it against quantity, being the preference felt by those who, in their opportunities of experience, to which must be added their habits of self-consciousness and self-observation, are best furnished with the means of comparison. This, being, according to the utilitarian opinion, the end of human action, is necessarily also the standard of morality; which may accordingly be defined, the rules and precepts for human conduct, by the observance of which an existence such as has been described might be, to the greatest extent possible, secured to all mankind; and not to them only, but, so far as the nature of things admits, to the whole sentient creation.

Against this doctrine, however, arises another class of objectors, who say that happiness, in any form, cannot be the rational purpose of human life and action; because, in the first place, it is unattainable: and they contemptuously ask, What right hast thou to be happy? A question which Mr Carlyle clenches by the addition, What right, a short time ago, hadst thou even *to be*? Next, they say, that men can do *without* happiness; that all noble human beings have felt this, and could not have become noble but by learning the lesson of *Entsagen*, or renunciation; which lesson, thoroughly learnt and submitted to, they affirm to be the beginning and necessary condition of all virtue.

The first of these objections would go to the root of the matter were it well founded; for if no happiness is to be had at all by human beings, the attainment of it cannot be the end of morality, or of any rational conduct. Though, even in that case, something might still be said for the utilitarian theory; since utility includes not solely the pursuit of happiness, but the prevention or mitigation of unhappiness; and if the former aim be chimerical, there will be all the greater scope and more imperative need for the latter, so long at least as mankind think fit to live, and do not take refuge in the simultaneous act of suicide recommended under certain conditions by Novalis. When, however, it is thus positively asserted to be impossible that human life should be happy, the assertion, if not something like a verbal quibble, is at least an exaggeration. If by happiness be meant a continuity of highly pleasurable excitement, it is evident enough that this is impossible. A state of exalted pleasure lasts only moments, or in some cases, and with some intermissions, hours or days, and is the occasional brilliant flash of enjoyment, not its permanent and steady flame. Of this the philosophers who have taught that happiness is the end of life were as fully aware as those who taunt them. The happiness which they meant was not a life of rapture; but moments of such, in an existence made up of few and transitory pains, many and various pleasures, with a decided predominance of the active over the passive, and having as the foundation of the whole, not to expect more from life than it is capable of bestowing. A life thus composed, to those who have been fortunate enough to obtain it, has always appeared worthy of the name of happiness. And such an existence is even now the lot of many, during some considerable portion of their lives. The present wretched education, and wretched social arrangements, are the only real hindrance to its being attainable by almost all.

The objectors perhaps may doubt whether human beings, if taught to consider happiness as the end of life, would be satisfied with such a moderate share of it. But great numbers of mankind have been satisfied with much less. The main constituents of a satisfied life appear to be two, either of which by itself is often found sufficient for the purpose: tranquillity, and excitement. With much tranquillity, many find that they can be content with very little pleasure: with much excitement, many can reconcile themselves to a considerable quantity of pain. There is assuredly no inherent impossibility in enabling even the mass of mankind to unite both; since the two are so far from being incompatible that they are in natural alliance, the prolongation of either being a preparation for, and exciting a wish for, the other. It is only those in whom indolence amounts to a vice, that do not desire excitement after an interval of repose; it is only those in whom the need of excitement is a disease, that feel the tranquillity which follows excitement dull and insipid, instead of pleasurable in direct proportion to the excitement which preceded it. When people who are tolerably fortunate in their outward lot do not find in life sufficient enjoyment to make it valuable to them, the cause generally is caring for nobody but themselves. To those who have neither public nor private affections, the excitements of life are much curtailed, and in any case dwindle in value as the time approaches when all selfish interests must be terminated by death: while those who leave after them objects of personal affection, and especially those who have also cultivated a fellow feeling with the collective interests of mankind, retain as lively an interest in life on the eve of death as in the vigour of youth and health. Next to selfishness, the principal cause which makes life unsatisfactory, is want of mental cultivation. A cultivated mind – I do not mean that of a philosopher, but any mind to which the fountains of knowledge have been opened, and which has been taught, in any tolerable degree, to exercise its faculties – finds sources of inexhaustible interest in all that surrounds it; in the objects of nature, the achievements of art, the imaginations of poetry, the incidents of history, the ways of mankind past and present, and their prospects in the future. It is possible, indeed, to become indifferent to all this, and that too without having exhausted a thousandth part of it; but only when one has had from the beginning no moral or human interest in these things, and has sought in them only the gratification of curiosity.

Now there is absolutely no reason in the nature of things why an amount of mental culture sufficient to give an intelligent interest in these objects of contemplation, should not be the inheritance of every one born in a civilized country. As little is there an inherent necessity that any human being should be a selfish egotist, devoid of every feeling or care but those which centre in his own miserable individuality. Something far superior to this is sufficiently common even now, to give ample earnest of what the human species may be made. Genuine private affections, and a sincere interest in the public good, are possible, though in unequal degrees, to every rightly brought-up human being. In a world in which there is so much to interest, so much to enjoy, and so much also to correct and improve, every one who has this moderate amount of moral and intellectual requisites is capable of an existence which may be called enviable; and unless such a person, through bad laws, or subjection to the will of others, is denied the liberty to use the sources of happiness within his reach, he will not fail to find this enviable existence, if he escape the positive evils of life, the great sources of physical and mental suffering – such as indigence, disease, and the unkindness, worthlessness or premature loss of objects of affection. The main stress of the problem lies, therefore, in the contest with these calamities, from which it is a rare good fortune entirely to escape; which, as things now are, cannot be obviated, and often cannot be in any material degree mitigated. Yet no one whose opinion deserves a moment's consideration can doubt that most of the great positive evils of the world are in themselves removable, and will, if human affairs continue to improve, be in the end reduced within narrow limits. Poverty, in any sense implying suffering, may be completely extinguished by the wisdom of society, combined with the good sense and providence of individuals. Even that most intractable of enemies, disease, may be indefinitely reduced in dimensions by good physical and moral education, and proper control of noxious influences; while the progress of science holds out a promise for the future of still more direct conquests over this detestable foe. And every advance in that direction relieves us from some, not only of the chances which cut short our own lives, but, what concerns us still more, which deprive us of those in whom our happiness is wrapped up. As for vicissitudes of fortune, and other disappointments connected with worldly circumstances, these are principally the effect either of gross imprudence, of ill-regulated desires, or of bad or imperfect social institutions. All the grand sources, in short, of human suffering are in a great degree, many of them almost entirely, conquerable by human care and effort; and though their removal is grievously slow – though a long succession of generations will perish in the breach before the conquest is completed, and this world becomes all that, if will and knowledge were not wanting, it might easily be made – yet every mind sufficiently intelligent and generous to bear a part, however small and unconspicuous, in the endeavour, will draw a noble enjoyment from the contest itself, which he would not for any bribe in the form of selfish indulgence consent to be without.

And this leads to the true estimation of what is said by the objectors concerning the possibility, and the obligation, of learning to do without happiness. Unquestionably it is possible to do without happiness; it is done involuntarily by nineteen twentieths of mankind, even in those parts of our present world which are least deep in barbarism; and it often has to be done voluntarily by the hero or the martyr, for the sake of something which he prizes more than his individual happiness. But this something, what is it, unless the happiness of others, or some of the requisites of happiness? It is noble to be capable of resigning entirely one's own portion of happiness, or chances of it: but, after all, this self-sacrifice must be for some end; it is not its own end; and if we are told that its end is not happiness, but virtue, which is better than happiness, I ask, would the sacrifice be made if the hero or martyr did not believe that it would earn for others immunity from similar sacrifices? Would it be made, if he thought that his renunciation of happiness for himself would produce no fruit for any of his fellow creatures, but to make their lot like his, and place them also in the condition of persons who have renounced happiness? All honour to those who can abnegate for themselves the personal enjoyment of life, when by such renunciation they contribute worthily to increase the amount of happiness in the world; but he who does it, or professes to do it, for any other purpose, is no more deserving of admiration than the ascetic mounted on his pillar. He may be an inspiriting proof of what men *can* do, but assuredly not an example of what they *should*.

Though it is only in a very imperfect state of the world's arrangements that any one can best serve the happiness of others by the absolute sacrifice of his own, yet so long as the world is in that imperfect state, I fully acknowledge that the readiness to make such a sacrifice is the highest virtue which can be found in man. I will add, that in this condition of the world, paradoxical as the assertion may be, the conscious ability to do without happiness gives the best prospect of realizing such happiness as is attainable. For nothing except that consciousness can raise a person above the chances of life, by making him feel that, let fate and fortune do their worst, they have not power to subdue him: which, once felt, frees him from excess of anxiety concerning the evils of life, and enables him, like many a Stoic in the worst times of the Roman Empire, to cultivate in tranquillity the sources of satisfaction accessible to him, without concerning himself about the uncertainty of their duration, any more than about their inevitable end.

Meanwhile, let utilitarians never cease to claim the morality of self-devotion as a possession which belongs by as good a right to them, as either to the Stoic or to the Transcendentalist. The utilitarian morality does recognize in human beings the power of sacrificing their own greatest good for the good of others. It only refuses to admit that the sacrifice is itself a good. A sacrifice which does not increase, or tend to increase, the sum total of happiness, it considers as wasted. The only self-renunciation which it applauds, is devotion to the happiness, or to some of the means of happiness, of others; either of mankind collectively, or of individuals within the limits imposed by the collective interests of mankind.

I must again repeat, what the assailants of utilitarianism seldom have the justice to acknowledge, that the happiness which forms the utilitarian standard of what is right in conduct, is not the agent's own happiness, but that of all concerned. As between his own happiness and that of others, utilitarianism requires him to be as strictly impartial as a disinterested and benevolent spectator. In the golden rule of Jesus of Nazareth, we read the complete spirit of the ethics of utility. To do as one would be done by, and to love one's neighbour as oneself, constitute the ideal perfection of utilitarian morality. As the means of making the nearest approach to this ideal, utility would enjoin, first, that laws and social arrangements should place the happiness, or (as speaking practically it may be called) the interest, of every individual, as nearly as possible in harmony with the interest of the whole; and secondly, that education and opinion, which have so vast a power over human character, should so use that power as to establish in the mind of every individual an indissoluble association between his own happiness and the good of the whole; especially between his own happiness and the practice of such modes of conduct, negative and positive, as regard for the universal happiness prescribes: so that not only he may be unable to conceive the possibility of happiness to himself, consistently with conduct opposed to the general good, but also that a direct impulse to promote the general good may be in every individual one of the habitual motives of action, and the sentiments connected therewith may fill a large and prominent place in every human being's sentient existence. If the impugners of the utilitarian morality represented it to their own minds in this its true character, I know not what recommendation possessed by any other morality they could possibly affirm to be wanting to it: what more beautiful or more exalted developments of human nature any other ethical system can be supposed to foster, or what springs of action, not accessible to the utilitarian, such systems rely on for giving effect to their mandates.

The objectors to utilitarianism cannot always be charged with representing it in a discreditable light. On the contrary, those among them who entertain anything like a just idea of its disinterested character, sometimes find fault with its standard as being too high for humanity. They say it is exacting too much to require that people shall always act from the inducement of promoting the general interests of society. But this is to mistake the very meaning of a standard of morals, and to confound the rule of action with the motive of it. It is the business of ethics to tell us what are our duties, or by what test we may know them; but no system of ethics requires that the sole motive of all we do shall be a feeling of duty; on the contrary, ninety-nine hundredths of all our actions are done from other motives, and rightly so done, if the rule of duty does not condemn them. It is the more unjust to utiliarianism that this particular misapprehension should be made a ground of objection to it, inasmuch as utilitarian moralists have gone beyond almost all others in affirming that the motive has nothing to do with the morality of the action, though much with the worth of the agent. He who saves a fellow creature from drowning does what is morally right, whether his motive be duty, or the hope of being paid for his trouble: he who betrays the friend that trusts him, is guilty of a crime, even if his object be to serve another friend to whom he is under greater obligations.* But to speak only of actions done from the motive of duty, and in direct obedience to principle: it is a misapprehension of the utilitarian mode of thought, to conceive it as implying that people should fix their minds upon so wide a generality as the world, or society at large. The great majority of good actions are intended, not for the benefit of the world, but for that of individuals, of which the good of the world is made up; and the

*An opponent, whose intellectual and moral fairness it is a pleasure to acknowledge (the Rev. J. Llewellyn Davies), has objected to this passage, saying, 'Surely the rightness or wrongness of saving a man from drowning does depend very much upon the motive with which it is done. Suppose that a tyrant, when his enemy jumped into the sea to escape from him, saved him from drowning simply in order that he might inflict upon him more exquisite tortures, would it tend to clearness to speak of that rescue as "a morally right action?" Or suppose again, according to one of the stock illustrations of ethical inquiries, that a man betrayed a trust received from a friend, because the discharge of it would fatally injure that friend himself or some one belonging to him, would utilitarianism compel one to call the betrayal "a crime" as much as if it had been done from the meanest motive?'

I submit, that he who saves another from drowning in order to kill him by torture afterwards, does not differ only in motive from him who does the same thing from duty or benevolence; the act itself is different. The rescue of the man is, in the case supposed, only the necessary first step of an act far more atrocious than leaving him to drown would have been. Had Mr Davies said, 'The rightness or wrongness of saving a man from drowning does depend very much' – not upon the motive, but – 'upon the *intention*,' no utilitarian would have differed from him. Mr Davies, by an oversight too common not to be quite venial, has in this case confounded the very different ideas of Motive and Intention. There is no point which utilitarian thinkers (and Bentham pre-eminently) have taken more pains to illustrate than this. The morality of the action depends entirely upon the intention – that is, upon what the agent *wills to do*. But the motive, that is, the feeling which makes him will so to do, when it makes no difference in the act, makes none in the morality: though it makes a great difference in our moral estimation of the agent, especially if it indicates a good or a bad habitual *disposition* – a bent of character from which useful, or from which hurtful actions are likely to arise.

thoughts of the most virtuous man need not on these occasions travel beyond the particular persons concerned, except so far as is necessary to assure himself that in benefiting them he is not violating the rights – that is, the legitimate and authorized expectations – of any one else. The multiplication of happiness is, according to the utilitarian ethics, the object of virtue: the occasions on which any person (except one in a thousand) has it in his power to do this on an extended scale, in other words, to be a public benefactor, are but exceptional; and on these occasions alone is he called on to consider public utility; in every other case, private utility, the interest or happiness of some few persons, is all he has to attend to. Those alone the influence of whose actions extends to society in general, need concern themselves habitually about so large an object. In the case of abstinences indeed – of things which people forbear to do, from moral considerations, though the consequences in the particular case might be beneficial – it would be unworthy of an intelligent agent not to be consciously aware that the action is of a class which, if practised generally, would be generally injurious, and that this is the ground of the obligation to abstain from it. The amount of regard for the public interest implied in this recognition, is no greater than is demanded by every system of morals; for they all enjoin to abstain from whatever is manifestly pernicious to society.

The same considerations dispose of another reproach against the doctrine of utility, founded on a still grosser misconception of the purpose of a standard of morality, and of the very meaning of the words right and wrong. It is often affirmed that utilitarianism renders men cold and unsympathizing; that it chills their moral feelings towards individuals; that it makes them regard only the dry and hard consideration of the consequences of actions, not taking into their moral estimate the qualities from which those actions emanate. If the assertion means that they do not allow their judgement respecting the rightness or wrongness of an action to be influenced by their opinion of the qualities of the person who does it, this is a complaint not against utilitarianism, but against having any standard of morality at all; for certainly no known ethical standard decides an action to be good or bad because it is done by a good or a bad man, still less because done by an amiable, a brave, or a benevolent man, or the contrary. These considerations are relevant, not to the estimation of actions, but of persons; and there is nothing in the utilitarian theory inconsistent with the fact that there are other things which interest us in persons besides the rightness and wrongness of their actions. The Stoics, indeed, with the paradoxical misuse of language which was part of their system, and by which they strove to raise themselves above all concern about anything but virtue, were fond of saying that he who has that has everything; that he, and only he, is rich, is beautiful, is a king. But no claim of this description is made for the virtuous man by the utilitarian doctrine. Utilitarians are quite aware that there are other desirable possessions and qualities besides virtue, and are perfectly willing to allow to all of them their full worth. They are also aware that a right action does not necessarily indicate a virtuous character, and that actions which are blameable often proceed from qualities entitled to praise. When this is apparent in any particular case, it modifies their estimation, not certainly of the act, but of the agent. I grant that they are, notwithstanding, of opinion, that in the long run the best proof of a good character is good actions; and resolutely refuse to consider any mental disposition as good, of which the predominant tendency is to produce bad conduct. This makes them unpopular with many people; but it is an unpopularity which they must share with every one who regards the distinction between right and wrong in a serious light; and the reproach is not one which a conscientious utilitarian need be anxious to repel.

If no more be meant by the objection than that many utilitarians look on the morality of actions, as measured by the utilitarian standard, with too exclusive a regard, and do not lay sufficient stress upon the other beauties of character which go towards making a human being lovable or admirable, this may be admitted. Utilitarians who have cultivated their moral feelings, but not their sympathies nor their artistic perceptions, do fall into this mistake; and so do all other moralists under the same conditions. What can be said in excuse for other moralists is equally available for them, namely, that if there is to be any error, it is better that it should be on that side. As a matter of fact, we may affirm that among utilitarians as among adherents of other systems, there is every imaginable degree of rigidity and of laxity in the application of their standard: some are even puritanically rigorous, while others are as indulgent as can possibly be desired by sinner or by sentimentalist. But on the whole, a doctrine which brings prominently forward the interest that mankind have in the repression and prevention of conduct which violates the moral law, is likely to be inferior to no other in turning the sanctions of opinion against such violations. It is true, the question, What does violate the moral law? is one on which those who recognize different standards of morality are likely now and then to differ. But difference of opinion on moral questions was not first introduced into the world by utilitarianism, while that doctrine does supply, if not always an easy, at all events a tangible and intelligible mode of deciding such differences.

It may not be superfluous to notice a few more of the common misapprehensions of utilitarian ethics, even those which are so obvious and gross that it might appear impossible for any person of candour and intelligence to fall into them: since persons, even of considerable mental endowments, often give themselves so little trouble to understand the bearings of any opinion against which they entertain a prejudice, and men are in general so little conscious of this voluntary ignorance as a defect, that the vulgarest misunderstandings of ethical doctrines are continually met with in the deliberate writings of persons of the greatest pretensions both to high principle and to philosophy. We not uncommonly hear the doctrine of utility inveighed against as a *godless* doctrine. If it be necessary to say anything at all against so mere an assumption, we may say that the question depends upon what idea we have formed of the moral character of the Deity. If it be a true belief that God desires, above all things, the happiness of his creatures, and that this was his purpose in their creation, utility is not only not a godless doctrine, but more profoundly religious than any other. If it be meant that utilitarianism does not recognize the revealed will of God as the supreme law of morals, I answer that a utilitarian who believes in the perfect goodness and wisdom of God necessarily believes that whatever God has thought fit to reveal on the subject of morals, must fulfil the requirements of utility in a supreme degree. But others besides utilitarians have been of opinion that the Christian revelation was intended, and is fitted, to inform the hearts and minds of mankind with a spirit which should enable them to find for themselves what is right, and incline them to do it when found, rather than to tell them, except in a very general way, what it is: and that we need a doctrine of ethics, carefully followed out, to *interpret* to us the will of God. Whether this opinion is correct or not, it is superfluous here to discuss; since whatever aid religion, either natural or revealed, can afford to ethical investigation, is as open to the utilitarian moralist as to any other. He can use it as the testimony of God to the usefulness or hurtfulness of any given course of action, by as good a right as others can use it for the indication of a transcendental law, having no connection with usefulness or with happiness.

Again, Utility is often summarily stigmatized as an immoral doctrine by giving it the name of Expediency, and taking advantage of the popular use of that term to contrast it with Principle. But the Expedient, in the sense in which it is opposed to the Right, generally means that which is expedient for the particular interest of the agent himself; as when a minister sacrifices the interest of his country to keep himself in place. When it means anything better than this, it means that which is expedient for some immediate object, some temporary purpose, but which violates a rule whose observance is expedient in a much higher degree. The Expedient, in this sense, instead of being the same thing with the useful, is a branch of the hurtful. Thus, it would often be expedient, for the purpose of getting over some momentary embarrassment, or attaining some object immediately useful to ourselves or others, to tell a lie. But inasmuch as the cultivation in ourselves of a sensitive feeling on the subject of veracity is one of the most useful, and the enfeeblement of that feeling one of the most hurtful, things to which our conduct can be instrumental; and inasmuch as any, even unintentional, deviation from truth does that much towards weakening the trustworthiness of human assertion, which is not only the principal support of all present social well-being, but the insufficiency of which does more than any one thing that can be named to keep back civilization, virtue, everything on which human happiness on the largest scale depends; we feel that the violation, for a present advantage, of a rule of such transcendent expediency, is not expedient, and that he who, for the sake of a convenience to himself or to some other individual, does what depends on him to deprive mankind of the good, and inflict upon them the evil, involved in the greater or less reliance which they can place in each other's word, acts the part of one of their worst enemies. Yet that even this rule, sacred as it is, admits of possible exceptions, is acknowledged by all moralists; the chief of which is when the withholding of some fact (as of information from a malefactor, or of bad news from a person dangerously ill) would preserve some one (especially a person other than oneself) from great and unmerited evil, and when the withholding can only be effected by denial. But in order that the exception may not extend itself beyond the need, and may have the least possible effect in weakening reliance on veracity, it ought to be recognized, and, if possible, its limits defined; and if the principle of utility is good for anything, it must be good for weighing these conflicting utilities against one another, and marking out the region within which one or the other preponderates.

Again, defenders of utility often find themselves called upon to reply to such objections as this – that there is not time, previous to action, for calculating and weighing the effects of any line of conduct on the general happiness. This is exactly as if any one were to say that it is impossible to guide our conduct by Christianity, because there is not time, on every occasion on which anything has to be done, to read through the Old and New Testaments. The answer to the objection is, that there has been ample time, namely, the whole past duration of the human species. During all that time mankind have been learning by experience the tendencies of actions; on which experience all the prudence, as well as all the morality of life, is dependent. People talk as if the commencement of this course of experience had hitherto been put off, and as if, at the moment when some man feels tempted to meddle with the property or life of another, he had to begin considering for the first time whether murder and theft are injurious to human happiness. Even then I do not think that he would find the question very puzzling; but, at all events, the matter is now done to his hand. It is truly a whimsical supposition that if mankind were agreed in considering utility to be the test of morality, they would remain without any agreement as to what *is* useful, and would take no measures for having their notions on the subject taught to the young, and enforced by law and opinion. There is no difficulty in proving any ethical standard whatever to work ill, if we suppose universal idiocy to be conjoined with it; but on any hypothesis short of that, mankind must by this time have acquired positive beliefs as to the effects of some actions on their happiness; and the beliefs which have thus come down are the rules of morality for the multitude, and for the philosopher until he has succeeded in finding better. That philosophers might easily do this, even now, on many subjects; that the received code of ethics is by no means of divine right; and that mankind have still much to learn as to the effects of actions on the general happiness, I admit, or rather, earnestly maintain. The corollaries from the principle of utility, like the precepts of every practical art, admit of indefinite improvement, and, in a progressive state of human mind, their improvement is perpetually going on. But to consider the rules of morality as improvable, is one thing; to pass over the intermediate generalizations entirely, and endeavour to test each individual action directly by the first principle, is another. It is a strange notion that the acknowledgement of a first principle is inconsistent with the admission of secondary ones. To inform a traveller respecting the place of his ultimate destination, is not to forbid the use of landmarks and direction-posts on the way. The proposition that happiness is the end and aim of morality, does not mean that no road ought to be laid down to that goal, or that persons going thither should not be advised to take one direction rather than another. Men really ought to leave off talking a kind of nonsense on this subject, which they would neither talk nor listen to on other matters of practical concernment. Nobody argues that the art of navigation is not founded on astronomy, because sailors cannot wait to calculate the Nautical Almanack. Being rational creatures, they go to sea with it ready calculated; and all rational creatures go out upon the sea of life with their minds made up on the common questions of right and wrong, as well as on many of the far more difficult questions of wise and foolish. And this, as long as foresight is a human quality, it is to be presumed they will continue to do. Whatever we adopt as the fundamental principle of morality, we require subordinate principles to apply it by: the impossibility of doing without them, being common to all systems, can afford no argument against any one in particular: but gravely to argue as if no such secondary principles could be had, and as if mankind had remained till now, and always must remain, without drawing any general conclusions from the experience of human life, is as high a pitch, I think, as absurdity has ever reached in philosophical controversy.

The remainder of the stock arguments against utilitarianism mostly consist in laying to its charge the common infirmities of human nature, and the general difficulties which embarrass conscientious persons in shaping their course through life. We are told that a utilitarian will be apt to make his own particular case an exception to moral rules, and, when under temptation, will see a utility in the breach of a rule, greater than he will see in its observance. But is utility the only creed which is able to furnish us with excuses for evil doing, and means of cheating our own conscience? They are afforded in abundance by all doctrines which recognize as a fact in morals the existence of conflicting considerations; which all doctrines do, that have been believed by sane persons. It is not the fault of any creed, but of the complicated nature of human affairs, that rules of conduct cannot be so framed as to require no exceptions, and that hardly any kind of action can safely be laid down as either always obligatory or always condemnable. There is no ethical creed which does not temper the rigidity of its laws, by giving a certain latitude, under the moral responsibility of the agent, for accommodation to peculiarities of circumstances; and under every creed, at the opening thus made, self-deception and dishonest casuistry get in. There exists no moral system under which there do not arise unequivocal cases of conflicting obligation. These are the real difficulties, the knotty points both in the theory of ethics, and in the conscientious guidance of personal conduct. They are overcome practically with greater or with less success according to the intellect and virtue of the individual; but it can hardly be pretended that anyone will be the less qualified for dealing with them, from possessing an ultimate standard to which conflicting rights and duties can be referred. If utility is the ultimate source of moral obligations, utility may be invoked to decide between them when their demands are incompatible. Though the application of the standard may be difficult, it is better than none at all: while in other systems, the moral laws all claiming independent authority, there is no common umpire entitled to interfere between them; their claims to precedence one over another rest on little better than sophistry, and unless determined, as they generally are, by the unacknowledged influence of considerations of utility, afford a free scope for the action of personal desires and partialities. We must remember that only in these cases of conflict between secondary principles is it requisite that first principles should be appealed to. There is no case of moral obligation in which some secondary principle is not involved; and if only one, there can seldom be any real doubt which one it is in the mind of any person by whom the principle itself is recognized.

Chapter III
Of the Ultimate Sanction
of the Principle of Utility

The question is often asked, and properly so, in regard to any supposed moral standard – What is its sanction? what are the motives to obey it? or more specifically, what is the source of its obligation? whence does it derive its binding force? It is a necessary part of moral philosophy to provide the answer to this question; which, though frequently assuming the shape of an objection to the utilitarian morality, as if it had some special applicability to that above others, really arises in regard to all standards. It arises, in fact, whenever a person is called on to *adopt* a standard, or refer morality to any basis on which he has not been accustomed to rest it. For the customary morality, that which education and opinion have consecrated, is the only one which presents itself to the mind with the feeling of being *in itself* obligatory; and when a person is asked to believe that this morality *derives* its obligation from some general principle round which custom has not thrown the same halo, the assertion is to him a paradox; the supposed corollaries seem to have a more binding force than the original theorem; the superstructure seems to stand better without, than with, what is represented as its foundation. He says to himself, I feel that I am bound not to rob or murder, betray or deceive; but why am I bound to promote the general happiness? If my own happiness lies in something else, why may I not give that the preference?

If the view adopted by the utilitarian philosophy of the nature of the moral sense be correct, this difficulty will always present itself, until the influences which form moral character have taken the same hold of the principle which they have taken of some of the consequences – until, by the improvement of education, the feeling of unity with our fellow creatures shall be (what it cannot be doubted that Christ intended it to be) as deeply rooted in our character, and to our own consciousness as completely a part of our nature, as the horror of crime is in an ordinarily well brought-up young person. In the mean time, however, the difficulty has no peculiar application to the doctrine of utility, but is inherent in every attempt to analyse morality and reduce it to principles; which, unless the principle is already in men's minds invested with as much sacredness as any of its applications, always seems to divest them of a part of their sanctity.

The principle of utility either has, or there is no reason why it might not have, all the sanctions which belong to any other system of morals. Those sanctions are either external or internal. Of the external sanctions it is not necessary to speak at any length. They are, the hope of favour and the fear of displeasure from our fellow creatures or from the Ruler of the Universe, along with whatever we may have of sympathy or affection for them, or of love and awe of Him, inclining us to do his will independently of selfish consequences. There is evidently no reason why all these motives for observance should not attach themselves to the utilitarian morality, as completely and as powerfully as to any other. Indeed, those of them which refer to our fellow creatures are sure to do so, in proportion to the amount of general intelligence; for whether there be any other ground of moral obligation than the general happiness or not, men do desire happiness; and however imperfect may be their own practice, they desire and commend all conduct in others towards themselves, by which they think their happiness is promoted. With regard to the religious motive, if men believe, as most profess to do, in the goodness of God, those who think that conduciveness to the general happiness is the essence, or even only the criterion, of good, must necessarily believe that it is also that which God approves. The whole force therefore of external reward and punishment, whether physical or moral, and whether proceeding from God or from our fellow men, together with all that the capacities of human nature admit, of disinterested devotion to either, become available to enforce the utilitarian morality, in proportion as that morality is recognized; and the more powerfully, the more the appliances of education and general cultivation are bent to the purpose.

So far as to external sanctions. The internal sanction of duty, whatever our standard of duty may be, is one and the same – a feeling in our own mind; a pain, more or less intense, attendant on violation of duty, which in properly cultivated moral natures rises, in the more serious cases, into shrinking from it as an impossibility. This feeling, when disinterested, and connecting itself with the pure idea of duty, and not with some particular form of it, or with any of the merely accessory circumstances, is the essence of Conscience; though in that complex phenomenon as it actually exists, the simple fact is in general all encrusted over with collateral associations, derived from sympathy, from love, and still more from fear; from all the forms of religious feeling; from the recollections of childhood and of all our past life; from self-esteem, desire of the esteem of others, and occasionally even self-abasement. This extreme complication is, I apprehend, the origin of the sort of mystical character which, by a tendency of the human mind of which there are many other examples, is apt to be attributed to the idea of moral obligation, and which leads people to believe that the idea cannot possibly attach itself to any other objects than those which, by a supposed mysterious law, are found in our present experience to excite it. Its binding force, however, consists in the existence of a mass of feeling which must be broken through in order to do what violates our standard of right, and which, if we do nevertheless violate that standard, will probably have to be encountered afterwards in the form of remorse. Whatever theory we have of the nature or origin of conscience, that is what essentially constitutes it.

The ultimate sanction, therefore, of all morality (external motives apart) being a subjective feeling in our own minds, I see nothing embarrassing to those whose standard is utility, in the question, what is the sanction of that particular standard? We may answer, the same as of all other moral standards – the conscientious feelings of mankind. Undoubtedly this sanction has no binding efficacy on those who do not possess the feelings it appeals to; but neither will these persons be more obedient to any other moral principle than to the utilitarian one. On them morality of any kind has no hold but through the external sanctions. Meanwhile the feelings exist, a fact in human nature, the reality of which, and the great power with which they are capable of acting on those in whom they have been duly cultivated, are proved by experience. No reason has ever been shown why they may not be cultivated to as great intensity in connection with the utilitarian, as with any other rule of morals.

There is, I am aware, a disposition to believe that a person who sees in moral obligation a transcendental fact, an objective reality belonging to the province of 'Things in themselves', is likely to be more obedient to it than one who believes it to be entirely subjective, having its seat in human consciousness only. But whatever a person's opinion may be on this point of ontology, the force he is really urged by is his own subjective feeling, and is exactly measured by its strength. No one's belief that duty is an objective reality is stronger than the belief that God is so; yet the belief in God, apart from the expectation of actual reward and punishment, only operates on conduct through, and in proportion to, the subjective religious feeling. The sanction, so far as it is disinterested, is always in the mind itself; and the notion therefore of the transcendental moralists must be, that this sanction will not exist *in* the mind unless it is believed to have its root out of the mind; and that if a person is able to say to himself, This which is restraining me, and which is called my conscience, is only a feeling in my own mind, he may possibly draw the conclusion that when the feeling ceases the obligation ceases, and that if he find the feeling inconvenient, he may disregard it, and endeavour to get rid of it. But is this danger confined to the utilitarian morality? Does the belief that moral obligation has its seat outside the mind make the feeling of it too strong to be got rid of? The fact is so far otherwise, that all moralists admit and lament the ease with which, in the generality of minds, conscience can be silenced or stifled. The question, Need I obey my conscience? is quite as often put to themselves by persons who never heard of the principle of utility, as by its adherents. Those whose conscientious feelings are so weak as to allow of their asking this question, if they answer it affirmatively, will not do so because they believe in the transcendental theory, but because of the external sanctions.

It is not necessary, for the present purpose, to decide whether the feeling of duty is innate or implanted. Assuming it to be innate, it is an open question to what objects it naturally attaches itself; for the philosophic supporters of that theory are now agreed that the intuitive perception is of principles of morality, and not of the details. If there be anything innate in the matter, I see no reason why the feeling which is innate should not be that of regard to the pleasures and pains of others. If there is any principle of morals which is intuitively obligatory, I should say it must be that. If so, the intuitive ethics would coincide with the utilitarian, and there would be no further quarrel between them. Even as it is, the intuitive moralists, though they believe that there are other intuitive moral obligations, do already believe this to be one; for they unanimously hold that a large *portion* of morality turns upon the consideration due to the interests of our fellow creatures. Therefore, if the belief in the transcendental origin of moral obligation gives any additional efficacy to the internal sanction, it appears to me that the utilitarian principle has already the benefit of it.

On the other hand, if, as is my own belief, the moral feelings are not innate, but acquired, they are not for that reason the less natural. It is natural to man to speak, to reason, to build cities, to cultivate the ground, though these are acquired faculties. The moral feelings are not indeed a part of our nature, in the sense of being in any perceptible degree present in all of us; but this, unhappily, is a fact admitted by those who believe the most strenuously in their transcendental origin. Like the other acquired capacities above referred to, the moral faculty, if not a part of our nature, is a natural outgrowth from it; capable, like them in a certain small degree, of springing up spontaneously; and susceptible of being brought by cultivation to a high degree of development. Unhappily it is also susceptible, by a sufficient use of the external sanctions and of the force of early impressions, of being cultivated in almost any direction: so that there is hardly anything so absurd or so mischievous that it may not, by means of these influences, be made to act on the human mind with all the authority of conscience. To doubt that the same potency might be given by the same means to the principle of utility, even if it had no foundation in human nature, would be flying in the face of all experience.

But moral associations which are wholly of artificial creation, when intellectual culture goes on, yield by degrees to the dissolving force of analysis: and if the feeling of duty, when associated with utility, would appear equally arbitrary, if there were no leading department of our nature, no powerful class of sentiments, with which that association would harmonize, which would make us feel it congenial, and incline us not only to foster it in others (for which we have abundant interested motives), but also to cherish it in ourselves, if there were not, in short, a natural basis of sentiment for utilitarian morality, it might well happen that this association also, even after it had been implanted by education, might be analysed away.

But there *is* this basis of powerful natural sentiment; and this it is which, when once the general happiness is recognized as the ethical standard, will constitute the strength of the utilitarian morality. This firm foundation is that of the social feelings of mankind; the desire to be in unity with our fellow creatures, which is already a powerful principle in human nature, and happily one of those which tend to become stronger, even without express inculcation, from the influences of advancing civilization.

The social state is at once so natural, so necessary, and so habitual to man, that, except in some unusual circumstances or by an effort of voluntary abstraction, he never conceives himself otherwise than as a member of a body; and this association is riveted more and more, as mankind are further removed from the state of savage independence. Any condition, therefore, which is essential to a state of society, becomes more and more an inseparable part of every person's conception of the state of things which he is born into, and which is the destiny of a human being. Now, society between human beings, except in the relation of master and slave, is manifestly impossible on any other footing than that the interests of all are to be consulted. Society between equals can only exist on the understanding that the interests of all are to be regarded equally. And since in all states of civilization, every person, except an absolute monarch, has equals, every one is obliged to live on these terms with somebody; and in every age some advance is made towards a state in which it will be impossible to live permanently on other terms with anybody. In this way people grow up unable to conceive as possible to them a state of total disregard of other people's interests. They are under a necessity of conceiving themselves as at least abstaining from all the grosser injuries, and (if only for their own protection) living in a state of constant protest against them. They are also familiar with the fact of co-operating with others, and proposing to themselves a collective, not an individual, interest, as the aim (at least for the time being) of their actions. So long as they are co-operating, their ends are identified with those of others; there is at least a temporary feeling that the interests of others are their own interests. Not only does all strengthening of social ties, and all healthy growth of society, give to each individual a stronger personal interest in practically consulting the welfare of others; it also leads him to identify his *feelings* more and more with their good, or at least with an ever greater degree of practical consideration for it. He comes, as though instinctively, to be conscious of himself as a being who *of course* pays regard to others. The good of others becomes to him a thing naturally and necessarily to be attended to, like any of the physical conditions of our existence. Now, whatever amount of this feeling a person has, he is urged by the strongest motives both of interest and of sympathy to demonstrate it, and to the utmost of his power encourage it in others; and even if he has none of it himself, he is as greatly interested as anyone else that others should have it. Consequently, the smallest germs of the feeling are laid hold of and nourished by the contagion of sympathy and the influences of education; and a complete web of corroborative association is woven round it, by the powerful agency of the external sanctions. This mode of conceiving ourselves and human life, as civilization goes on, is felt to be more and more natural. Every step in political improvement renders it more so, by removing the sources of opposition of interest, and levelling those inequalities of legal privilege between individuals or classes, owing to which there are large portions of mankind whose happiness it is still practicable to disregard. In an improving state of the human mind, the influences are constantly on the increase, which tend to generate in each individual a feeling of unity with all the rest; which feeling, if perfect, would make him never think of, or desire, any beneficial condition for himself, in the benefits of which they are not included. If we now suppose this feeling of unity to be taught as a religion, and the whole force of education, of institutions, and of opinion, directed, as it once was in the case of religion, to make every person grow up from infancy surrounded on all sides both by the profession and by the practice of it, I think that no one, who can realize this conception, will feel any misgiving about the sufficiency of the ultimate sanction for the Happiness morality. To any ethical student who finds the realization difficult, I recommend, as a means of facilitating it, the second of M. Comte's two principal works, the *Système de Politique Positive*. I entertain the strongest objections to the system of politics and morals set forth in that treatise; but I think it has superabundantly shown the possibility of giving to the service of humanity, even without the aid of belief in a Providence, both the psychical power and the social efficacy of a religion; making it take hold of human life, and colour all thought, feeling and action in a manner of which the greatest ascendancy ever exercised by any religion may be but a type and foretaste; and of which the danger is, not that it should be insufficient, but that it should be so excessive as to interfere unduly with human freedom and individuality.

Neither is it necessary to the feeling which constitutes the binding force of the utilitarian morality on those who recognize it, to wait for those social influences which would make its obligation felt by mankind at large. In the comparatively early state of human advancement in which we now live, a person cannot indeed feel that entireness of sympathy with all others, which would make any real discordance in the general direction of their conduct in life impossible; but already a person in whom the social feeling is at all developed, cannot bring himself to think of the rest of his fellow creatures as struggling rivals with him for the means of happiness, whom he must desire to see defeated in their object in order that he may succeed in his. The deeply rooted conception which every individual even now has of himself as a social being, tends to make him feel it one of his natural wants that there should be harmony between his feelings and aims and those of his fellow creatures. If differences of opinion and of mental culture make it impossible for him to share many of their actual feelings – perhaps make him denounce and defy those feelings – he still needs to be conscious that his real aim and theirs do not conflict; that he is not opposing himself to what they really wish for, namely, their own good, but is, on the contrary, promoting it. This feeling in most individuals is much inferior in strength to their selfish feelings, and is often wanting altogether. But to those who have it, it possesses all the characters of a natural feeling. It does not present itself to their minds as a superstition of education, or a law despotically imposed by the power of society, but as an attribute which it would not be well for them to be without. This conviction is the ultimate sanction of the greatest-happiness morality. This it is which makes any mind, of well developed feelings, work with, and not against, the outward motives to care for others, afforded by what I have called the external sanctions; and when those sanctions are wanting, or act in an opposite direction, constitutes in itself a powerful internal binding force, in proportion to the sensitiveness and thoughtfulness of the character; since few but those whose mind is a moral blank, could bear to lay out their course of life on the plan of paying no regard to others except so far as their own private interest compels.

Chapter IV
Of What Sort of Proof the
Principle of Utility Is Susceptible

It has already been remarked, that questions of ultimate ends do not admit of proof, in the ordinary acceptation of the term. To be incapable of proof by reasoning is common to all first principles; to the first premises of our knowledge, as well as to those of our conduct. But the former, being matters of fact, may be the subject of a direct appeal to the faculties which judge of fact – namely, our senses and our internal consciousness. Can an appeal be made to the same faculties on questions of practical ends? Or by what other faculty is cognizance taken of them?

Questions about ends are, in other words, questions about what things are desirable. The utilitarian doctrine is that happiness is desirable, and the only thing desirable, as an end; all other things being only desirable as means to that end. What ought to be required of this doctrine – what conditions is it requisite that the doctrine should fulfil – to make good its claim to be believed?

The only proof capable of being given that an object is visible, is that people actually see it. The only proof that a sound is audible, is that people hear it: and so of the other sources of our experience. In like manner, I apprehend, the sole evidence it is possible to produce that anything is desirable, is that people do actually desire it. If the end which the utilitarian doctrine proposes to itself were not, in theory and in practice, acknowledged to be an end, nothing could ever convince any person that it was so. No reason can be given why the general happiness is desirable, except that each person, so far as he believes it to be attainable, desires his own happiness. This, however, being a fact, we have not only all the proof which the case admits of, but all which it is possible to require, that happiness is a good: that each person's happiness is a good to that person, and the general happiness, therefore, a good to the aggregate of all persons. Happiness has made out its title as *one* of the ends of conduct, and consequently one of the criteria of morality.

But it has not, by this alone, proved itself to be the sole criterion. To do that, it would seem, by the same rule, necessary to show, not only that people desire happiness, but that they never desire anything else. Now it is palpable that they do desire things which, in common language, are decidedly distinguished from happiness. They desire, for example, virtue and the absence of vice, no less really than pleasure and the absence of pain. The desire of virtue is not as universal, but it is as authentic a fact, as the desire of happiness. And hence the opponents of the utilitarian standard deem that they have a right to infer that there are other ends of human action besides happiness, and that happiness is not the standard of approbation and disapprobation.

But does the utilitarian doctrine deny that people desire virtue, or maintain that virtue is not a thing to be desired? The very reverse. It maintains not only that virtue is to be desired, but that it is to be desired disinterestedly, for itself. Whatever may be the opinion of utilitarian moralists as to the original conditions by which virtue is made virtue; however they may believe (as they do) that actions and dispositions are only virtuous because they promote another end than virtue; yet this being granted, and it having been decided, from considerations of this description, what *is* virtuous, they not only place virtue at the very head of the things which are good as means to the ultimate end, but they also recognize as a psychological fact the possibility of its being, to the individual, a good in itself, without looking to any end beyond it; and hold, that the mind is not in a right state, not in a state conformable to Utility, not in the state most conducive to the general happiness, unless it does love virtue in this manner – as a thing desirable in itself, even although, in the individual instance, it should not produce those other desirable consequences which it tends to produce, and on account of which it is held to be virtue. This opinion is not, in the smallest degree, a departure from the Happiness principle. The ingredients of happiness are very various, and each of them is desirable in itself, and not merely when considered as swelling an aggregate. The principle of utility does not mean that any given pleasure, as music, for instance, or any given exemption from pain, as for example health, are to be looked upon as means to a collective something termed happiness, and to be desired on that account. They are desired and desirable in and for themselves; besides being means, they are a part of the end. Virtue, according to the utilitarian doctrine, is not naturally and originally part of the end, but it is capable of becoming so; and in those who love it disinterestedly it has become so, and is desired and cherished, not as a means to happiness, but as a part of their happiness.

To illustrate this farther, we may remember that virtue is not the only thing, originally a means, and which if it were not a means to anything else, would be and remain indifferent, but which by association with what it is a means to, comes to be desired for itself, and that too with the utmost intensity. What, for example, shall we say of the love of money? There is nothing originally more desirable about money than about any heap of glittering pebbles. Its worth is solely that of the things which it will buy; the desires for other things than itself, which it is a means of gratifying. Yet the love of money is not only one of the strongest moving forces of human life, but money is, in many cases, desired in and for itself; the desire to possess it is often stronger than the desire to use it, and goes on increasing when all the desires which point to ends beyond it, to be compassed by it, are falling off. It may be then said truly, that money is desired not for the sake of an end, but as part of the end. From being a means to happiness, it has come to be itself a principal ingredient of the individual's conception of happiness. The same may be said of the majority of the great objects of human life – power, for example, or fame; except that to each of these there is a certain amount of immediate pleasure annexed, which has at least the semblance of being naturally inherent in them; a thing which cannot be said of money. Still, however, the strongest natural attraction, both of power and of fame, is the immense aid they give to the attainment of our other wishes; and it is the strong association thus generated between them and all our objects of desire, which gives to the direct desire of them the intensity it often assumes, so as in some characters to surpass in strength all other desires. In these cases the means have become a part of the end, and a more important part of it than any of the things which they are means to. What was once desired as an instrument for the attainment of happiness, has come to be desired for its own sake. In being desired for its own sake it is, however, desired as *part* of happiness. The person is made, or thinks he would be made, happy by its mere possession; and is made unhappy by failure to obtain it. The desire of it is not a different thing from the desire of happiness, any more than the love of music, or the desire of health. They are included in happiness. They are some of the elements of which the desire of happiness is made up. Happiness is not an abstract idea, but a concrete whole; and these are some of its parts. And the utilitarian standard sanctions and approves their being so. Life would be a poor thing, very ill provided with sources of happiness, if there were not this provision of nature, by which things originally indifferent, but conducive to, or otherwise associated with, the satisfaction of our primitive desires, become in themselves sources of pleasure more valuable than the primitive pleasures, both in permanency, in the space of human existence that they are capable of covering, and even in intensity.

Virtue, according to the utilitarian conception, is a good of this description. There was no original desire of it, or motive to it, save its conduciveness to pleasure, and especially to protection from pain. But through the association thus formed, it may be felt a good in itself, and desired as such with as great intensity as any other good; and with this difference between it and the love of money, of power, or of fame, that all of these may, and often do, render the individual noxious to the other members of the society to which he belongs, whereas there is nothing which makes him so much a blessing to them as the cultivation of the disinterested love of virtue. And consequently, the utilitarian standard, while it tolerates and approves those other acquired desires, up to the point beyond which they would be more injurious to the general happiness than promotive of it, enjoins and requires the cultivation of the love of virtue up to the greatest strength possible, as being above all things important to the general happiness.

It results from the preceding considerations, that there is in reality nothing desired except happiness. Whatever is desired otherwise than as a means to some end beyond itself, and ultimately to happiness, is desired as itself a part of happiness, and is not desired for itself until it has become so. Those who desire virtue for its own sake, desire it either because the consciousness of it is a pleasure, or because the consciousness of being without it is a pain, or for both reasons united; as in truth the pleasure and pain seldom exist separately, but almost always together, the same person feeling pleasure in the degree of virtue attained, and pain in not having attained more. If one of these gave him no pleasure, and the other no pain, he would not love or desire virtue, or would desire it only for the other benefits which it might produce to himself or to persons whom he cared for.

We have now, then, an answer to the question, of what sort of proof the principle of utility is susceptible. If the opinion which I have now stated is psychologically true – if human nature is so constituted as to desire nothing which is not either a part of happiness or a means of happiness, we can have no other proof, and we require no other, that these are the only things desirable. If so, happiness is the sole end of human action, and the promotion of it the test by which to judge of all human conduct; from whence it necessarily follows that it must be the criterion of morality, since a part is included in the whole.

And now to decide whether this is really so; whether mankind do desire nothing for itself but that which is a pleasure to them, or of which the absence is a pain; we have evidently arrived at a question of fact and experience, dependent, like all similar questions, upon evidence. It can only be determined by practised self-consciousness and self-observation, assisted by observation of others. I believe that these sources of evidence, impartially consulted, will declare that desiring a thing and finding it pleasant, aversion to it and thinking of it as painful, are phenomena entirely inseparable, or rather two parts of the same phenomenon; in strictness of language, two different modes of naming the same psychological fact: that to think of an object as desirable (unless for the sake of its consequences), and to think of it as pleasant, are one and the same thing; and that to desire anything, except in proportion as the idea of it is pleasant, is a physical and metaphysical impossibility.

So obvious does this appear to me, that I expect it will hardly be disputed: and the objection made will be, not that desire can possibly be directed to anything ultimately except pleasure and exemption from pain, but that the will is a different thing from desire; that a person of confirmed virtue, or any other person whose purposes are fixed, carries out his purposes without any thought of the pleasure he has in contemplating them, or expects to derive from their fulfilment; and persists in acting on them, even though these pleasures are much diminished, by changes in his character or decay of his passive sensibilities, or are outweighed by the pains which the pursuit of the purposes may bring upon him. All this I fully admit, and have stated it elsewhere,* as positively and emphatically as any one. Will, the active phenomenon, is a different thing from desire, the state of passive sensibility, and though originally an offshoot from it, may in time take root and detach itself from the parent stock; so much so, that in the case of an habitual purpose, instead of willing the thing because we desire it, we often desire it only because we will it. This, however, is but an instance of that familiar fact, the power of habit, and is nowise confined to the case of virtuous actions. Many indifferent things, which men originally did from a motive of some sort, they continue to do from habit. Sometimes this is done unconsciously, the consciousness coming only after the action: at other times with conscious volition, but volition which has became habitual, and is put into operation by the force of habit, in opposition perhaps to the deliberate preference, as often happens with those who have contracted habits of vicious or hurtful indulgence. Third and last comes the case in which the habitual act of will in the individual instance is not in contradiction to the general intention prevailing at other times, but in fulfilment of it; as in the case of the person of confirmed virtue,

*A System of Logic, Book VI, Ch. II, Section 4, above pp. 119–21.

and of all who pursue deliberately and consistently any determinate end. The distinction between will and desire thus understood, is an authentic and highly important psychological fact; but the fact consists solely in this – that will, like all other parts of our constitution, is amenable to habit, and that we may will from habit what we no longer desire for itself, or desire only because we will it. It is not the less true that will, in the beginning, is entirely produced by desire; including in that term the repelling influence of pain as well as the attractive one of pleasure. Let us take into consideration, no longer the person who has a confirmed will to do right, but him in whom that virtuous will is still feeble, conquerable by temptation, and not to be fully relied on; by what means can it be strengthened? How can the will to be virtuous, where it does not exist in sufficient force, be implanted or awakened? Only by making the person *desire* virtue – by making him think of it in a pleasurable light, or of its absence in a painful one. It is by associating the doing right with pleasure, or the doing wrong with pain, or by eliciting and impressing and bringing home to the person's experience the pleasure naturally involved in the one or the pain in the other, that it is possible to call forth that will to be virtuous, which, when confirmed, acts without any thought of either pleasure or pain. Will is the child of desire, and passes out of the dominion of its parent only to come under that of habit. That which is the result of habit affords no presumption of being intrinsically good; and there would be no reason for wishing that the purpose of virtue should become independent of pleasure and pain, were it not that the influence of the pleasurable and painful associations which prompt to virtue is not sufficiently to be depended on for unerring constancy of action until it has acquired the support of habit. Both in feeling and in conduct, habit is the only thing which imparts certainty; and it is because of the importance to others of being able to rely absolutely on one's feelings and conduct, and to oneself of being able to rely on one's own, that the will to do right ought to be cultivated into this habitual independence. In other words, this state of the will is a means to good, not intrinsically a good; and does not contradict the doctrine that nothing is a good to human beings but in so far as it is either itself pleasurable, or a means of attaining pleasure or averting pain.

But if this doctrine be true, the principle of utility is proved. Whether it is so or not, must now be left to the consideration of the thoughtful reader.

Chapter V
On the Connection between
Justice and Utility

In all ages of speculation, one of the strongest obstacles to the reception of the doctrine that Utility or Happiness is the criterion of right and wrong, has been drawn from the idea of Justice. The powerful sentiment, and apparently clear perception, which that word recalls with a rapidity and certainty resembling an instinct, have seemed to the majority of thinkers to point to an inherent quality in things; to show that the Just must have an existence in Nature as something absolute – generically distinct from every variety of the Expedient, and, in idea, opposed to it, though (as is commonly acknowledged) never, in the long run, disjoined from it in fact.

In the case of this, as of our other moral sentiments, there is no necessary connection between the question of its origin, and that of its binding force. That a feeling is bestowed on us by Nature, does not necessarily legitimate all its promptings. The feeling of justice might be a peculiar instinct, and might yet require, like our other instincts, to be controlled and enlightened by a higher reason. If we have intellectual instincts, leading us to judge in a particular way, as well as animal instincts that prompt us to act in a particular way, there is no necessity that the former should be more infallible in their sphere than the latter in theirs: it may as well happen that wrong judgements are occasionally suggested by those, as wrong actions by these. But though it is one thing to believe that we have natural feelings of justice, and another to acknowledge them as an ultimate criterion of conduct, these two opinions are very closely connected in point of fact. Mankind are always predisposed to believe that any subjective feeling, not otherwise accounted for, is a revelation of some objective reality.

Our present object is to determine whether the reality, to which the feeling of justice corresponds, is one which needs any such special revelation; whether the justice or injustice of an action is a thing intrinsically peculiar, and distinct from all its other qualities, or only a combination of certain of those qualities, presented under a peculiar aspect. For the purpose of this inquiry, it is practically important to consider whether the feeling itself, of justice and injustice, is *sui generis* like our sensations of colour and taste, or a derivative feeling, formed by a combination of others. And this it is the more essential to examine, as people are in general willing enough to allow, that objectively the dictates of justice coincide with a part of the field of General Expediency; but inasmuch as the subjective mental feeling of Justice is different from that which commonly attaches to simple expediency, and, except in extreme cases of the latter, is far more imperative in its demands, people find it difficult to see, in Justice, only a particular kind or branch of general utility, and think that its superior binding force requires a totally different origin.

To throw light upon this question, it is necessary to attempt to ascertain what is the distinguishing character of justice, or of injustice: what is the quality, or whether there is any quality, attributed in common to all modes of conduct designated as unjust (for justice, like many other moral attributes, is best defined by its opposite), and distinguishing them from such modes of conduct as are disapproved, but without having that particular epithet of disapprobation applied to them. If, in everything which men are accustomed to characterize as just or unjust, some one common attribute or collection of attributes is always present, we may judge whether this particular attribute or combination of attributes would be capable of gathering round it a sentiment of that peculiar character and intensity by virtue of the general laws of our emotional constitution, or whether the sentiment is inexplicable, and requires to be regarded as a special provision of Nature. If we find the former to be the case, we shall, in resolving this question, have resolved also the main problem: if the latter, we shall have to seek for some other mode of investigating it.

To find the common attributes of a variety of objects, it is necessary to begin by surveying the objects themselves in the concrete. Let us therefore advert successively to the various modes of action, and arrangements of human affairs, which are classed, by universal or widely spread opinion, as Just or as Unjust. The things well known to excite the sentiments associated with those names, are of a very multifarious character. I shall pass them rapidly in review, without studying any particular arrangement.

In the first place, it is mostly considered unjust to deprive any one of his personal liberty, his property, or any other thing which belongs to him by law. Here, therefore, is one instance of the application of the terms just and unjust in a perfectly definite sense, namely, that it is just to respect, unjust to violate, the *legal rights* of anyone. But this judgement admits of several exceptions, arising from the other forms in which the notions of justice and injustice present themselves. For example, the person who suffers the deprivation may (as the phrase is) have *forfeited* the rights which he is so deprived of: a case to which we shall return presently. But also,

Secondly; the legal rights of which he is deprived, may be rights which *ought* not to have belonged to him; in other words, the law which confers on him these rights, may be a bad law. When it is so, or when (which is the same thing for our purpose) it is supposed to be so, opinions will differ as to the justice or injustice of infringing it. Some maintain that no law, however bad, ought to be disobeyed by an individual citizen; that his opposition to it, if shown at all, should only be shown in endeavouring to get it altered by competent authority. This opinion (which condemns many of the most illustrious benefactors of mankind, and would often protect pernicious institutions against the only weapons which, in the state of things existing at the time, have any chance of succeeding against them) is defended, by those who hold it, on grounds of expediency; principally on that of the importance, to the common interest of mankind, of maintaining inviolate the sentiment of submission to law. Other persons, again, hold the directly contrary opinion, that any law, judged to be bad, may blamelessly be disobeyed, even though it be not judged to be unjust, but only inexpedient; while others would confine the licence of disobedience to the case of unjust laws: but again, some say, that all laws which are inexpedient are unjust; since every law imposes some restriction on the natural liberty of mankind, which restriction is an injustice, unless legitimated by tending to their good. Among these diversities of opinion, it seems to be universally admitted that there may be unjust laws, and that law, consequently, is not the ultimate criterion of justice, but may give to one person a benefit, or impose on another an evil, which justice condemns. When, however, a law is thought to be unjust, it seems always to be regarded as being so in the same way in which a breach of law is unjust, namely, by infringing somebody's right; which, as it cannot in this case be a legal right, receives a different appellation, and is called a moral right. We may say, therefore, that a second case of injustice consists in taking or withholding from any person that to which he has a *moral right*.

Thirdly, it is universally considered just that each person should obtain that (whether good or evil) which he *deserves*; and unjust that he should obtain a good, or be made to undergo an evil, which he does not deserve. This is, perhaps, the clearest and most emphatic form in which the idea of justice is conceived by the general mind. As it involves the notion of desert, the question arises, what constitutes desert? Speaking in a general way, a person is understood to deserve good if he does right, evil if he does wrong; and in a more particular sense, to deserve good from those to whom he does or has done good, and evil from those to whom he does or has done evil. The precept of returning good for evil has never been regarded as a case of the fulfilment of justice, but as one in which the claims of justice are waived, in obedience to other considerations.

Fourthly, it is confessedly unjust to *break faith* with any one: to violate an engagement, either express or implied, or disappoint expectations raised by our own conduct, at least if we have raised those expectations knowingly and voluntarily. Like the other obligations of justice already spoken of, this one is not regarded as absolute, but as capable of being overruled by a stronger obligation of justice on the other side; or by such conduct on the part of the person concerned as is deemed to absolve us from our obligation to him, and to constitute a *forfeiture* of the benefit which he has been led to expect.

Fifthly, it is, by universal admission, inconsistent with justice to be *partial*; to show favour or preference to one person over another, in matters to which favour and preference do not properly apply. Impartiality, however, does not seem to be regarded as a duty in itself, but rather as instrumental to some other duty; for it is admitted that favour and preference are not always censurable, and indeed the cases in which they are condemned are rather the exception than the rule. A person would be more likely to be blamed than applauded for giving his family or friends no superiority in good offices over strangers, when he could do so without violating any other duty; and no one thinks it unjust to seek one person in preference to another as a friend, connection, or companion. Impartiality where rights are concerned is of course obligatory, but this is involved in the more general obligation of giving to everyone his right. A tribunal, for example, must be impartial, because it is bound to award, without regard to any other consideration, a disputed object to the one of two parties who has the right to it. There are other cases in which impartiality means, being solely influenced by desert; as with those who, in the capacity of judges, preceptors, or parents, administer reward and punishment as such. There are cases, again, in which it means, being solely influenced by consideration for the public interest; as in making a selection among candidates for a government employment. Impartiality, in short, as an obligation of justice, may be said to mean, being exclusively influenced by the considerations which it is supposed ought to influence the particular case in hand; and resisting the solicitation of any motives which prompt to conduct different from what those considerations would dictate.

Nearly allied to the idea of impartiality, is that of *equality*; which often enters as a component part both into the conception of justice and into the practice of it, and, in the eyes of many persons, constitutes its essence. But in this, still more than in any other case, the notion of justice varies in different persons, and always conforms in its variations to their notion of utility. Each person maintains that equality is the dictate of justice, except where he thinks that expediency requires inequality. The justice of giving equal protection to the rights of all, is maintained by those who support the most outrageous inequality in the rights themselves. Even in slave countries it is theoretically admitted that the rights of the slave, such as they are, ought to be as sacred as those of the master; and that a tribunal which fails to enforce them with equal strictness is wanting in justice; while, at the same time, institutions which leave to the slave scarcely any rights to enforce, are not deemed unjust, because they are not deemed inexpedient. Those who think that utility requires distinctions of rank, do not consider it unjust that riches and social privileges should be unequally dispensed; but those who think this inequality inexpedient, think it unjust also. Whoever thinks that government is necessary, sees no injustice in as much inequality as is constituted by giving to the magistrate powers not granted to other people. Even among those who hold levelling doctrines, there are as many questions of justice as there are differences of opinion about expediency. Some Communists consider it unjust that the produce of the labour of the community should be shared on any other principle than that of exact equality; others think it just that those should receive most whose needs are greatest; while others hold that those who work harder, or who produce more, or whose services are more valuable to the community, may justly claim a larger quota in the division of the produce. And the sense of natural justice may be plausibly appealed to in behalf of every one of these opinions.

Among so many diverse applications of the term Justice, which yet is not regarded as ambiguous, it is a matter of some difficulty to seize the mental link which holds them together, and on which the moral sentiment adhering to the term essentially depends. Perhaps, in this embarrassment, some help may be derived from the history of the word, as indicated by its etymology.

In most, if not in all, languages, the etymology of the word which corresponds to Just, points to an origin connected either with positive law, or with that which was in most cases the primitive form of law – authoritative custom. *Justum* is a form of *jussum*, that which has been ordered. *Jus* is of the same origin. Δίκαιον comes from δίκη, of which the principal meaning, at least in the historical ages of Greece, was a suit at law. Originally, indeed, it meant only the mode or *manner* of doing things, but it early came to mean the *prescribed* manner; that which the recognized authorities, patriarchal, judicial, or political, would enforce. *Recht*, from which came *right* and *righteous*, is synonymous with law. The original meaning indeed of *recht* did not point to law, but to physical straightness; as *wrong* and its Latin equivalents meant twisted or *tortuous*; and from this it is argued that right did not originally mean law, but on the contrary law meant right. But however this may be, the fact that *recht* and *droit* became restricted in their meaning to positive law, although much which is not required by law is equally necessary to moral straightness or rectitude, is as significant of the original character of moral ideas as if the derivation had been the reverse way. The courts of justice, the administration of justice, are the courts and the administration of law. *La justice*, in French, is the established term for judicature. There can, I think, be no doubt that the *idée mère*, the primitive element, in the formation of the notion of justice, was conformity to law. It constituted the entire idea among the Hebrews, up to the birth of Christianity; as might be expected in the case of a people whose laws attempted to embrace all subjects on which precepts were required, and who believed those laws to be a direct emanation from the Supreme Being. But other nations, and in particular the Greeks and Romans, who knew that their laws had been made originally, and still continued to be made, by men, were not afraid to admit that those men might make bad laws; might do, by law, the same things, and from the same motives, which, if done by individuals without the sanction of law, would be called unjust. And hence the sentiment of injustice came to be attached, not to all violations of law, but only to violations of such laws as *ought* to exist, including such as ought to exist but do not; and to laws themselves, if supposed to be contrary to what ought to be law. In this manner the idea of law and of its injunctions was still predominant in the notion of justice, even when the laws actually in force ceased to be accepted as the standard of it.

It is true that mankind consider the idea of justice and its obligations as applicable to many things which neither are, nor is it desired that they should be, regulated by law. Nobody desires that laws should interfere with the whole detail of private life; yet everyone allows that in all daily conduct a person may and does show himself to be either just or unjust. But even here, the idea of the breach of what ought to be law, still lingers in a modified shape. It would always give us pleasure, and chime in with our feelings of fitness, that acts which we deem unjust should be punished, though we do not always think it expedient that this should be done by the tribunals. We forgo that gratification on account of incidental inconveniences. We should be glad to see just conduct enforced and injustice repressed, even in the minutest details, if we were not, with reason, afraid of trusting the magistrate with so unlimited an amount of power over individuals. When we think that a person is bound in justice to do a thing, it is an ordinary form of language to say, that he ought to be compelled to do it. We should be gratified to see the obligation enforced by anybody who had the power. If we see that its enforcement by law would be inexpedient, we lament the impossibility, we consider the impunity given to injustice as an evil, and strive to make amends for it by bringing a strong expression of our own and the public disapprobation to bear upon the offender. Thus the idea of legal constraint is still the generating idea of the notion of justice, though undergoing several transformations before that notion, as it exists in an advanced state of society, becomes complete.

The above is, I think, a true account, as far as it goes, of the origin and progressive growth of the idea of justice. But we must observe, that it contains, as yet, nothing to distinguish that obligation from moral obligation in general. For the truth is, that the idea of penal sanction, which is the essence of law, enters not only into the conception of injustice, but into that of any kind of wrong. We do not call anything wrong, unless we mean to imply that a person ought to be punished in some way or other for doing it; if not by law, by the opinion of his fellow creatures; if not by opinion, by the reproaches of his own conscience. This seems the real turning point of the distinction between morality and simple expediency. It is a part of the notion of Duty in every one of its forms, that a person may rightfully be compelled to fulfil it. Duty is a thing which may be *exacted* from a person, as one exacts a debt. Unless we think that it might be exacted from him, we do not call it his duty. Reasons of prudence, or the interest of other people, may militate against actually exacting it; but the person himself, it is clearly understood, would not be entitled to complain. There are other things, on the contrary, which we wish that people should do, which we like or admire them for doing, perhaps dislike or despise them for not doing, but yet admit that they are not bound to do; it is not a case of moral obligation; we do not blame them, that is, we do not think that they are proper objects of punishment. How we come by these ideas of deserving and not deserving punishment, will appear, perhaps, in the sequel; but I think there is no doubt that this distinction lies at the bottom of the notions of right and wrong; that we call any conduct wrong, or employ, instead, some other term of dislike or disparagement, according as we think that the person ought, or ought not, to be punished for it; and we say that it would be right to do so and so, or merely that it would be desirable or laudable, according as we would wish to see the person whom it concerns, compelled, or only persuaded and exhorted, to act in that manner.

This, therefore, being the characteristic difference which marks off, not justice, but morality in general, from the remaining provinces of Expediency and Worthiness; the character is still to be sought which distinguishes justice from other branches of morality. Now it is known that ethical writers divide moral duties into two classes, denoted by the ill-chosen expressions, duties of perfect and of imperfect obligation; the latter being those in which, though the act is obligatory, the particular occasions of performing it are left to our choice; as in the case of charity or beneficence, which we are indeed bound to practise, but not towards any definite person, nor at any prescribed time. In the more precise language of philosophic jurists, duties of perfect obligation are those duties in virtue of which a correlative *right* resides in some person or persons; duties of imperfect obligation are those moral obligations which do not give birth to any right. I think it will be found that this distinction exactly coincides with that which exists between justice and the other obligations of morality. In our survey of the various popular acceptations of justice, the term appeared generally to involve the idea of a personal right – a claim on the part of one or more individuals, like that which the law gives when it confers a proprietary or other legal right. Whether the injustice consists in depriving a person of a possession, or in breaking faith with him, or in treating him worse than he deserves, or worse than other people who have no greater claims, in each case the supposition implies two things – a wrong done, and some assignable person who is wronged. Injustice may also be done by treating a person better than others; but the wrong in this case is to his competitors, who are also assignable persons. It seems to me that this feature in the case – a right in some person, correlative to the moral obligation – constitutes the specific difference between justice, and generosity or beneficence. Justice implies something which it is not only right to do, and wrong not to do, but which some individual person can claim from us as his moral right. No one has a moral right to our generosity or beneficence, because we are not morally bound to practise those virtues towards any given individual. And it will be found with respect to this as with respect to every correct definition, that the instances which seem to conflict with it are those which most confirm it. For if a moralist attempts, as some have done, to make out that mankind generally, though not any given individual, have a right to all the good we can do them, he at once, by that thesis, includes generosity and beneficence within the category of justice. He is obliged to say, that our utmost exertions are *due* to our fellow creatures, thus assimilating them to a debt; or that nothing less can be a sufficient *return* for what society does for us, thus classing the case as one of gratitude; both of which are acknowledged cases of justice. Wherever there is a right, the case is one of justice, and not of the virtue of beneficence: and whoever does not place the distinction between justice and morality in general where we have now placed it, will be found to make no distinction between them at all, but to merge all morality in justice.

Having thus endeavoured to determine the distinctive elements which enter into the composition of the idea of justice, we are ready to enter on the inquiry, whether the feeling, which accompanies the idea, is attached to it by a special dispensation of nature, or whether it could have grown up, by any known laws, out of the idea itself; and in particular, whether it can have originated in considerations of general expediency.

I conceive that the sentiment itself does not arise from anything which would commonly, or correctly, be termed an idea of expediency, but that though the sentiment does not, whatever is moral in it does.

We have seen that the two essential ingredients in the sentiment of justice are, the desire to punish a person who has done harm, and the knowledge or belief that there is some definite individual or individuals to whom harm has been done.

Now it appears to me, that the desire to punish a person who has done harm to some individual, is a spontaneous outgrowth from two sentiments, both in the highest degree natural, and which either are or resemble instincts; the impulse of self-defence, and the feeling of sympathy.

It is natural to resent, and to repel or retaliate, any harm done or attempted against ourselves, or against those with whom we sympathize. The origin of this sentiment it is not necessary here to discuss. Whether it be an instinct or a result of intelligence, it is, we know, common to all animal nature; for every animal tries to hurt those who have hurt, or who it thinks are about to hurt, itself or its young. Human beings, on this point, only differ from other animals in two particulars. First, in being capable of sympathizing, not solely with their offspring, or, like some of the more noble animals, with some superior animal who is kind to them, but with all human, and even with all sentient, beings. Secondly, in having a more developed intelligence, which gives a wider range to the whole of their sentiments, whether self-regarding or sympathetic. By virtue of his superior intelligence, even apart from his superior range of sympathy, a human being is capable of apprehending a community of interest between himself and the human society of which he forms a part, such that any conduct which threatens the security of the society generally, is threatening to his own, and calls forth his instinct (if instinct it be) of self-defence. The same superiority of intelligence, joined to the power of sympathizing with human beings generally, enables him to attach himself to the collective idea of his tribe, his country, or mankind, in such a manner that any act hurtful to them rouses his instinct of sympathy, and urges him to resistance.

The sentiment of justice, in that one of its elements which consists of the desire to punish, is thus, I conceive, the natural feeling of retaliation or vengeance, rendered by intellect and sympathy applicable to those injuries, that is, to those hurts, which wound us through, or in common with, society at large. This sentiment, in itself, has nothing moral in it; what is moral is, the exclusive subordination of it to the social sympathies, so as to wait on and obey their call. For the natural feeling tends to make us resent indiscriminately whatever any one does that is disagreeable to us; but when moralized by the social feeling, it only acts in the directions conformable to the general good: just persons resenting a hurt to society, though not otherwise a hurt to themselves, and not resenting a hurt to themselves, however painful, unless it be of the kind which society has a common interest with them in the repression of.

It is no objection against this doctrine to say, that when we feel our sentiment of justice outraged, we are not thinking of society at large, or of any collective interest, but only of the individual case. It is common enough certainly, though the reverse of commendable, to feel resentment merely because we have suffered pain; but a person whose resentment is really a moral feeling, that is, who considers whether an act is blameable before he allows himself to resent it – such a person, though he may not say expressly to himself that he is standing up for the interest of society, certainly does feel that he is asserting a rule which is for the benefit of others as well as for his own. If he is not feeling this – if he is regarding the act solely as it affects him individually – he is not consciously just; he is not concerning himself about the justice of his actions. This is admitted even by anti-utilitarian moralists. When Kant (as before remarked) propounds as the fundamental principle of morals, 'So act, that thy rule of conduct might be adopted as a law by all rational beings,' he virtually acknowledges that the interest of mankind collectively, or at least of mankind indiscriminately, must be in the mind of the agent when conscientiously deciding on the morality of the act. Otherwise he uses words without a meaning: for, that a rule even of utter selfishness could not *possibly* be adopted by all rational beings – that there is any insuperable obstacle in the nature of things to its adoption – cannot be even plausibly maintained. To give any meaning to Kant's principle, the sense put upon it must be, that we ought to shape our conduct by a rule which all rational beings might adopt *with benefit to their collective interest*.

To recapitulate: the idea of justice supposes two things; a rule of conduct, and a sentiment which sanctions the rule. The first must be supposed common to all mankind, and intended for their good. The other (the sentiment) is a desire that punishment may be suffered by those who infringe the rule. There is involved, in addition, the conception of some definite person who suffers by the infringement; whose rights (to use the expression appropriated to the case) are violated by it. And the sentiment of justice appears to me to be the animal desire to repel or retaliate a hurt or damage to oneself, or to those with whom one sympathizes, widened so as to include all persons, by the human capacity of enlarged sympathy, and the human conception of intelligent self-interest. From the latter elements, the feeling derives its morality; from the former, its peculiar impressiveness, and energy of self-assertion.

I have, throughout, treated the idea of a *right* residing in the injured person, and violated by the injury, not as a separate element in the composition of the idea and sentiment, but as one of the forms in which the other two elements clothe themselves. These elements are, a hurt to some assignable person or persons on the one hand, and a demand for punishment on the other. An examination of our own minds, I think, will show, that these two things include all that we mean when we speak of violation of a right. When we call anything a person's right, we mean that he has a valid claim on society to protect him in the possession of it, either by the force of law, or by that of education and opinion. If he has what we consider a sufficient claim, on whatever account, to have something guaranteed to him by society, we say that he has a right to it. If we desire to prove that anything does not belong to him by right, we think this done as soon as it is admitted that society ought not to take measures for securing it to him, but should leave it to chance, or to his own exertions. Thus, a person is said to have a right to what he can earn in fair professional competition; because society ought not to allow any other person to hinder him from endeavouring to earn in that manner as much as he can. But he has not a right to three hundred a year, though he may happen to be earning it; because society is not called on to provide that he shall earn that sum. On the contrary, if he owns ten thousand pounds three per cent stock, he *has* a right to three hundred a year; because society has come under an obligation to provide him with an income of that amount.

To have a right, then, is, I conceive, to have something which society ought to defend me in the possession of. If the objector goes on to ask why it ought, I can give him no other reason than general utility. If that expression does not seem to convey a sufficient feeling of the strength of the obligation, nor to account for the peculiar energy of the feeling, it is because there goes to the composition of the sentiment, not a rational only but also an animal element, the thirst for retaliation; and this thirst derives its intensity, as well as its moral justification, from the extraordinarily important and impressive kind of utility which is concerned. The interest involved is that of security, to every one's feelings the most vital of all interests. Nearly all other earthly benefits are needed by one person, not needed by another; and many of them can, if necessary, be cheerfully forgone, or replaced by something else; but security no human being can possibly do without; on it we depend for all our immunity from evil, and for the whole value of all and every good, beyond the passing moment; since nothing but the gratification of the instant could be of any worth to us, if we could be deprived of everything the next instant by whoever was momentarily stronger than ourselves. Now this most indispensable of all necessaries, after physical nutriment, cannot be had, unless the machinery for providing it is kept unintermittedly in active play. Our notion, therefore, of the claim we have on our fellow creatures to join in making safe for us the very groundwork of our existence, gathers feelings round it so much more intense than those concerned in any of the more common cases of utility, that the difference in degree (as is often the case in psychology) becomes a real difference in kind.

The claim assumes that character of absoluteness, that apparent infinity, and incommensurability with all other considerations, which constitute the distinction between the feeling of right and wrong and that of ordinary expediency and inexpediency. The feelings concerned are so powerful, and we count so positively on finding a responsive feeling in others (all being alike interested), that *ought* and *should* grow into *must*, and recognized indispensability becomes a moral necessity, analogous to physical, and often not inferior to it in binding force.

If the preceding analysis, or something resembling it, be not the correct account of the notion of justice; if justice be totally independent of utility, and be a standard *per se*, which the mind can recognize by simple introspection of itself; it is hard to understand why that internal oracle is so ambiguous, and why so many things appear either just or unjust, according to the light in which they are regarded.

We are continually informed that Utility is an uncertain standard, which every different person interprets differently, and that there is no safety but in the immutable, ineffaceable, and unmistakable dictates of Justice, which carry their evidence in themselves, and are independent of the fluctuations of opinion. One would suppose from this that on questions of justice there could be no controversy; that if we take that for our rule, its application to any given case could leave us in as little doubt as a mathematical demonstration. So far is this from being the fact, that there is as much difference of opinion, and as fierce discussion, about what is just, as about what is useful to society. Not only have different nations and individuals different notions of justice, but, in the mind of one and the same individual, justice is not some one rule, principle, or maxim, but many, which do not always coincide in their dictates, and in choosing between which, he is guided either by some extraneous standard, or by his own personal predilections.

For instance, there are some who say, that it is unjust to punish anyone for the sake of example to others; that punishment is just, only when intended for the good of the sufferer himself. Others maintain the extreme reverse, contending that to punish persons who have attained years of discretion, for their own benefit, is despotism and injustice, since if the matter at issue is solely their own good, no one has a right to control their own judgement of it; but that they may justly be punished to prevent evil to others, this being an exercise of the legitimate right of self-defence. Mr Owen, again, affirms that it is unjust to punish at all; for the criminal did not make his own character; his education, and the circumstances which surround him, have made him a criminal, and for these he is not responsible. All these opinions are extremely plausible; and so long as the question is argued as one of justice simply, without going down to the principles which lie under justice and are the source of its authority, I am unable to see how any of these reasoners can be refuted. For, in truth, every one of the three builds upon rules of justice confessedly true. The first appeals to the acknowledged injustice of singling out an individual, and making him a sacrifice, without his consent, for other people's benefit. The second relies on the acknowledged justice of self-defence, and the admitted injustice of forcing one person to conform to another's notions of what constitutes his good. The Owenite invokes the admitted principle, that it is unjust to punish anyone for what he cannot help. Each is triumphant so long as he is not compelled to take into consideration any other maxims of justice than the one he has selected; but as soon as their several maxims are brought face to face, each disputant seems to have exactly as much to say for himself as the others. No one of them can carry out his own notion of justice without trampling upon another equally binding. These are difficulties; they have always been felt to be such; and many devices have been invented to turn rather than to overcome them. As a refuge from the last of the three, men imagined what they called the freedom of the will; fancying that they could not justify punishing a man whose will is in a thoroughly hateful state, unless it be supposed to have come into that state through no influence of anterior circumstances. To escape from the other difficulties, a favourite contrivance has been the fiction of a contract, whereby at some unknown period all the members of society engaged to obey the laws, and consented to be punished for any disobedience to them; thereby giving to their legislators the right, which it is assumed they would not otherwise have had, of punishing them, either for their own good or for that of society. This happy thought was considered to get rid of the whole difficulty, and to legitimate the infliction of punishment, in virtue of another received maxim of justice, *volenti non fit injuria*; that is not unjust which is done with the consent of the person who is supposed to be hurt by it. I need hardly remark, that even if the consent were not a mere fiction, this maxim is not superior in authority to the others which it is brought in to supersede. It is, on the contrary, an instructive specimen of the loose and irregular manner in which supposed principles of justice grow up. This particular one evidently came into use as a help to the coarse exigencies of courts of law, which are sometimes obliged to be content with very uncertain presumptions, on account of the greater evils which would often arise from any attempt on their part to cut finer. But even courts of law are not able to adhere consistently to the maxim, for they allow voluntary engagements to be set aside on the ground of fraud, and sometimes on that of mere mistake or misinformation.

Again, when the legitimacy of inflicting punishment is admitted, how many conflicting conceptions of justice come to light in discussing the proper apportionment of punishment to offences. No rule on this subject recommends itself so strongly to the primitive and spontaneous sentiment of justice, as the *lex talionis*, an eye for an eye and a tooth for a tooth. Though this principle of the Jewish and of the Mahomedan law has been generally abandoned in Europe as a practical maxim, there is, I suspect, in most minds, a secret hankering after it; and when retribution accidentally falls on an offender in that precise shape, the general feeling of satisfaction evinced, bears witness how natural is the sentiment to which this repayment in kind is acceptable. With many the test of justice in penal infliction is that the punishment should be proportioned to the offence; meaning that it should be exactly measured by the moral guilt of the culprit (whatever be their standard for measuring moral guilt): the consideration, what amount of punishment is necessary to deter from the offence, having nothing to do with the question of justice, in their estimation: while there are others to whom that consideration is all in all; who maintain that it is not just, at least for man, to inflict on a fellow creature, whatever may be his offences, any amount of suffering beyond the least that will suffice to prevent him from repeating, and others from imitating, his misconduct.

To take another example from a subject already once referred to. In a co-operative industrial association, is it just or not that talent or skill should give a title to superior remuneration? On the negative side of the question it is argued, that whoever does the best he can, deserves equally well, and ought not in justice to be put in a position of inferiority for no fault of his own; that superior abilities have already advantages more than enough, in the admiration they excite, the personal influence they command, and the internal sources of satisfaction attending them, without adding to these a superior share of the world's goods; and that society is bound in justice rather to make compensation to the less favoured, for this unmerited inequality of advantages, than to aggravate it. On the contrary side it is contended, that society receives more from the more efficient labourer; that his services being more useful, society owes him a larger return for them; that a greater share of the joint result is actually his work, and not to allow his claim to it is a kind of robbery; that if he is only to receive as much as others, he can only be justly required to produce as much, and to give a smaller amount of time and exertion, proportioned to his superior efficiency. Who shall decide between these appeals to conflicting principles of justice? Justice has in this case two sides to it, which it is impossible to bring into harmony, and the two disputants have chosen opposite sides; the one looks to what it is just that the individual should receive, the other to what it is just that the community should give. Each, from his own point of view, is unanswerable; and any choice between them, on grounds of justice, must be perfectly arbitrary. Social utility alone can decide the preference.

How many, again, and how irreconcilable, are the standards of justice to which reference is made in discussing the repartition of taxation. One opinion is, that payment to the State should be in numerical proportion to pecuniary means. Others think that justice dictates what they term graduated taxation; taking a higher percentage from those who have more to spare. In point of natural justice a strong case might be made for disregarding means altogether, and taking the same absolute sum (whenever it could be got) from every one: as the subscribers to a mess, or to a club, all pay the same sum for the same privileges, whether they can all equally afford it or not. Since the protection (it might be said) of law and government is afforded to, and is equally required by, all, there is no injustice in making all buy it at the same price. It is reckoned justice, not injustice, that a dealer should charge to all customers the same price for the same article, not a price varying according to their means of payment. This doctrine, as applied to taxation, finds no advocates, because it conflicts strongly with men's feelings of humanity and perceptions of social expediency; but the principle of justice which it invokes is as true and as binding as those which can be appealed to against it. Accordingly, it exerts a tacit influence on the line of defence employed for other modes of assessing taxation. People feel obliged to argue that the State does more for the rich than for the poor, as a justification for its taking more from them: though this is in reality not true, for the rich would be far better able to protect themselves, in the absence of law or government, than the poor, and indeed would probably be successful in converting the poor into their slaves. Others, again, so far defer to the same conception of justice, as to maintain that all should pay an equal capitation tax for the protection of their persons (these being of equal value to all), and an unequal tax for the protection of their property, which is unequal. To this others reply, that the all of one man is as valuable to him as the all of another. From these confusions there is no other mode of extrication than the utilitarian.

Is, then, the difference between the Just and the Expedient a merely imaginary distinction? Have mankind been under a delusion in thinking that justice is a more sacred thing than policy, and that the latter ought only to be listened to after the former has been satisfied? By no means. The exposition we have given of the nature and origin of the sentiment, recognizes a real distinction; and no one of those who profess the most sublime contempt for the consequences of actions as an element in their morality, attaches more importance to the distinction than I do. While I dispute the pretensions of any theory which sets up an imaginary standard of justice not grounded on utility, I account the justice which is grounded on utility to be the chief part, and incomparably the most sacred and binding part, of all morality. Justice is a name for certain classes of moral rules, which concern the essentials of human well-being more nearly, and are therefore of more absolute obligation, than any other rules for the guidance of life; and the notion which we have found to be of the essence of the idea of justice, that of a right residing in an individual, implies and testifies to this more binding obligation.

The moral rules which forbid mankind to hurt one another (in which we must never forget to include wrongful interference with each other's freedom) are more vital to human well-being than any maxims, however important, which only point out the best mode of managing some department of human affairs. They have also the peculiarity, that they are the main element in determining the whole of the social feelings of mankind. It is their observance which alone preserves peace among human beings: if obedience to them were not the rule, and disobedience the exception, every one would see in every one else a probable enemy, against whom he must be perpetually guarding himself. What is hardly less important, these are the precepts which mankind have the strongest and the most direct inducements for impressing upon one another. By merely giving to each other prudential instruction or exhortation, they may gain, or think they gain, nothing: in inculcating in each other the duty of positive beneficence they have an unmistakable interest, but far less in degree: a person may possibly not need the benefits of others; but he always needs that they should not do him hurt. Thus the moralities which protect every individual from being harmed by others, either directly or by being hindered in his freedom of pursuing his own good, are at once those which he himself has most at heart, and those which he has the strongest interest in publishing and enforcing by word and deed. It is by a person's observance of these, that his fitness to exist as one of the fellowship of human beings, is tested and decided; for on that depends his being a nuisance or not to those with whom he is in contact. Now it is these moralities primarily, which compose the obligations of justice. The most marked cases of injustice, and those which give the tone to the feeling of repugnance which characterizes the sentiment, are acts of wrongful aggression, or wrongful exercise of power over some one; the next are those which consist in wrongfully withholding from him something which is his due; in both cases, inflicting on him a positive hurt, either in the form of direct suffering, or of the privation of some good which he had reasonable ground, either of a physical or of a social kind, for counting upon.

The same powerful motives which command the observance of these primary moralities, enjoin the punishment of those who violate them; and as the impulses of self-defence, of defence of others, and of vengeance, are all called forth against such persons, retribution, or evil for evil, becomes closely connected with the sentiment of justice, and is universally included in the idea. Good for good is also one of the dictates of justice; and this, though its social utility is evident, and though it carries with it a natural human feeling, has not at first sight that obvious connection with hurt or injury, which, existing in the most elementary cases of just and unjust, is the source of the characteristic intensity of the sentiment. But the connection, though less obvious, is not less real. He who accepts benefits, and denies a return of them when needed, inflicts a real hurt, by disappointing one of the most natural and reasonable of expectations, and one which he must at least tacitly have encouraged, otherwise the benefits would seldom have been conferred. The important rank, among human evils and wrongs, of the disappointment of expectation, is shown in the fact that it constitutes the principal criminality of two such highly immoral acts as a breach of friendship and a breach of promise. Few hurts which human beings can sustain are greater, and none wound more, than when that on which they habitually and with full assurance relied, fails them in the hour of need; and few wrongs are greater than this mere withholding of good; none excite more resentment, either in the person suffering, or in a sympathizing spectator. The principle, therefore, of giving to each what they deserve, that is, good for good as well as evil for evil, is not only included within the idea of Justice as we have defined it, but is a proper object of that intensity of sentiment, which places the Just, in human estimation, above the simply Expedient.

Most of the maxims of justice current in the world, and commonly appealed to in its transactions, are simply instrumental to carrying into effect the principles of justice which we have now spoken of. That a person is only responsible for what he has done voluntarily, or could voluntarily have avoided; that it is unjust to condemn any person unheard; that the punishment ought to be proportioned to the offence, and the like, are maxims intended to prevent the just principle of evil for evil from being perverted to the infliction of evil without that justification. The greater part of these common maxims have come into use from the practice of courts of justice, which have been naturally led to a more complete recognition and elaboration than was likely to suggest itself to others, of the rules necessary to enable them to fulfil their double function, of inflicting punishment when due, and of awarding to each person his right.

That first of judicial virtues, impartiality, is an obligation of justice, partly for the reason last mentioned; as being a necessary condition of the fulfilment of the other obligations of justice. But this is not the only source of the exalted rank, among human obligations, of those maxims of equality and impartiality, which, both in popular estimation and in that of the most enlightened, are included among the precepts of justice. In one point of view, they may be considered as corollaries from the principles already laid down. If it is a duty to do to each according to his deserts, returning good for good as well as repressing evil by evil, it necessarily follows that we should treat all equally well (when no higher duty forbids) who have deserved equally well of us, and that society should treat all equally well who have deserved equally well of it, that is, who have deserved equally well absolutely. This is the highest abstract standard of social and distributive justice; towards which all institutions, and the efforts of all virtuous citizens, should be made in the utmost possible degree to converge. But this great moral duty rests upon a still deeper foundation, being a direct emanation from the first principle of morals, and not a mere logical corollary from secondary or derivative doctrines. It is involved in the very meaning of Utility, or the Greatest Happiness Principle. That principle is a mere form of words without rational signification, unless one person's hap-

piness, supposed equal in degree (with the proper allowance made for kind), is counted for exactly as much as another's. Those conditions being supplied, Bentham's dictum, 'everybody to count for one, nobody for more than one', might be written under the principle of utility as an explanatory commentary.*
The equal claim of everybody to happiness in the estimation of the moralist and the legislator, involves an equal claim to all the means of happiness, except in so far as the inevitable conditions of human life, and the general interest, in which that of every individual is included, set limits to the maxim; and those limits ought to be strictly construed. As every other maxim of justice,

*This implication, in the first principle of the utilitarian scheme, of perfect impartiality between persons, is regarded by Mr Herbert Spencer (in his *Social Statics*) as a disproof of the pretensions of utility to be a sufficient guide to right; since (he says) the principle of utility presupposes the anterior principle that everybody has an equal right to happiness. It may be more correctly described as supposing that equal amounts of happiness are equally desirable, whether felt by the same or by different persons. This, however, is not a presupposition; not a premise needful to support the principle of utility, but the very principle itself; for what is the principle of utility, if it be not that 'happiness' and 'desirable' are synonymous terms? If there is any anterior principle implied, it can be no other than this, that the truths of arithmetic are applicable to the valuation of happiness, as of all other measurable quantities.

Mr Herbert Spencer, in a private communication on the subject of the preceding Note, objects to being considered an opponent of Utilitarianism, and states that he regards happiness as the ultimate end of morality; but deems that end only partially attainable by empirical generalizations from the observed results of conduct, and completely attainable only by deducing, from the laws of life and the conditions of existence, what kinds of action necessarily tend to produce happiness and what kinds to produce unhappiness. With the exception of the word 'necessarily', I have no dissent to express from this doctrine; and (omitting that word) I am not aware that any modern advocate of utilitarianism is of a different opinion. Bentham, certainly, to whom in the *Social Statics* Mr Spencer particularly referred, is, least of all writers, chargeable with unwillingness to deduce the effect of actions on happiness from the laws of human nature and the universal conditions of human life. The common charge against him is of relying too exclusively upon such deductions, and declining altogether to be bound by the generalizations from specific experience which Mr Spencer thinks that utilitarians generally confine themselves to. My own opinion (and, as I collect, Mr Spencer's) is, that in ethics, as in all other branches of scientific study, the consilience of the results of both these processes, each corroborating and verifying the other, is requisite to give to any general proposition the kind and degree of evidence which constitutes scientific proof.

so this, is by no means applied or held applicable universally; on the contrary, as I have already remarked, it bends to every person's ideas of social expediency. But in whatever case it is deemed applicable at all, it is held to be the dictate of justice. All persons are deemed to have a *right* to equality of treatment, except when some recognized social expediency requires the reverse. And hence all social inequalities which have ceased to be considered expedient, assume the character not of simple inexpediency, but of injustice, and appear so tyrannical, that people are apt to wonder how they ever could have been tolerated; forgetful that they themselves perhaps tolerate other inequalities under an equally mistaken notion of expediency, the correction of which would make that which they approve seem quite as monstrous as what they have at last learnt to condemn. The entire history of social improvement has been a series of transitions, by which one custom or institution after another, from being a supposed primary necessity of social existence, has passed into the rank of a universally stigmatized injustice and tyranny. So it has been with the distinctions of slaves and freemen, nobles and serfs, patricians and plebeians; and so it will be, and in part already is, with the aristocracies of colour, race, and sex.

It appears from what has been said, that justice is a name for certain moral requirements, which, regarded collectively, stand higher in the scale of social utility, and are therefore of more paramount obligation, than any others; though particular cases may occur in which some other social duty is so important, as to overrule any one of the general maxims of justice. Thus to save a life, it may not only be allowable, but a duty, to steal, or take by force, the necessary food or medicine, or to kidnap, and compel to officiate the only qualified medical practitioner. In such cases, as we do not call anything justice which is not a virtue, we usually say, not that justice must give way to some other moral principle, but that what is just in ordinary cases is, by reason of that other principle, not just in the particular case. By this useful accommodation of language, the character of indefeasibility attributed to justice is kept up, and we are saved from the necessity of maintaining that there can be laudable injustice.

The considerations which have now been adduced resolve,

I conceive, the only real difficulty in the utilitarian theory of morals. It has always been evident that all cases of justice are also cases of expediency: the difference is in the peculiar sentiment which attaches to the former, as contradistinguished from the latter. If this characteristic sentiment has been sufficiently accounted for; if there is no necessity to assume for it any peculiarity of origin; if it is simply the natural feeling of resentment, moralized by being made co-extensive with the demands of social good; and if this feeling not only does but ought to exist in all the classes of cases to which the idea of justice corresponds; that idea no longer presents itself as a stumbling-block to the utilitarian ethics. Justice remains the appropriate name for certain social utilities which are vastly more important, and therefore more absolute and imperative, than any others are as a class (though not more so than others may be in particular cases); and which, therefore, ought to be, as well as naturally are, guarded by a sentiment not only different in degree, but also in kind; distinguished from the milder feeling which attaches to the mere idea of promoting human pleasure or convenience, at once by the more definite nature of its commands, and by the sterner character of its sanctions.

Further Reading

The literature by and on Mill is so voluminous that any selection is invidious. The serious student of Mill will want to turn first to the *Collected Works* which have been appearing for twenty years from the University of Toronto Press under the general editorship of John M. Robson with admirable textual and topical introductions. *The Mill Newsletter* (from the same source) carries a constantly updated bibliography of articles on every aspect of Mill's work as well as essays and reviews. Material up to 1978 appears in Michael Laine (ed.), *Bibliography of Works on John Stuart Mill* (University of Toronto Press, Toronto, 1982). The standard, though flawed, biography of Mill is Michael Packe, *The Life of John Stuart Mill* (Secker and Warburg, London, 1954). William Thomas's *J. S. Mill* in the Oxford 'Past Masters' series (Oxford University Press, Oxford, 1985) is very brief and very useful. Longer and very good is John M. Robson's *The Improvement of Mankind* (University of Toronto Press, Toronto, 1968). Alan Ryan, *J. S. Mill* (Routledge and Kegan Paul, London, 1974) and John Halliday, *John Stuart Mill* (Allen & Unwin, London, 1974) cover Mill's ethics and politics. An excellent recent book almost entirely devoted to Mill's ethics is Fred Berger, *Happiness, Justice and Freedom* (University of California Press, Berkeley, California, 1985). Well worth reading in addition are John Gray, *Mill on Liberty: A Defence* (Routledge and Kegan Paul, London, 1983), *New Essays on John Stuart Mill and Utilitarianism* (*Canadian Journal of Philosophy*, supplement, 1979), Alan Ryan, *The Philosophy of John Stuart Mill* (Macmillan, London, 1970), David Lyons, *Forms and Limits of Utilitarianism* (Oxford University Press, Oxford, 1965).

Index

342

READ MORE IN PENGUIN

In every corner of the world, on every subject under the sun, Penguin represents quality and variety – the very best in publishing today.

For complete information about books available from Penguin – including Puffins, Penguin Classics and Arkana – and how to order them, write to us at the appropriate address below. Please note that for copyright reasons the selection of books varies from country to country.

In the United Kingdom: Please write to *Dept. EP, Penguin Books Ltd, Bath Road, Harmondsworth, West Drayton, Middlesex UB7 ODA*

In the United States: Please write to *Consumer Sales, Penguin USA, P.O. Box 999, Dept. 17109, Bergenfield, New Jersey 07621-0120.* VISA and MasterCard holders call 1-800-253-6476 to order Penguin titles

In Canada: Please write to *Penguin Books Canada Ltd, 10 Alcorn Avenue, Suite 300, Toronto, Ontario M4V 3B2*

In Australia: Please write to *Penguin Books Australia Ltd, P.O. Box 257, Ringwood, Victoria 3134*

In New Zealand: Please write to *Penguin Books (NZ) Ltd, Private Bag 102902, North Shore Mail Centre, Auckland 10*

In India: Please write to *Penguin Books India Pvt Ltd, 706 Eros Apartments, 56 Nehru Place, New Delhi 110 019*

In the Netherlands: Please write to *Penguin Books Netherlands bv, Postbus 3507, NL-1001 AH Amsterdam*

In Germany: Please write to *Penguin Books Deutschland GmbH, Metzlerstrasse 26, 60594 Frankfurt am Main*

In Spain: Please write to *Penguin Books S. A., Bravo Murillo 19, 1° B, 28015 Madrid*

In Italy: Please write to *Penguin Italia s.r.l., Via Felice Casati 20, I–20124 Milano*

In France: Please write to *Penguin France S. A., 17 rue Lejeune, F–31000 Toulouse*

In Japan: Please write to *Penguin Books Japan, Ishikiribashi Building, 2–5–4, Suido, Bunkyo-ku, Tokyo 112*

In South Africa: Please write to *Longman Penguin Southern Africa (Pty) Ltd, Private Bag X08, Bertsham 2013*

PENGUIN AUDIOBOOKS

A Quality of Writing that Speaks for Itself

Penguin Books has always led the field in quality publishing. Now you can listen at leisure to your favourite books, read to you by familiar voices from radio, stage and screen. Penguin Audiobooks are ideal as gifts, for when you are travelling or simply to enjoy at home. They are produced to an excellent standard, and abridgements are always faithful to the original texts. From thrillers to classic literature, biography to humour, with a wealth of titles in between, Penguin Audiobooks offer you quality, entertainment and the chance to rediscover the pleasure of listening.

You can order Penguin Audiobooks through Penguin Direct by telephoning (0181) 899 4036. The lines are open 24 hours every day. Ask for Penguin Direct, quoting your credit card details.

Published or forthcoming:

Emma by Jane Austen, read by Fiona Shaw

Persuasion by Jane Austen, read by Joanna David

Pride and Prejudice by Jane Austen, read by Geraldine McEwan

The Tenant of Wildfell Hall by Anne Brontë, read by Juliet Stevenson

Jane Eyre by Charlotte Brontë, read by Juliet Stevenson

Villette by Charlotte Brontë, read by Juliet Stevenson

Wuthering Heights by Emily Brontë, read by Juliet Stevenson

The Woman in White by Wilkie Collins, read by Nigel Anthony and Susan Jameson

Heart of Darkness by Joseph Conrad, read by David Threlfall

Tales from the One Thousand and One Nights, read by Souad Faress and Raad Rawi

Moll Flanders by Daniel Defoe, read by Frances Barber

Great Expectations by Charles Dickens, read by Hugh Laurie

Hard Times by Charles Dickens, read by Michael Pennington

Martin Chuzzlewit by Charles Dickens, read by John Wells

The Old Curiosity Shop by Charles Dickens, read by Alec McCowen

PENGUIN AUDIOBOOKS

Crime and Punishment by Fyodor Dostoyevsky, read by Alex Jennings

Middlemarch by George Eliot, read by Harriet Walter

Silas Marner by George Eliot, read by Tim Pigott-Smith

The Great Gatsby by F. Scott Fitzgerald, read by Marcus D'Amico

Madame Bovary by Gustave Flaubert, read by Claire Bloom

Jude the Obscure by Thomas Hardy, read by Samuel West

The Return of the Native by Thomas Hardy, read by Steven Pacey

Tess of the D'Urbervilles by Thomas Hardy, read by Eleanor Bron

The Iliad by Homer, read by Derek Jacobi

Dubliners by James Joyce, read by Gerard McSorley

The Dead and Other Stories by James Joyce, read by Gerard McSorley

On the Road by Jack Kerouac, read by David Carradine

Sons and Lovers by D. H. Lawrence, read by Paul Copley

The Fall of the House of Usher by Edgar Allan Poe, read by Andrew Sachs

Wide Sargasso Sea by Jean Rhys, read by Jane Lapotaire and Michael Kitchen

The Little Prince by Antoine de Saint-Exupéry, read by Michael Maloney

Frankenstein by Mary Shelley, read by Richard Pasco

Of Mice and Men by John Steinbeck, read by Gary Sinise

Travels with Charley by John Steinbeck, read by Gary Sinise

The Pearl by John Steinbeck, read by Hector Elizondo

Dr Jekyll and Mr Hyde by Robert Louis Stevenson, read by Jonathan Hyde

Kidnapped by Robert Louis Stevenson, read by Robbie Coltrane

The Age of Innocence by Edith Wharton, read by Kerry Shale

The Buccaneers by Edith Wharton, read by Dana Ivey

Mrs Dalloway by Virginia Woolf, read by Eileen Atkins

READ MORE IN PENGUIN

A CHOICE OF CLASSICS

READ MORE IN PENGUIN

A CHOICE OF CLASSICS

William Hazlitt	**Selected Writings**
George Herbert	**The Complete English Poems**
Thomas Hobbes	**Leviathan**
Samuel Johnson/	
James Boswell	**A Journey to the Western Islands of Scotland and The Journal of a Tour of the Hebrides**
Charles Lamb	**Selected Prose**
George Meredith	**The Egoist**
Thomas Middleton	**Five Plays**
John Milton	**Paradise Lost**
Samuel Richardson	**Clarissa**
	Pamela
Earl of Rochester	**Complete Works**
Richard Brinsley	
Sheridan	**The School for Scandal and Other Plays**
Sir Philip Sidney	**Selected Poems**
Christopher Smart	**Selected Poems**
Adam Smith	**The Wealth of Nations**
Tobias Smollett	**The Adventures of Ferdinand Count Fathom**
	Humphrey Clinker
Laurence Sterne	**The Life and Opinions of Tristram Shandy**
	A Sentimental Journey Through France and Italy
Jonathan Swift	**Gulliver's Travels**
	Selected Poems
Thomas Traherne	**Selected Poems and Prose**
Sir John Vanbrugh	**Four Comedies**

READ MORE IN PENGUIN

A CHOICE OF CLASSICS

Matthew Arnold	**Selected Prose**
Jane Austen	**Emma**
	Lady Susan/The Watsons/Sanditon
	Mansfield Park
	Northanger Abbey
	Persuasion
	Pride and Prejudice
	Sense and Sensibility
William Barnes	**Selected Poems**
Anne Brontë	**Agnes Grey**
	The Tenant of Wildfell Hall
Charlotte Brontë	**Jane Eyre**
	Shirley
	Villette
Emily Brontë	**Wuthering Heights**
Samuel Butler	**Erewhon**
	The Way of All Flesh
Thomas Carlyle	**Selected Writings**
Arthur Hugh Clough	**Selected Poems**
Wilkie Collins	**The Moonstone**
	The Woman in White
Charles Darwin	**The Origin of Species**
	The Voyage of the *Beagle*
Benjamin Disraeli	**Sybil**
George Eliot	**Adam Bede**
	Daniel Deronda
	Felix Holt
	Middlemarch
	The Mill on the Floss
	Romola
	Scenes of Clerical Life
	Silas Marner
Elizabeth Gaskell	**Cranford/Cousin Phillis**
	The Life of Charlotte Brontë
	Mary Barton
	North and South
	Wives and Daughters

READ MORE IN PENGUIN

A CHOICE OF CLASSICS

Charles Dickens	**American Notes for General Circulation**
	Barnaby Rudge
	Bleak House
	The Christmas Books (in two volumes)
	David Copperfield
	Dombey and Son
	Great Expectations
	Hard Times
	Little Dorrit
	Martin Chuzzlewit
	The Mystery of Edwin Drood
	Nicholas Nickleby
	The Old Curiosity Shop
	Oliver Twist
	Our Mutual Friend
	The Pickwick Papers
	Selected Short Fiction
	A Tale of Two Cities
Edward Gibbon	**The Decline and Fall of the Roman Empire**
George Gissing	**New Grub Street**
	The Odd Women
William Godwin	**Caleb Williams**
Thomas Hardy	**The Distracted Preacher and Other Tales**
	Far from the Madding Crowd
	Jude the Obscure
	The Mayor of Casterbridge
	A Pair of Blue Eyes
	The Return of the Native
	Tess of the d'Urbervilles
	The Trumpet-Major
	Under the Greenwood Tree
	The Woodlanders

READ MORE IN PENGUIN

A CHOICE OF CLASSICS

Lord Macaulay	**The History of England**
Henry Mayhew	**London Labour and the London Poor**
John Stuart Mill	**The Autobiography**
	On Liberty
William Morris	**News from Nowhere** and **Selected Writings and Designs**
John Henry Newman	**Apologia Pro Vita Sua**
Robert Owen	**A New View of Society and Other Writings**
Walter Pater	**Marius the Epicurean**
John Ruskin	**'Unto This Last' and Other Writings**
Walter Scott	**Ivanhoe**
	Heart of Midlothian
Robert Louis Stevenson	**Kidnapped**
	Dr Jekyll and Mr Hyde and Other Stories
William Makepeace Thackeray	**The History of Henry Esmond**
	The History of Pendennis
	Vanity Fair
Anthony Trollope	**Barchester Towers**
	Can You Forgive Her?
	The Eustace Diamonds
	Framley Parsonage
	He Knew He Was Right
	The Last Chronicle of Barset
	Phineas Finn
	The Prime Minister
	The Small House at Allington
	The Warden
	The Way We Live Now
Oscar Wilde	**Complete Short Fiction**
Mary Wollstonecraft	**A Vindication of the Rights of Woman**
	Mary and Maria
	Matilda
Dorothy and William Wordsworth	**Home at Grasmere**